*Frances D. Castello*

# READINGS IN
# AMERICAN CULTURES

## Volume I

## Michael Hardy
## Barry Grossbach

*Of the thought are
consistent w/the way
Reader's level ...*

**AMERICAN HERITAGE ■ CUSTOM PUBLISHING GROUP**
A Division of Forbes Inc.
60 Fifth Avenue
New York, New York 10011

Excerpts from *The Diary of Samuel Sewall 1674–1729* by Samuel Sewall, edited by M. Halsey Thomas. Copyright © 1973 by Farrar, Straus, and Giroux, Inc.

Excerpts from *The Present State of Virginia,* by Hugh Jones, edited by Richard L. Morton. Copyright © 1956 by The University of North Carolina Press.

Excerpts from *The Secret Diary of William Byrd of Westover,* by William Byrd, edited by Louis B. Wright and Marion Tinling. Copyright © 1941 Louis B. Wright and Marion Tinling.

Excerpts from "Equiano's Travels" by Olaudah Equiano, abridged and edited by Paul Edwards. Copyright © 1967 Paul Edwards. Reprinted by permission of Heinemann Publishers (Oxford) Ltd.

Selected excerpts from "The Autobiography," by Benjamin Franklin from *Benjamin Franklin: The Autobiography and Other Writings,* edited by L. Jesse Lemisch. Published by The New American Library. Copyright © 1961 by L. Jesse Lemisch.

"A Proposal for Promoting Useful Knowledge Among the British Plantations in America, May 14, 1743," by Benjamin Franklin. Copyright © 1987 by Literary Classics of the United States, Inc. Reprinted by permission of The Library of America.

Selected excerpts from "Travels through North and South Carolina" by William Bartram, edited by Mark Van Doren. Copyright © 1955 by Dover Publications, Inc. Reprinted by permission.

"Thomas Jefferson: The Object of the Declaration of Independence, a letter to Henry Lee" by Thomas Jefferson. Copyright © 1984 by Literary Classics of the United States, Inc. Reprinted by permission of The Library of America.

CIP Data is available.
Printed in the United States of America
10  9  8  7  6  5  4  3  2

ISBN 0–8281–0532–4

# SYLLABUS AND STUDY ASSIGNMENTS

# INTRODUCTION

The materials for this course in American history are meant to reveal the views of reality held by a series of cultures in the American past, not the image of reality as we would like it to have been, but reality as defined by those past societies themselves. Instead of being told what the participants in these past cultures considered reality, you will be asked to read and consider their own descriptions of life and experience as they conceived it. Thus you will be using only primary materials, documents and items created by the particular societies we shall be studying.

The great bulk of these materials are included in these *Readings in American Cultures*. Additionally, before the semester ends, you must obtain Benjamin Franklin's *Autobiography and other Writings* (New American Library Paperback). All these materials are available at the school bookstore. The audio-visual programs referred to in the Syllabus and Study Assignments will be made available in class.

For each assignment there is an introduction and series of study questions. These contain crucial information about the material and its background together with questions which furnish a framework for studying the assignment. In order for the materials to fulfill their function, i.e., to reveal the signal features of the culture being studied, they must be subjected to *intensive* analysis. In short, they must not only be *read or viewed* but *dissected*.

The study questions were designed to assist you in performing this operation. Some questions were included to elicit simple data to insure that you are aware of the basic argument presented, others are more complex, requiring critical consideration of the readings. A suggested study procedure would be to skim through the required assignment, noting its general organization or structure and then, using the questions on the data sheet, to systematically analyze the material. But, do not expect to be able to satisfactorily answer these questions by viewing or reading through the assignment and then taking up the questions *in toto*. Instead, the questions are arranged in an order which generally parallels the sequential logic of the material being studied, thus with each paragraph of questions it is necessary to return to the materials to obtain the answers.

You must perform this study assignment before the topic is discussed in class. In most instances you may expect that each of the topics on the syllabus (and any study assignments listed) will be covered in one class session. Additionally, this volume of readings has been designed for insertion in a loose leaf binder so that you can interleave your notes on each selection with each set of study questions. You can then bring all of these items to class.

The materials included in this volume have been edited with a view to retaining their original arguments and characteristics. The spelling and punctuation used, in most instances, are the original authors' own. Any later additions are included in brackets and a series of dots (i.e. . . . . ) appears whenever a portion of the original has been deleted.

While there is no other text, as such, required for this course, you may need or desire a reference work to supply additional background information. Any standard college text, of which there are many adequate examples found in the library, will serve this need. If you desire to pursue any of the topics of this course at a more intensive level, ask your instructor to supply you with a select bibliography of works to consult. If you have any questions regarding particular subjects or the course in general do not hesitate to approach him.

# INTRODUCTION & QUESTIONS

## THE PURITAN SYSTEM— A DUE FORM OF GOVERNMENT

To a large extent the political outlines of Puritan New England can be illustrated in the life, both private and public, of John Winthrop (1588–1649). That life is synonymous with the early years of the founding and development of the Puritan state of Massachusetts. If one considers Winthrop's career not as an idiosyncratic personal expression, but as representative of much larger social developments, one observes many of the wellsprings of Puritanism.

For our purposes, an analysis of Winthrop's life—at least those features which illustrate the dynamics of American Puritanism—should begin by noting that his grandfather was a London cloth maker. In 1534, this Winthrop purchased a manor, or landed estate, then the property of a Catholic monastery. This acquisition was made possible by King Henry VIII's dissolution of the monasteries and confiscation and sale of their properties, in keeping with his Reformation of the Church in England. The Winthrop family's primary social role as members of the gentry or landed class came about in conjunction with that Reformation.

Yet Henry's reform consisted mainly of dispersing church property and installing the King, rather than the Pope, as head of the newly formed Church of England. Church and State remained unified and the new Anglican Church retained a great deal of its "Catholic" character. Its institutional structure, forms of worship, and doctrinal emphases followed guidelines laid down during the years under the papacy. Only with Henry's successors did the process of religious reformation erratically proceed.

That process was again in motion by the time of John Winthrop's birth in 1588 into a family now well-established in the gentry. By the age of eighteen, John had assumed the expected roles of administrator of the Winthrop estate, justice of the peace, and responsible social leader. Only his two years of schooling at Cambridge saw a disruption in the established pattern. During that time, John Winthrop became a Puritan.

Puritanism, in its simplest, most concrete form, was a radical program to rid the Church of England of its "Romish" or "papish" elements and to reinstall the religious forms and formulas Puritans observed in the Bible. This included rejecting the prevailing "Catholic" ritual and ceremony of the Church, including the use of vestments, the prayer book, kneeling at communion, the celebration of "holy days" and the symbolic use of the crucifix. Puritans not only demanded that such forms be changed, but that church membership be "purified." On the one hand, former Catholic priests and other "incompetents" must be dismissed from the ministry; while those lay church members whose desolate behavior indicated an obvious lack of religious commitment would also be rejected.

1

It was this crusade to cleanse the Church, and through it the world, that infected Winthrop as a young man. And by the 1620's he, as a Puritan, saw much in his world in need of cleansing. He and his associates faced a monarchy, in the Stuart family, distinctly hostile to their proposals. In 1625 Charles I became the second Stuart to ascend the English throne. Following his father, James I, he continued to battle the Puritan forces entrenched in Parliament. Also like his predecessor, Charles maintained a conspicuously extravagant court and insisted on strict adherence to and retention of royal prerogatives against any assertions of parliamentary power. This last concern resulted in Charles' dissolution of Parliament in 1629 and an eleven year rule of England without a Representative assembly.

The Puritan, therefore, saw his world of the late 1620s as a corrupt society, presided over by a licentious and tyrannical monarch bent on destroying the state, rejecting, if not silencing, the only valid religious reform program. He witnessed, too, a society which seemed increasingly to favor individual acquisitiveness and materialistic rewards at the expense of community responsibility and attention to spiritual concerns. He beheld, also, the retreat of European Protestantism in its violent struggle with a now militant Roman Catholicism. While one can not say that men like Winthrop were personally persecuted, many did, given these signs, envision an impending catastrophe in the form of divine judgement. This climate of opinion was expressed in one of John Winthrop's letters to his wife when he assured her:

> It is a great favour that we may enjoye so much comfort and peace in these so evill and declininge tymes and when the increasinge of our sinnes gives us go great cause to looke for some heavy Scourge and Judgment to be comminge upon us: the Lorde hath admonished, threatened, corrected, and astonished us, yet we growe worse and worse, so as his spirit will not allwayes strive with us, he must needs give waye to his furye at last; he hath smitten all the other Churches [of Protestant Europe] before our eyes, and hath made them to drinke of the bitter cuppe of tribulation, even unto death; we sawe this, and humbled not ourselves, to turne from our evill wayes, but have provoked him more than all the nations rounde about us: therefore he is turning the cuppe towards us also, and because we are the last, our portion must be, to drinke the very dreggs which remaine: my dear wife, I am veryly perswaded, God will bringe some heavye Affliction upon this lande,  and that speedylye.

Given such a vision, the idea of emigrating from England was being seriously considered by those of John Winthrop's persuasion, *if* such a departure could be made under the correct circumstances.

In 1629, such conditions arose when a group of Puritans secured financial control of a joint-stock company chartered as "The Governor and Company of Massachusetts Bay in New England." This joint-stock company was not unlike the East India or Virginia Companies, that is, trading organizations, monopolistic corporations given, by the King's charter, the powers of ownership and government over a specified economic or geographical area.

Normally required to meet in either of the great seaports of London or Plymouth, these colonial companies were administered by a governor, deputy-governor and "assistants" (essentially a "board of directors") chosen yearly by the company's "freemen" (stockholders) meeting collectively as the General Court. Under the royal patent or charter such companies enjoyed extremely broad authority, essentially the power, in their holdings, to establish any governmental forms, pass any legislation, install any officials they deemed desirable. They worked under one royal restriction—that such arrangements "be not contrary to the laws of this our realm of England."

Such joint-stock corporations were designed primarily to encourage and develop England's trade and to assist in the economic exploitation of her newly acquired overseas territories. Yet, in this instance, the Puritans intended conducting a very special social experiment, establishing in the New World a "Holy Commonwealth," a successfully functioning model of the true Church and community which might be emulated by England and, ultimately, by the world. This, then, was no simple flight from persecution, but an exodus to found, as Winthrop described it, "a city set upon a hill, the eyes of all people are upon us."

Having convinced Winthrop to join the Company, the proponents of this utopian vision forced out the non-Puritan stockholders and hand-picked the initial settlers who sailed for New England in April, 1630. Yet if their company had been identical to all others, this project would have suffered from the continuing intervention of hostile English authorities, particularly when these unsympathetic officials observed and supervised the Company's affairs at the periodic convocations of the General Court. But such was not to be a problem, as the Puritans' charter was in one way unique. Either through calculation or bureaucratic oversight, no meeting place had been designated. Given this extraordinary opportunity for independence from English restraint, the Puritans simply decided to hold the next meeting of the General Court in Massachusetts, taking both Company and charter to the New World.

Two major alterations were made in the governing apparatus of the Company to make it meet the special political requirements demanded by the Puritans. First, the privileges and responsibilities of freemen were extended only to Puritan church members. These religiously screened and certified individuals, as represented by the General Court, now became for all the inhabitants of Massachusetts, the final legislative, judicial and executive authority. Since this initial arrangement greatly extended the number of freemen, the General Court became a representative body. Bicameral after 1640, it was made up of governor, deputy-governor and assistants sitting as one house and popularly elected deputies, two from each of the Bay Colony's towns, making up the other.

Agent and proponent of these founding activities, Winthrop continued to enjoy the confidence of Massachusetts' citizenry for the nineteen years remaining to him in the colony, a period which witnessed the arrival of over 20,000 other immigrants. Despite this influx, rarely did he fall from political favor, receiving the governorship for fifteen of those years and at least an assistantship for all of them.

Winthrop's "Speech to the General Court" was delivered in 1645 while he was serving as deputy-governor. He had just been tried and acquitted by the General Court of the charge of exceeding his authority as a political official (magistrate) and going beyond the basic law of the land. This charge was originally levied against him after he intervened in a dispute over the election of a local official. His reply provides more than a justification for his actions. It reveals some of the fundamental assumptions of Puritan political theory. Some of these premises may be revealed by answering the following questions:

1.  What motivates Winthrop to present this speech? There may indeed be more than one reason. To whom is it addressed, both literally and theoretically?

2.  Why, if Winthrop has been acquitted, should he feel "humiliation"? Does this indicate anything concerning his attitudes toward authority?

3.  By what process are magistrates selected? Does this process provide them with their authority? What is the source of that authority?

4.  What relationship exists, according to Winthrop, between the magistrates and the people? What other kinds of social relationships does he cite as being analogous to this one?

5.  What should the people's response be to human "failings" on the magistrate's part? Do these failings in any way affect his authority? If not, what possible limits can there be to that authority? In this context, what is implied in the distinction he draws between "skill" and "Faithfulness"?

6.  How does Winthrop categorize "liberty"? What are the characteristics of "natural liberty"? Under such conditions, does man display any particular inclinations? What quality of freedom does he enjoy in this condition?

7.  What freedoms does man enjoy under "civil liberty"? Note the alternate term used to refer to political constitutions. Does a relationship similar to that which should prevail between the people and political authority exist in any other social contexts?

8.  In Winthrop's argument, what is the essential relationship between liberty and authority?

# A SPEECH TO THE GENERAL COURT

*John Winthrop*

I suppose something may be expected from me, upon this charge that is befallen me, which moves me to speak now to you; yet I intend not to intermeddle in the proceedings of the court, or with any of the persons concerned therein. Only I bless God, that I see an issue[1] of this troublesome business. I also acknowledge the justice of the court, and, for mine own part, I am well satisfied, I was publicly charged, and I am publicly and legally acquitted, which is all I did expect or desire. And though this be sufficient for my justification before men, yet not so before the God, who hath seen so much amiss in my dispensations[2] (and even in this affair) as calls me to be humble. For to be publicly and criminally charged in this court, is a matter of humiliation, (and I desire to make a right use of it,) notwithstanding I be thus acquitted. . . . I am unwilling to stay you from your urgent affairs, yet give me leave (upon this special occasion) to speak a little more to this assembly. It may be of some good use, to inform and rectify the judgements of some of the people, and may prevent such distempers[3] as have arisen amongst us. The great questions that have troubled the country, are about the authority of the magistrates and the liberty of the people. It is yourselves who have called us to this office, and being called by you, we have our authority from God . . . the contempt and violation whereof hath been vindicated with examples of divine vengence. I entreat you to consider, that when you choose magistrates, you take them from among yourselves, men subject to like passions as you are. Therefore when you see infirmities[4] in us, you should reflect upon your own, and that would make you bear the more with us, and not be severe censurers of the failings of your magistrates, when you have continual experience of the like infirmities in yourselves and others. We account him a good servant, who breaks not his covenant. The covenant between you and us is the oath you have taken of us, which is to this purpose, that we shall govern you and judge your causes by the rules of God's laws and our own, according to our best

---

1. issue—end, conclusion.
2. dispensations—administration, stewardship.
3. distempers—disorders
4. infirmities—illness, weakness

skill. When you agree with a workman to build you a ship or house, etc., he undertakes as well for his skill as for his faithfulness, for it is his profession, and you pay him for both. But when you call one to be a magistrate, he doth not profess nor undertake to have sufficient skill for that office, nor can you furnish him with gifts, etc., therefore you must run the hazard of his skill and ability. But if he fail in faithfulness, which by his oath he is bound unto, that he must answer for. If it fall out that the case be clear to common apprehension, and the rule clear also, if he transgress here, the error is not in the skill, but in the evil of the will: it must be required of him. But if the case be doubtful, or the rule doubtful, to men of such understanding and parts as your magistrates are, if your magistrates should err here, yourselves must bear it.

For the other point concerning liberty, I observe a great mistake in the country about that. There is a twofold liberty, natural (I mean as our nature is now corrupt) and civil or federal. The first is common to man with beasts and other creatures. By this, man . . . hath liberty to do what he lists; it is a liberty to evil as well as to good. This liberty is incompatible and inconsistent with authority, and cannot endure the least restraint of the most just authority. The exercise and maintaining of this liberty makes men grow more evil, and in time to be worse than brute beasts: *omnes sumus licentia deteriores*.[5] This is that great enemy of truth and peace, that wild beast, which all ordinances of God are bent against, to restrain and subdue it. The other kind of liberty I call civil or federal, it may also be termed moral, in reference to the covenant between God and man, in the moral law, and the politic covenants and constitutions, amongst men themselves. This liberty is the proper end and object of authority, and cannot subsist without it; and it is a liberty to that only which is good, just, and honest. . . . This liberty is maintained and exercised in a way of subjection to authority; it is of the same kind of liberty wherewith Christ hath made us free. The woman's own choice makes such a man her husband; yet being so chosen, he is her lord, and she is to be subject to him, yet in a way of liberty, not of bondage; and a true wife accounts her subjection her honor and freedom, and would not think her condition safe and free, but in her subjection to her husband's authority. Such is the liberty of the church under the authority of Christ, her king and husband; his yoke is so easy and sweet to her as a bride's ornaments; and if through frowardness or wantonness, etc., she shake it off, at any time, she is at no rest in her spirit, until she take it up again; and whether her lord smiles upon her, and embraceth her in his arms, or whether he frowns, or rebukes, or smites her, she apprehends the sweetness of his love in all, and is refreshed, supported, and instructed by every such dispensation of his authority over her. On the other side, ye know who they are that complain of this yoke and say, let us break their bands, etc., we will not have this man to rule over us. Even so, brethren, it will be between you and your magistrates. If you stand for your

---

5. *omnes sumus licentia deteriores*—Latin for: "We are all the worse for liberty."

natural corrupt liberties, and will do what is good in your own eyes, you will not endure the least weight of authority, but will murmur, and oppose, and be always striving to shake off that yoke; but if you will be satisfied to enjoy such civil and lawful liberties, such as Christ allows you, then will you quietly and cheerfully submit unto that authority which is set over you, in all the administrations of it, for your good. Wherein, if we fail at any time, we hope we shall be willing (by God's assistance) to hearken to good advice from any of you, or in any other way of God; so shall your liberties be preserved, in upholding the honor and power of authority amongst you.

# INTRODUCTION & QUESTIONS

## THE RELIGION OF THE VISIBLE SAINTS

Some of the basic premises of the Puritans' theology, that is, their assumptions about God, Humanity and their relationship to each other, can be found in the work of the premier poet among Puritan ranks in New England. He was Michael Wigglesworth (1631–1705), a Harvard graduate and minister at Malden, Massachusetts for nearly fifty years.

His magnum opus, *The Day of Doom, or a Description of the Great and Last Judgment, with a short discourse about Eternity,* was based on a reading in the book of Ecclesiastes, which declared "For God shall bring every work into judgment with every secret thing, whether it be good, or whether it be evil." Published in 1662, it went through eleven editions within the next hundred years, its tremendous popularity attesting to its sympathetic resonance to the theological commitments of the Puritans.

In reviewing this portion, which depicts men of "good works" and those who died in infancy pleading their cases at the last judgment, asking admission to Heaven, and being answered by God, the great Judge, consider:

1. What shared characteristic underlies the way the "company of civil honest men" describe themselves? How does God's response make use of that characteristic? What then, for God, is the worth of "good works" in Humanity's acquiring salvation?

2. What cases do the infants make for admission into Heaven? What faults does God find in their arguments?

3. How does God represent himself and his gift of "grace"? Is it bestowed on mankind in general or only on select individuals? On what basis is it granted?

# THE DAY OF DOOM

*Michael Wigglesworth*

. . . . . . . . . . . . . . . . . . . . . . .

*Then were brought nigh a Company*
      *of Civil honest Men,*
*That lov'd true dealing, and hated stealing,*
      *ne'r wrong'd their Bretheren;*
*Who pleaded thus, Thou knowest us*
      *that we were blameless livers;*
*No Whoremongers, no Murderers,*
      *no quarrellers nor strivers.*

*Idolaters, Adulterers,*
      *Church-robbers we were none,*
*Nor false-dealers, no couzeners,*[1]
      *but paid each man his own.*
*Our way was fair, our dealing square,*
      *we were no wasteful spenders,*
*No lewd toss-pots*[2]*, no drunken sots,*
      *no scandalous offenders. . . .*

. . . . . . . . . . . . . . . . . . . . . . .

*Thus to obey, hath been our way;*
      *let our good deeds, we pray,*
*Find some regard and some reward*
      *with thee, O Lord, this day. . . .*

*Then answered unto their dread,*
      *the Judge: . . . .*

---

1. couzeners—swindlers
2. toss-pots—drunkards

. . . . . . . . . . . . . . . . . . . . . .

*However fair, however square,*
*        your way and work hath been,*
*Before mens eyes, yet God espies*
*        iniquity therein.*

*God looks upon th' affection*
*        and temper of the heart;*
*Not only on the action,*
*        and the external part.*
*Whatever end vain men pretend,*
*        God knows the verity;*
*And by the end which they intend*
*        their words and deeds doth try.*

. . . . . . . . . . . . . . . . . . . . . .

*Your argument shews your intent,*
*        in all that you have done:*
*You thought to scale Heav'ns lofty Wall*
*        by Ladders of your own.*

*Your blinded spirit, hoping to merit*
*        by your own Righteousness,*
*Needed no Saviour, but your behaviour,*
*        and blameless carriages;*
*You trusted to what you could do,*
*        and in no need you stood:*
*Your haughty pride laid me aside,*
*        and trampled on my Blood.*

. . . . . . . . . . . . . . . . . . . . . .

*Again you thought and mainly sought*
*        a name with men t'acquire;*
*Pride bare the Bell, that made you swell,*
*        and your own selves admire.*
*Mean fruit it is, and vile, I wiss,*
*        that springs from such a root:*
*Vertue divine and genuine*
*        wonts not from pride to shoot.*

*Such deeds as your are worse than poor;*
*        they are but sins guilt over*

*With silver dross, whose glistering gloss*
*can them no longer cover.*

. . . . . . . . . . . . . . . . . . . . . . . . .

*Your Gold is brass, your silver dross,*
*your righteousness is sin:*
*And think you by such honesty*
*eternal life to win?*
*You much mistake, if for its sake*
*you dream of acceptation;*
*Whereas the same deserveth shame,*
*and meriteth Damnation.*

. . . . . . . . . . . . . . . . . . . . . . . . .

*Then to the Bar, all they drew near*
*who dy'd in Infancy,*
*And never had or good or bad*
*effected pers'nally,*
*But from the womb unto the tomb*
*were straightway carried, . . .*
*who thus began to plead:*

. . . . . . . . . . . . . . . . . . . . . . . . .

*Not we, but he, ate of the Tree,*
*whose fruit was interdicted:[3]*
*Yet on us all of his sad Fall,*
*the punishment's inflicted.*
*How could we sin that had not been,*
*or how is his sin our,*
*Without consent, which to prevent,*
*we never had a pow'r?*

*O great Creator, why was our Nature*
*depraved and forlorn?*
*Why so defil'd, and made so vild*
*whilst we were yet unborn?*
*If it be just, and needs we must*
*transgressors reck'ned be,*
*Thy Mercy, Lord, to us afford,*
*which sinners hath set free.*

. . . . . . . . . . . . . . . . . . . . . . . . .

---

3. interdicted—forbidden

*Then answered the Judge most dread,*
    *God doth such doom forbid,*
*That men should dye eternally*
    *for what they never did.*
*But what you call old Adam's Fall,*
    *and only his Trespass,*
*You call amiss to call it his,*
    *both his and yours it was.*

*He was design'd of all Mankind*
    *to be a publick Head,*
*A common Root, whence all should shoot,*
    *and stood in all their stead.*
*He stood and fell, did ill or well,*
    *not for himself alone,*
*But for you all, who now his Fall,*
    *and Trespass would disown.*

. . . . . . . . . . . . . . . . . . . . . . . .

*Hence you were born in state forlorn,*
    *with Natures so depraved:*
*Death was your due, because that you*
    *had thus your selves behaved.*

. . . . . . . . . . . . . . . . . . . . . . . .

*Am I alone of what's my own,*
    *no Master or no Lord?*
*Or if I am, how can you claim*
    *what I to some afford?*
*Will you demand Grace at my hand,*
    *and challenge what is mine?*
*Will you teach me whom to set free,*
    *and thus my Grace confine?*

*You sinners are, and such a share*
    *as sinners may expect,*
*Such you shall have; for I do save*
    *none but mine own Elect.*
*Yet to compare your sin with their,*
    *who liv'd a longer time,*
*I do confess yours is much less,*
    *though every sin's a crime.*
*A crime it is, therefore in bliss*

*you may not hope to dwell;*
But unto you I shall allow
    *the easiest room in Hell.*
*The glorious King thus answering,*
    *they cease, and plead no longer:*
*Their Consciences must needs confess*
    *his Reasons are the stronger.*

*Thus all mens Pleas the Judge with ease*
    *doth answer and confute,*
*Until that all, both great and small,*
    *are silenced and mute.*
*Vain hopes are cropt,*[4] *all mouths are stopt,*
    *sinners have nought to say,*
*But that 'tis just, and equal most*
    *they should be damn'd for ay.*

. . . . . . . . . . . . . . . . . . . . . . . . .

---

4. cropt—cut short

# INTRODUCTION & QUESTIONS

## SELECTIONS FROM THE LAUUES AND LIBERTYES OF MASSACHUSETTS

*The Book of the General Lauues and Libertyes concerning the Inhabitants of the Massachusetts* was published in 1648. Various attempts were made previous to this to design an ideal legal code, both by ministers and laymen. This work of 1648 was the final product and included all legislation in effect in the colony as of that date. (The dates following each section indicate the date of the law's establishment.) You have here only representative selections from that work but more than enough to describe some of the major outlines of Puritan culture.

*The Lauues and Libertyes of Massachusetts* were arranged in alphabetical order. For this first of three assignments into the religion of the Puritan, you should read *only* the following sections of the *Lauues and Libertyes* which bear the headings which appear in quotation marks below.

### "TO OUR BELOVED BRETHREN AND NEIGHBORS"

1. From what sources do the Puritans derive their laws? How are they comparable to other national law codes?

2. What similarities do church and state in Massachusetts have? What relationship do they have to each other? How does this differ from previous arrangements?

### "ANA-BAPTISTS"

1. What specific ideas, if expressed publically, are here defined as illegal? What is the punishment for such offenses? Does this form of punishment suggest anything regarding the Puritans' ideas of community?

2. What are the most heinous activities indulged in by the Anabaptists? Which are the most dangerous, their theological speculations of their social and political ideas?

### "BURGLARIE AND THEFT"

1. How is "Burglarie" defined? What punishment is levied upon first offenders? Upon second offenders? Does the punishment appear to have more than one purpose? What is the presumption about individuals who

*THE*
BOOK OF THE GENERAL

# LAUUES AND LIBERTYES

CONCERNING THE INHABITANTS OF THE MASSACHUSETS

*COLLECTED OUT OF THE RECORDS OF THE GENERAL COURT*
*FOR THE SEVERAL YEARS WHERIN THEY WERE MADE*
*AND ESTABLISHED,*

And now revifed by the fame Court and difpofed into an Alphabetical order
and publifhed by the fame Authoritie in the General Court
held at *Bofton* the fourteenth of the
firft month *Anno*
1647.

---

*VVhofoever therefore refifteth the power, refifteth the ordinance of God,*
*and they that refift receive to themfelves damnation. Romanes 13.2.*

---

---

*CAMBRIDGE.*
Printed according to order of the *GENERAL COURT.*
1648.

---

And are to be folde at the fhop of *Hezekiah Ufher*
in *Bofton.*

commit a "like offence" a third time? Under what circumstances might different punishments be meted out?

## "CAPITAL LAWES"

1. What crimes are deemed punishable by death? What justification appears to be given for so designating a crime? Note the comparison between the length of this listing and the number of capital offenses in England, more than fifty in the seventeenth century and over one hundred in the eighteenth.

## "ECCLESIASTICALL"

1. Do churches in Massachusetts need any authorization from the state? What legal standards must they meet?

2. In what areas of concern do the churches have freedom from state control? In what ways are they limited in making decisions about such matters? How well-defined are the standards for setting these limits?

3. What arrangements are referred to that would tend to insure uniformity among the churches? How sure are these to achieve such uniformity?

4. What authority does a church have over political officials who are its members? What limits are there on this power?

5. What is the function of the "Assemblie"? What authority does it have to impose its decisions on its member churches and their members? What then is the relationship among the churches?

6. What is declared to be the "chief ordinary means" of acquiring salvation? By what authority does the minister execute his responsibility?

7. What actions may be taken by the government against those who disrupt religious services or falsely charge the ministers with errors? What appear to be the objectives of the punishments used?

8. What obligations to the churches are required of all members of the community? What agency ensures compliance with these regulations?

## "FORNICATION"

1. What are the critical determinants of crime under this provision? What kinds of punishment are prescribed? Who determines the punishment? What guide lines are used?

## "HERESIE"

1. How is "heresie" defined? What circumstances must exist for one to be charged under this statute? What responsibility does the state have in such cases? What is the nature of the punishment provided?

**"JESUITS"**

    1. What assumption is made about the Jesuits? What is the colony's policy regarding them? What punishment(s) befall(s) an individual discovered to be (or suspected of being) a Jesuit? Were any exceptions provided for?

**"MARRIAGE"**

    1. By the requirements of part four of this section, who is authorized to conduct marriages? How is this different from present American practice? What prerequisites for legal marriage are there? What purpose could these prerequisites have?

**"PROFANE SWEARING"**

    1. What appears to be the ultimate justification for this legislation? Who has the authority to impose penalties? What forms of punishment are authorized for such offenses?

# THE BOOK OF THE GENERAL LAUUES AND LIBERTYES CONCERNING THE INHABITANTS OF THE MASSACHUSETTS

**TO OUR BELOVED BRETHREN AND NEIGHBOURS THE INHABITANTS OF THE MASSACHUSETTS, THE GOVERNOUR, ASSISTANTS AND DEPUTIES ASSEMBLED IN THE GENERALL COURT OF THAT JURISDICTION WITH GRACE AND PEACE IN OUR LORD JESUS CHRIST.**

So soon as God had set up Politicall Government among his people Israel he gave them a body of laws for judgement both in civil and criminal causes. These were brief and fundamental principles, yet withall so full and comprehensive as out of them clear deductions were to be drawne to all particular cases in future times. For a Common-wealth without lawes is like a Ship without rigging and steerage. Nor is it sufficient to have principles or fundamentalls, but these are to be drawn out into so many of their deductions as the time and condition of that people may have use of. And it is very unsafe & injurious to the body of the people to put them to learn their duty and libertie from generall rules, nor is it enough to have lawes except they be also just. Therefore among other priviledges which the Lord bestowed upon his peculiar people, these he calls them specially to consider of, that God was neerer to them and their lawes were more righteous than other nations. God was sayd to be amongst them or neer to them because of his Ordnances established by himselfe, and their lawes righteous because himselfe was their Law-giver: yet in the comparison are implyed two things, first that other nations had somthing of Gods presence amongst them. Secondly that there was also somwhat of equitie in their lawes, for it pleased the Father (upon the Covenant of Redemption with his Son) to restore so much of his Image to lost man as whereby all nations are disposed to worship God, and to advance righteousnes: which appears in that of the Apostle *Rom.* 1.21.[1] They knew God etc: and in the 2.14. They did by nature the things conteined in the law of God. But the nations corrupting his Ordnances (both of Religion, and Justice) God withdrew his presence from them proportionably whereby they were given up to abominable lusts *Rom.* 2.21. Whereas if they had

---

1. *Rom.* 1.21—citations such as this refer to books, chapters and verses in the Bible. The reference here is to Romans, chapter I, verse 21.

walked according to that light & law of nature they might have been preserved from such moral evils and might have enjoyed a common blessing in all their natural and civil Ordinances: now, if it might have been so with the nations who were so much strangers to the Covenant of Grace, what advantage have they who have interest in this Covenant, and may injoye the special presence of God in the puritie and native simplicitie of all his Ordinances by which he is so neer to his owne people. This hath been no small priviledge, and advantage to us in New-England that our Churches, and civil State have been planted, and growne up (like two twinnes) together like that of Israel in the wildernes by which wee were put in minde (and had opportunitie put into our hands) not only to gather our Churches, and set up the Ordinances of Christ Jesus in them according to the Apostolick patterne[2] by such lights as the Lord graciously afforded us: but also withall to frame our civil Politie,[3] and lawes according to the rules of his most holy word whereby each do help and strengthen other (the Churches the civil Authoritie, and the civil Authoritie the Churches) and so both prosper the better without such aemulation,[4] and contention for priviledges or priority as have proved the misery (if not ruine) of both in some other places. . . .

## AGE

It is ordered by this Court & the Authoritie thereof, that the age for passing away of lands, or such kinde of hereditaments,[5] or for giving of votes, verdicts or sentences in any civil courts or causes, shal be twenty and one years: but in case of chusing of Guardions, fourteen years. [1641—1647]

## ANA-BAPTISTS[6]

Forasmuch as experience hath plentifully & often proved that since the first arising of the Ana-baptists about a hundred years past they have been the Incediaries of Common-wealths . . . & the Troublers of Churches in most places where they have been, . . . and wheras divers[7] of this kinde have since our coming into New-England appeared amongst our selvs. . . .

It is therfore ordered by this Court & Authoritie therof, that if any person or persons within this Jurisdiction shal either openly condemn or oppose the baptizing of Infants, or goe about secretly to seduce others from the approbation[8]

---

2. Apostolick patterne—the presumed pattern for the church established by Jesus' apostles.
3. civil Politie—the state.
4. aemulation—ambitious rivalry for power.
5. hereditaments—inheritances.
6. Ana-Baptists—a general name for those Protestant Christians who rejected infant baptism and were generally labeled heretics by most Protestants and Catholics alike.
7. divers—several.
8. approbation—approval, sanction.

or use therof, or shal purposely depart the Congregation at the administration of that Ordinance; or shal deny the Ordinance of Magistracy,[9] or their lawfull right or authoritie to make war, or to punish the outward breaches of the first Table,[10] and shal appear to the Court wilfully and obstinately to continue therein, after due meanes of conviction, everie such person or persons shal be sentenced to Banishment. . . . [1644]

## BAKERS

It is ordered by this Court and Authoritie therof, that henceforth every Baker shal have a distinct mark for his bread, & keep the true assizes[11] as heerafter is expressed *viz.* When wheat is ordinarily sold at these severall rates heerafter mentioned, the pennie white loaf by averdupois[12] weight shal weigh when wheat is by the bushell. . . .

| | The white | | wheaten | | household | |
|---|---|---|---|---|---|---|
| at 3 fs. 0d | 11 ounces | 1 qr. | 17 ounc. | 1 qr. | 23 ounc. | 0 |
| at 3 6 | 10 | 1 | 15 | 1 | 20 | 2. |
| at 4 0 | 09 | 1 | 14 | 0 | 18 | 2. |
| at 4 6 | 08 | 1 | 11 | 3 | 16 | 2. |
| at 5 0 | 07 | 3 | 11 | 2 | 15 | 2. |
| at 5 6 | 07 | 0 | 10 | 2 | 14 | 0. |
| at 6 0 | 06 | 2 | 10 | 0 | 13 | 0. |
| at 6 6 | 06 | 0 | 09 | 2 | 12 | 2. |

and so proportionably: under the penaltie of forfeiting all such bread as shal not be of the severall assizes as is aforementioned to the use of the poor of the towne where the offence is committed, and otherwise as is heerafter expressed: and for the better execution of this present Order; there shal be in everie market towne, and all other townes needfull, one or two able persons annually chosen by each town, who shal be sworn at the next county Court. or by the next Magistrate, unto the faithful discharge of his or their office; who are heerby authorized to enter into all houses, either with a Constable or without where they shal suspect or be informed of any bread baked for sale: & also to weigh the said bread as oft as they see cause: and to seize all such as they finde defective. As also to weigh all butter made up for sale; and bringing unto, or being in the towne or market to be solde by weight: which if found light after notice once given shal be forfeited in like manner. The like penaltie shal be for not marking

---

9. Ordinance of Magistracy—the authority of political officials.

10. first Table—the first four of the Ten Commandments, i.e. those inscribed on the two Tablets (Tables) of the Law.

11. assizes—regulated, fixed standards.

12. averdupois—English standard weight.

all bread made for sale, and the sayd officer shal have one third part of all forfeitures for his paines; the rest to the poor as aforesayd [1641]. . . .

## BOND-SLAVERY

It is ordered by this Court and authoritie thereof, that there shal never be any bond-slavery, villenage[13] or captivitie amongst us; unlesse it be lawfull captives, taken in just warrs, and such strangers as willingly sell themselves, or are solde to us: and such shal have the libertyes and christian usages, which the law of God established in Israel concerning such persons doth morally require, provided, this exempts none from servitude who shal be judged thereto by Authoritie. . . . (1641)

## BURGLARIE AND THEFT

Forasmuch as many persons of late years have been, and are apt to be injurious to the goods and lives of others, notwithstanding all care and meanes to prevent and punish the same;—

It is therefore ordered by this Court and Authoritie therof that if any person shal commit Burglarie by breaking up any dwelling house, or shal rob any person in the field, or high wayes; such a person so offending shal for the first offence be branded on the forehead with the letter (B) If he shal offend in the same kinde the second time, he shal be branded as before and also be severally whipped: and if he shal fall into the like offence the third time he shal be put to death, as being incorrigible. And if any person shal commit such Burglarie, or rob in the fields or house on the Lords day besides the former punishments, he shal for the first offence have one of his ears cut off. And for the second offence in the same kinde he shal loose his other ear in the same manner. And if he fall into the same offence a third time he shal be put to death if it appear to the Court he did it presumptuously [1642–1647]. . . .

## CAPITAL LAWES

1. If any man after legal conviction shal HAVE OR WORSHIP any other God, but the LORD GOD: he shal be put to death. *Exod.* 22.20. *Deut.* 13.6. & 10. *Deut.* 17. 2.6.

2. If any man or woman be a WITCH, that is, hath or consulteth with a familiar spirit,[14] they shal be put to death. *Exod.* 22.18. *Levit.* 20.27. *Deut.* 18.10.11.

3. If any person within this Jurisdiction whether Christian or Pagan shal wittingly and willingly presume to BLASPHEME the holy Name of God, Father, Son or Holy-Ghost, with direct, expresse, presumptuous, or high-

---

13. villenage—serfdom, tenure of land by bond-service rendered to a superior.
14. familiar spirit—a demon supposed to be under an individual's power.

handed blasphemy, either by wilfull or obstinate denying the true God, or his Creation, or Government of the world: or shal curse God in like manner, or reproach the holy Religion of God as if it were but a politick device to keep ignorant men in awe; or shal utter any other kinde of Blasphemy of the like nature & degree they shal be put to death. *Levit.* 24. 15. 16.

4. If any person shal commit any wilfull MURTHER, which is Man slaughter, committed upon premeditate malice, hatred, or crueltie not in a mans necessary and just defence, nor by meer casualty against his will, he shal be put to death. *Exod.* 21. 12. 13. *Numb.* 35. 31.

5. If any person slayeth another suddenly in his ANGER, or CRUELTY of passion, he shal be put to death. *Levit.* 24. 17. *Numb.* 35. 20. 21.

6. If any person shal slay another through guile, either by POYSONING, or other such devilish practice, he shal be put to death. *Exod.* 21. 14.

7. If any man or woman shal LYE WITH ANY BEAST, or bruit creature, by carnall copulation;they shal surely be put to death: and the beast shal be slain, & buried, and not eaten. *Lev.* 20. 15. 16.

8. If any man LYETH WITH MAN-KINDE, as he lieth with a woman, both of them have committed abomination, they both shal surely be put to death: unless the one partie were forced (or be under fourteen years of age in which case he shal be severely punished) *Levit.* 20. 13.

9. If any person commit ADULTERIE with a married, or espoused wife; the Adulterer & Adulteresse shal surely be put to death. *Lev.* 20. 19. & 18. 20. *Deu.* 22. 23. 27.

10. If any man STEALETH A MAN, or Man-kinde, he shal surely be put to death. *Exodus* 21. 16.

11. If any man rise up by FALSE-WITNES wittingly, and of purpose to take away any mans life: he shal be put to death. *Deut.* 19. 16. 18. 16.

12. If any man shal CONSPIRE, and attempt any Invasion, Insurrection, or publick Rebellion against our Common-Wealth: or shal indeavour to surprize any Town, or Townes, Fort, or Forts therein; or shal treacherously, & perfidiously attempt the Alteration and Subversion of our frame of Politie, or Government fundamentally he shal be put to death. *Numb.* 16 2 Sam. 3. 2 Sam. 18. 2 Sam. 20.

13. If any child, or children, above sixteen years old, and of sufficient understanding, shal CURSE, or SMITE their natural FATHER, or MOTHER; he or they shal be put to death: unless it can be sufficiently testified that the Parents have been very unchristianly negligent in the education of such

children; or so provoked them by extream, and cruel correction; that they have been forced therunto to preserve themselves from death or maiming. *Exod*. 21. 17. *Lev*. 20. 9. *Exod*. 21. 15.

14.  If a man have a stubborn or REBELLIOUS SON, of sufficient years & under-standing (*viz*) sixteen years of age, which will not obey the voice of his Father, or the voice of his Mother, and that when they have chastened him will not harken unto them: then shal his Father and Mother being his natural parents, lay hold on him, & bring him to the Magistrates assembled in Court & testifie unto them, that their Son is stubborn & rebellious & will not obey their voice and chastisement, but lives in sundry notorious crimes, such a son shal be put to death. *Deut*. 21. 20. 21.

15.  If any man shal RAVISH any maid or single woman, committing carnal copulation with her by force, against her own will; that is above the age of ten years he shal be punished either with death, or with some other greivous punishment according to circumstances as the Judges, or General court shal determin [1641]. . . .

## CATTEL. CORN-FIELDS. FENCES

1.  It is ordered by this Court and authoritie thereof, That in all corn-fields, which are inclosed in common: everie partie interested therein, shal from time to time make good his part of the fence, and shal not put in any cattel, so long as any corn shal be upon any part of it, upon payn to answer all the damage which shal come thereby. [1647]

2.  Wheras it is found by experience that there hath been much trouble & differ-ence in severall townes, about the fencing, planting, sowing, feeding & ordering of common fields, It is therfore ordered by this Court & authoritie thereof, that where the occupiers of the land, or of the greatest part thereof cannot agree about the fencing or improvment of such their said fields, that then the Select men[15] in the several towns shal order the same, or in case where no such are, then the major part of the Freemen (with what convenient speed they may) shal determin any such difference, as may arise upon any information given them by the said occupiers[1643–1647]shal . . .

3.  Whereas this Court hath long since provided that all men shal fence their corn, meadow ground and such like against great[16] cattle, to the end the increase of cattle especially of cowes and their breed should not be hindred, there being then but few horses in the countrie, which since are much increased, many wherof run in a sort wilde,[17] doing much damage in corn

---

15. Select men—a board of elected town officials who execute the orders of the town meeting.
16. great—pregnant.

and other things, notwithstanding fences made up according to the true intent of the order in that case established: many wherof are unknown, most so unruly that they can by no means be caught, or got into custodie, wherby their owners might answer damages: & if sometimes with much difficultie and charge they be; they are in danger of perishing before the owner appears or can be found out: all which to prevent,

It is ordered by this Court & authoritie therof; That everie towne and peculiar[18] in this Jurisdiction, shal henceforth give some distinct Brand-mark appointed by this court (a coppie of which marks each Clerk of writs in everie town shal keep a record of) upon the horn, or left buttock or shoulder of all their cattle which feed in open common without constant keepers, wherby it may be known to what town they doe belong. And if any trespasse not so marked they shal pay double damages: nor shal any person knowing, or after due notice given of any beast of his to be unruly in respect of fences, suffer him or them to go in common or against corn fields, or other impropriate inclosed grounds fenced as aforesaid, without such shackles or fetters, as may restrein and prevent trespasse therin by them from time to time. And if any horse or other beast trespasse in corn, or other inclosure being fenced in such sort as secures against cows, oxen and such like orderly cattel: the partie or parties trespassed shal procure two sufficient Inhabitants of that town, of good repute and credit to view and adjudge the harms, which the owner of the beast shal satisfie, when known, upon reasonable demand, whether the beast were impounded or not. But if the owner be known, or neer residing as in the same town or the like, he shal forthwith have notice of the trespasse and damage charged upon him, that if he approve not therof he may nominate one such man, who with one such other chosen by the partie damnified as aforesaid, shal review & adjudge the said harms, provided they agree of damage within one day after due notice given, & that no after harms intervene to hinder it. Which being forthwith discharged, together with the charge of the notice, former view and determination of damages, the first judgement shal be void, or else to stand good in law. And if any cattle be found damage faisant,[19] the partie damnified may impound or keep them in his own private close, or yard till he may give notice to the owner, and if they cannot agree, the owner may replevie[20] them, or the other partie may return them to the owner & take his remedie according to law [1647]. . . .

---

17. in a sort wilde—in a wild state.
18. peculiar—private property not part of a township.
19. damage faisant—doing damage.
20. replevie—to repossess goods taken from a person until the courts decide the case.

**CHARGES PUBLICK**

1. It is ordered by this Court that no Governour, Deputy Govern, Assistant, Associate, Grand, or Petty Jurie-man, at any court; nor any Deputie for the General court, nor any Comissioner for martial disciplin at the time of their publick meetings; shal at any time bear his own charges: but their necessary expences shal be defrayed either by the town, or the Shire[21] on whose service they are, or by the Country in generall. [1634–1641]

2. It is ordered by this Court that in all ordinary publick works of the Common-weal, one Assistant and the Overseer of the work shal have power to send their warrants to the Constables of the next towns to send so many labourers & artificers[22] as the warrant shal direct, which the Constable and two other or more of the Freemen which he shal take to himselfe shal forthwith execute: for which service such Assistant and Overseer aforesaid shal have power to give such extraordinary wages as they shal judge the work to deserve. Provided that for any ordinary work no man shal be compelled to work from home above a week together. And for all extraordinarie publick works it is ordered that one Assistant & the Overseer of the said work shal have power to send their warrants to the Constable of any town for so many men of any condition except Magistrates & Officers of Churches and Common-wealth, as the warrant shal direct, which the Constable & two or more that he shal chuse shal forthwith send: to advise & attend the same. [1634]

3. This Court taking into consideration the necessity of an equal contribution to all common charges in towns, and observing that the cheif occasion of the defect heerin ariseth from hence, that many of those who are not Freemen, nor members of any Church doe take advantage therby to withdraw their help in such voluntary contributions as are in use.

It is therfore ordered by this Court and Authoritie therof, That everie Inhabitant shal henceforth contribute to all charges both in Church & Commonwealth wherof he doth or may receive benefit: and every such Inhabitant who shal not voluntarily contribute proportionably to his ability with the Freemen of the same town to all comon charges both civil and ecclesiastical shal be compelled thereto by assessment & distresse[23] to be levied by the Constable or other Officer of the town as in other cases: and that the lands & estates of all men (wherever they dwell) shal be rated for all town charges both civil and ecclesiasticall as aforesaid where the lands and estates shal lye. . . . [1638, 1643, 1644]. . . .

---

21. Shire—county.
22. artificers—skilled workers
23. distresse—constraint, force.

## CHILDREN

For asmuch as the good education of children is of singular . . . benefit to any Common-wealth; and whereas many parents & masters are too indulgent and negligent of their duty in that kinde. It is therfore ordered that the Select men of everie town . . . shal have a vigilant eye over their brethren & neighbours, to see, first that none of them shal suffer so much barbarism in any of their families as not to indeavour to teach by themselves or others, their children & apprentices so much learning as may inable them perfectly to read the english-tongue, & knowledge of the Capital lawes: upon penaltie of twentie shillings for each neglect therin. Also that all masters of families doe once a week (at the least) catechize[24] their children and servants in the grounds & principles of Religion, & if any be unable to doe so much: that then at the least they procure such children or apprentices to learn some short orthodox catechism without book, that they may be able to answer unto the questions that shal be propounded to them out of such catechism by their parents or masters or any of the Select men when they shal call them to a tryall of what they have learned in this kinde. And further that all parents and masters do breed & bring up their children & apprentices in some honest lawful calling, labour or imployment, either in husbandry,[25] or some other trade profitable for themselves, and the Common-wealth if they will not or cannot train them up in learning to fit them for higher imployments. And if any of the Select men after admonition by them given to such masters of families shal finde them still negligent of their dutie in the particulars aforementioned, wherby children and servants become rude, stubborn & unruly; the said Select men with the help of two Magistrates, or the next County court for that Shire, shal take such children or apprentices from them & place them with some masters for years (boyes till they come to twenty one, and girls eighteen years of age compleat) which will more strictly look unto, and force them to submit unto government according to the rules of this order, if by fair means and former instructions they will not be drawn unto it.[1642]

## COLLEDGE

Wheras through the good hand of God upon us there is a Colledge founded in Cambridge in the County of Midlesex called Harvard College, for incouragement wherof this Court hath given the summe of four hundred pounds and also the revenue of the Ferrie betwixt Charlstown and Boston and that the well ordering and mannaging of the said Colledge is of great concernment,

It is therfore ordered by this Court and Authoritie therof, That the Governour & Deputie Govern: for the time being and all the Magistrates of this Jurisdiction together with the teaching Elders[26] of the six next adjoyning towns *viz:*

---

24. catechize—to give religious instruction by means of responding to questions in a catechism, a book summarizing religious doctrines.

25. husbandry—the cultivation of plants and animals.

Cambridge, Water-town, Charlstown, Boston, Roxburie and Dorchester, & the President of the said Colledge for the time being, shal from time to time have full power & authoritie to make and establish all such orders, statutes and constitutions, as they shal see necessary for the instituting, guiding and furthering of the said Colledge, and several members therof, from time to time, in Pietie, Moralitie & Learning, as also to dispose, order and manage to the use and behoof[27] of the said Colledge and members therof, all gifts, legacyes, bequeaths, revenues, lands and donations as either have been, are, or shal be conferred, bestowed, or any wayes shal fall or come to the sayd Colledge. . . . [1636, 1640, 1642]. . . .

## ECCLESIASTICALL

1. All the people of God within this Jurisdiction who are not in a Church way and be orthodox in judgement and not scandalous in life shal have full libertie to gather themselves into a Church estate, provided they doe it in a christian way with due observation of the rules of Christ revealed in his word. Provided also that the General Court doth not, nor will heerafter approve of any such companyes of men as shal joyne in any pretended way of Church fellowship unles they shal acquaint the Magistrates and the Elders of the neighbour Churches where they intend to joyn, & have their approbation[28] therin.

2. And it is farther ordered, that no person being a member of any Church which shal be gathered without the approbation of the Magistrates and the said Churches shal be admitted to the Freedom[29] of this Common-wealth.

3. Everie Church hath free liberty to exercise all the Ordinances of God according to the rules of the Scripture.

4. Everie Church hath free libertie of election and ordination of all her Officers from time to time. Provided they be able, pious and orthodox.

5. Everie Church hath also free libertie of admission, recommendation, dismission & expulsion or desposall of their Officers and members upon due cause, with free exercise of the disciplin and censures of Christ according to the rules of his word.

6. No injunction shal be put upon any Church, church Officer or member in point of doctrine, worship or disciplin, whether for substance or circumstance besides the institutions of the Lord.

---

26. teaching Elders—ministers.
27. behoof—advantage, profit.
28. approbation—approval.
29. Freedom—citizenship, political privileges.

7. Everie Church of Christ hath freedom to celebrate dayes of Fasting and prayer and of Thanksgiving according to the word of God.

8. The Elders of churches also have libertie to meet monthly, quarterly or otherwise in convenient numbers and places, for conference and consultations about christian and church questions and occasions.

9. All Churches also have libertie to deal with any their members in a church way that are in the hands of justice, so it be not to retard and hinder the course thereof.

10. Everie Church hath libertie to deal with any Magistrate, Deputy of court, or other Officer whatsoever that is a member of theirs, in a church way in case of apparent and just offence ... so it be done with due observance and respect.

11. Wee also allow private meetings for edification in Religion amongst christians of all sorts of people so it be without just offence, both for number, time, place and other circumstances.

12. For the preventing and removing of errour and offence that may grow and spread in any of the Churches in this Jurisdiction, and for the preserving of truth & peace in the severall Churches within themselves, and for the maintainance and exercise of brotherly communion amongst all the Churches in the country.

    It is allowed and ratified by the authoritie of this Court, as a lawfull libertie of the Churches of Christ, that once in every month of the year (when the season will bear it) it shal be lawfull for the Ministers and Elders of the Churches neer adjoyning, together with any other of the Brethren, with the consent of the Churches, to assemble by course in everie several church one after another, to the intent, that after the preaching of the word, by such a Minister as shal be requested therto, by the Elders of the Church where the Assembly is held, the rest of the day may be spent in publick christian conference, about the discussing and resolving of any such doubts & cases of conscience concerning matter of doctrine, or worship, or government of the Church as shal be propounded by any of the Brethren of that Church; with leave also to any other Brother to propound his objections, or answers, for further satisfaction according to the word of God. Provided that the whole action be guided and moderated by the Elders of the Church where the Assembly is held, or by such others as they shal appoint. And that nothing be concluded & imposed by way of Authoritie from one, or more Churches, upon another, but only by way of brotherly conference & consultations, that the truth may be searched out to the satisfying of every mans conscience in the sight of God according to his word. And because such an Assemblie and the work therof cannot be duly attended if other Lectures be held the same week, it is therfore agreed with the consent of the Churches, that in what week such an Assembly is held all the Lectures in all the neighbouring Churches for the week dayes shal be forborne, that so the publick service of Christ in this Assembly may be transacted with greater diligence & attention. [1641]

13. Forasmuch as the open contempt of Gods word and Messengers therof is the desolating sinne of civil States and Churches and that the preaching of the word by those whom God doth send, is the chief ordinary means ordained of God for the converting, edifying and saving the soules of the Elect through the presence and power of the Holy-Ghost, therunto promised: and that the ministry of the word, is set up by God in his Churches, for those holy ends; . . . . it is therfore ordered and decreed,

That if any christian (so called) within this Jurisdiction shal contemptuously behave himselfe toward the Word preached or the Messengers therof called to dispense the same in any Congregation; when he doth faithfully execute his Service and Office therin, according to the will and word of God, either by interrupting him in his preaching, or by charging him falsely with any errour which he hath not taught in the open face of the Church: or like a son of Korah[30] cast upon his true doctrine or himselfe any reproach, to the dishonour of the Lord Jesus who hath sent him and to the disparagement of that his holy Ordinance, and making Gods wayes contemptible and ridiculous: that everie such person or persons . . . shal for the first scandall be convented and reproved openly by the Magistrate at some Lecture, and bound to their good behavior. And if a second time they break forth into the like contemptuous carriages, they shal either pay five pounds to the publick Treasurie; or stand two hours openly upon a block or stool, four foot high on a lecture day with a paper fixed on his breast, written in Capital letters [AN OPEN AND OBSTINATE CONTEMNER OF GODS HOLY ORDINANCES] that others may fear and be ashamed of breaking out into the like wickednes. [1646]

14. It is ordered and decreed by this Court and Authoritie therof; that wheresoever the ministry of the word is established according to the order of the Gospell throughout this Jurisdiction every person shal duly resort and attend therunto respectively upon the Lords days & upon such publick Fast dayes, and dayes of Thanksgiving as are to be generally kept by the appointment of Authoritie: & if any person within this Jurisdiction shal without just and necessarie cause withdraw himselfe from hearing the publick ministry of the word after due meanes of conviction used, he shal forfeit for his absence from everie such publick meeting five shillings. All such offences to be heard and determined by any one Magistrate or more from time to time. [1646]

---

30. Korah—Biblical leader of an unsuccessful rebellion against the leadership of Moses and Aaron, later swallowed up by a providential earthquake (*Numbs.* 16, 17).

15. Forasmuch as the peace and prosperity of Churches and members therof as well as civil Rights & Liberties are carefully to be maintained, it is ordered by this Court & decreed, That the civil Authoritie heer established hath power and liberty to see the peace, ordinances and rules of Christ be observed in everie Church according to his word. As also to deal with any church-member in a way of civil justice notwithstanding any church relation, office, or interest; so it be done in a civil and not in an ecclesiastical way. Nor shal any church censure degrade or depose any men from any civil dignity, office or authoritie he shal have in the Common-wealth. (1641). . . .

## FORNICATION

It is ordered by this Court and Authoritie therof, That if any man shal commit Fornication with any single woman, they shal be punished either by enjoyning to Marriage, or Fine, or corporall punishment, or all or any of these as the Judges in the courts of Assistants shal appoint most agreeable to the word of God. And this Order to continue till the Court take further order. [1642]

## FREEMEN, NON-FREEMEN

Wheras there are within this Jurisdiction many members of Churches who to exempt themselves from all publick service in the Common-wealth will not come in, to be made Freemen, it is therfore ordered by this Court and the Authoritie thereof,

That all such members of Churches in the severall towns within this Jurisdiction shal not be exempted from such public service as they are from time to time chosen to by the Freemen of the severall towns; as Constables, Jurors, Select-men and Surveyors of high-wayes. And if any such person shal refuse to serve in, or take upon him any such Office being legally chosen therunto, he shal pay for every such refusall such Fine as the town shal impose, not exceeding twenty shillings as Freemen are lyable to in such cases. [1647]

## FUGITIVES, STRANGERS

It is ordered by this Court and Authoritie therof, That if any people of other nations professing the true Christian Religion shal flee to us from the tyranie or oppression of their persecutors, or from Famine, Wars, or the like necessarie and compulsarie cause, they shal be entertained and succoured amongst us according to that power and prudence God shal give us. [1641]

## GAMING

Upon complaint of great disorder by the use of the game called *Shuffle-board*, in houses of common entertainment, wherby much pretious time is spent unfruitfully and much wast of wine and beer occasioned, it is therfore ordered and enacted by the Authoritie of this Court;

That no person shal henceforth use the said game of Shuffle-board in any such house, nor in any other house used as common for such purpose, upon payn for every Keeper of such house to forfeit for every such offence twenty shillings: and for every person playing at the said game in any such house, to forfeit for everie such offence five shillings: Nor shal any person at any time play or game for any monie, or mony-worth upon penalty of forfeiting treble the value therof: one half to the partie informing, the other half to the Treasurie. And any Magistrate may hear and determin any offence against this Law (1646 1647). . . .

## HERESIE

Although no humane power be Lord over the Faith & Consciences of men, and therfore may not constrein them to beleive or professe against their Consciences: yet because such as bring in damnable heresies, tending to the subversion of the Christian Faith, and destruction of the soules of men, ought duly to be restreined from such notorius impiety, it is therfore ordered and decreed by this Court;

That if any Christian within this Jurisdiction shal go about to subvert and destroy the christian Faith and Religion, by broaching or mainteining any damnable heresie; as denying the immortalitie of the Soul, or the resurrection of the body, or any sin to be repented of in the Regenerate . . . or denying that Christ gave himself a Ransom for our sins, or shal affirm that wee are not justi-fied by his Death and Righteousnes, but by the perfection of our own works; or shal deny the moralitie of the fourth commandement, or shal indeavour to seduce others to any the herisies aforementioned, everie such person continuing obstinate therin after due means of conviction shal be sentenced to Banishment. [1646]

## IDLENES

It is ordered by this Court and Authoritie therof, that no person, Housholder or other shal spend his time idlely or unproffitably under pain of such punish-ment as the Court of Assistants or County Court shal . . . inflict. And for this end it is ordered that the Constable of everie place shal use speciall care and diligence to take knowledge of offenders in this kinde, especially of common coasters, unproffitable fowlers and tobacco takers,[31] and present the same unto the two next Assistants, who shal have power to hear and determin the case, or transfer it to the next Court. [1633]. . . .

---

31. common coasters, unproffitable fowlers and tobacco takers—these references to ordi-nary tobagganists, amateur hunters and smokers indicate the Puritans' idea of the kind of worthless activities promoted by leisure.

## INDIANS

1. It is ordered by Authoritie of this Court; that no person whatsoever shal henceforth buy land of any Indian, without licence first had & obtained of the General Court: and if any shal offend heerin, such land so bought shal be forfeited to the Countrie.

   Nor shal any man within this Jurisdiction directly or indirectly amend, repair, or cause to be amended or repaired any gun, small or great, belonging to any Indian. . . . Nor shal sell or give to any Indian, directly or indirectly anysuch gun, or any gun-powder, shot or lead, or shot-mould, or any militarie weapons or armour: upon payn of ten pounds fine, at the least for everie such offence: and that the court of Assistants shal have power to increase the Fine; or to impose corporall punishment (where a Fine cannot be had) at their discretion.

   It is also ordered by the Authoritie aforesaid that everie town shal have power to restrein all Indians from profaning the Lords day. [1633, 1637, 1641]

2. Wheras it appeareth to this Court that notwithstanding the former Laws, made against selling of guns, powder and Amunition to the Indians, they are yet supplyed by indirect means, it is therfore ordered by this Court and Authoritie therof;

   That if any person after publication heerof, shal sell, give or barter any gun or guns, powder, bullets, shot or lead to any Indian whatsoever, or unto any person inhabiting out of this Jurisdiction without licence of this Court, or the court of Assistants, or some two Magistrates, he shal forfeit for everie gun so sold, given or bartered ten pounds: and for everie pound of powder five pounds: and for everie pound of bullets, shot or lead fourty shillings: and so proportionably for any greater or lesser quantitie. [1642]

3. It is ordered by this Court and Authoritie therof, that in all places, the English and such others as co-inhabit within our Jurisdiction shal keep their cattle from destroying the Indians corn, in any ground where they have right to plant; and if any of their corn be destroyed for want of fencing, or hearding; the town shal make satisfaction, and shal have power among themselves to lay the charge where the occasion of the damage did arise. Provided that the Indians shal make proof that the cattle of such a town, farm, or person did the damage. And for encouragement of the Indians toward the fencing in of their corn fields, such towns, farms or persons, whose cattle may annoy them that way, shal direct, assist and help them in felling of trees, ryving,[32] and sharpening of rayls, & holding of posts: allowing one English-man to three or more Indians. And shal also draw the fencing into place for them, and allow one man a day or two toward the setting up the same, and either lend or sell them tools to finish it. Provided

---

32. ryving—riving, splitting.

that such Indians, to whom the Countrie, or any town hath given, or shal give ground to plant upon, or that shal purchase ground of the English shal fence such their corn fields or ground at their own charge as the English doe or should doe; and if any Indians refuse to fence their corn ground (being tendred help as aforesaid) in the presence and hearing of any Magistrate or selected Townsmen being met together they shal keep off all cattle or lose one half of their damages.

And it is also ordered that if any harm be done at any time by the Indians unto the English in their cattle; the Governour or Deputie Governour with two of the Assistants or any three Magistrates or any County Court may order satisfaction according to law and justice. [1640, 1648]

4. Considering that one end in planting these parts was to propagate the true Religion unto the Indians: and that divers of them are become subjects to the English and have ingaged themselves to be willing and ready to understand the Law of God, it is therfore ordered and decreed,

That such necessary and wholsom Laws, which are in force, and may be made from time to time, to reduce them to civilitie of life shal be once in the year (if the times be safe) made known to them, by such fit persons as the General Court shal nominate, having the help of some able Interpreter with them.

Considering also that interpretation of tongues is appointed of God for propagating the Truth: and may therfore have a blessed successe in the hearts of others in due season, it is therfore farther ordered and decreed,
That two Ministers shal be chosen by the Elders of the Churches everie year ... and so be sent with the consent of their Churches (with whomso-ever will freely offer themselves to accompany them in that service) to make known the heavenly counsell of God among the Indians in most familiar manner, by the help of some able Interpreter; as may be most available to bring them unto the knowledge of the truth, and their conversation to the Rules of Jesus Christ. And for that end that somthing be allowed them by the General Court, to give away freely unto those Indians whom they shal perceive most willing & ready to be instructed by them.

And it is farther ordered and decreed by this Court; that no Indian shal at any time *powaw*, , or performe outward worship to their false gods: or to the devil in any part of our Jurisdiction; whether they be such as shal dwell heer, or shal come hither: and if any shal transgresse this Law, the *Powawer* shal pay five pounds; the Procurer five pounds; and every other countenancing by his presence or otherwise being of age of discretion twenty shillings. [1646]. . . .

## JESUITS[33]

This Court taking into consideration the great wars, combustions and divisions which are this day in Europe: and that the same are observed to be raysed and formented chiefly by the secret underminings, and solicitations of those of the Jesuiticall Order, men brought up and devoted to the religion and court of Rome; which hath occasioned divers States to expell them their territories; for prevention wherof among ourselves, It is ordered and enacted by Authoritie of this Court, That no Jesuit, or spiritual or ecclesiastical person (as they are termed) ordained by the authoritie of the Pope . . . shal henceforth at any time repair to, or come within this Jurisdiction: And if any person shal give just cause of suspicion that he is one of such Societie or Order he shal be brought before some of the Magistrates, and if he cannot free himselfe of such suspicion he shal be committed to prison, or bound over to the next Court of Assistants, to be tryed and proceeded with by Banishment or otherwise as the Court shal see cause: and if any person so banished shal be taken the second time within this Jurisdiction upon lawfull tryall and conviction he shal be put to death. Provided this Law shal not extend to any such Jesuit, spiritual or ecclesiasticall person as shal be cast upon our shoars, by ship-wrack or other accident, so as he continue no longer then till he may have opportunitie of passage for his departure; nor to any such as shal come in company with any Messenger hither upon publick occasions, or any Merchant or Master of any ship, belonging to any place not in emnitie with the State of England, or our selves, so as they depart again with the same Messenger, Master or Merchant, and behave themselves inoffensively during their aboard heer [1647]. . . .

## MARRIAGE

1. For preventing all unlawfull marriages, it is ordered by this Court and Authoritie therof,

      That after due publication heerof no persons shal be joyned in marriage before the intention of the parties proceeding therin hath been three times published at some time of publick Lecture or Town-meeting, in both the towns where the parties or either of them doe ordinarily reside; or be set up in writing upon some post of their Meeting-house door in publick view, there to stand so as it may easily be read by the space of fourteen dayes. [1639]

2. And wheras God hath committed the care and power into the hands of Parents for the disposing their Children in marriage: so that it is against Rule to seek to draw away the affections of young maidens under pretence of purpose of marriage before their Parents have given way and allowance in that respect. And wheras it is a common practice in divers places for young men irregularly and disorderly to watch all advantages for their evil purposes to insinuate into the affections of young maidens, by coming to

33. Jesuits—members of the Society of Jesus, a Roman Catholic religious order charged with defending the papacy and Catholic dogma as well as undertaking missionary work among non-Catholics.

them in places, and seasons unknown to their Parents, for such ends; wherby much evil hath grown amongst us to the dishonour of God and damage of parties, for prevention wherof for time to come it is farther ordered by Authoritie of this Court,

That whatsoever person from henceforth shal indeavour directly, or indirectly to draw away the affections of any maid in this Jurisdiction under pretence of marriage, before he hath obtained libertie and allowance from her Parents or Governours (or in absence of such) of the neerest Magistrate; he shal forfeit for the first offence five pounds, for the second offence toward the same partie ten pounds, and be bound to forbear any farther attempt. . . . And for the third offence upon information, or complaint by such Parents or Governours to any Magistrate . . . he shal be committed to prison, and upon hearing and conviction by the next Court shal be adjudged to continue in prison untill the Court of Assistants shal see cause to release him [1647]. . . .

4. As the Ordinance of Marriage is honourable amongst all so should it be accordingly solemnized. It is therfore ordered by this Court and Authoritie therof;

That no person whatsoever in this Jurisdiction shal joyn any persons together in Marriage but the Magistrate, or such other as the General Court, or Court of Assistants shal authorize in such places where no Magistrate is neer. Nor shal any joyn themselves in Marriage but before some Magistrate, or person authorized as aforesaid. Nor shal any Magistrate, or other person authorized as aforesaid joyn any persons together in Marriage, or suffer them to joyn together in Marriage in their presence before the parties to be married have been published according to Law [1648]. . . .

## MASTERS, SERVANTS, LABOURERS

1. It is ordered by this Court and the Authoritie therof, that no servant, either man or maid shal either give, sell or *truck* any commoditie whatsoever without licence from their Masters, during the time of their service under pain of Fine, or corporal punishment at the discretion of the Court as the offence shal deserve.

2. And that all workmen shal work the whole day allowing convenient time for food and rest.

3. It is also ordered that when any servants shal run from their masters, or any other Inhabitants shal privily[34] goe away with suspicion of ill intentions, it shal be lawfull for the next Magistrate, or the Constable and two of the chief Inhabitants where no Magistrate is to presse men and boats or pinnaces[35] at

---

34. privily—stealthily, not openly or publicly.

the publick charge to pursue such persons by Sea or Land and bring them back by force of Arms.

4. It is also ordered by the Authoritie aforesaid, that the Free-men of everie town may from time to time as occasion shal require agree amongst themselves about the prizes, and rates of all workmens labours and servants wages. And everie person inhabiting in any town, whether workman, labourer or servant shal be bound to the same rates which the said Freemen, or the greater part shal binde themselves unto: and whosoever shal exceed those rates so agreed shal be punished by the discretion of the Court . . . according to the qualitie and measure of the offence. And if any town shal have cause of complaint against the Freemen of any other town for allowing greater rates, or wages than themselves, the Quarter Court . . . shal from time to time set order therin.

5. And for servants and workmens wages, it is ordered, that they may be paid in corn, to be valued by two indifferent Freemen, chosen the one by the Master, the other by the servant or workman, who also are to have respect to the value of the work or service, and if they cannot agree then a third man shal be chosen by the next Magistrate, or if no Magistrate be in the town  then by the next Constable, unles the parties agree the price themselves. Provided if any servant or workman agree for any particular payment, then to be payd *in specie*, or consideration for default therin. And for all other payments in corn, if the parties cannot agree they shal choos two indifferent men, and if they cannot agree then a third as before.

6. It is ordered, and by this Court declared, that if any servant shal flee from the tyrannie and crueltie of his, or her Master to the house of any Freeman of the same town, they shal be there protected and susteined till due order be taken for their releif. Provided due notice therof be speedily given to their Master from whom they fled, and to the next Magistrate or Constable where the partie so fled is harboured.

7. Also that no servant shal be put off for above a year to any other, neither in the life time of their Master, nor after their death by their Executors or Administrators, unles it be by consent of Authorite assembled in some Court, or two Assistants: otherwise all, and everie such Assignment to be void in Law.

8. And that if any man smite out the eye, or tooth of his man-servant, or maid-servant; or otherwise maim, or much disfigure them (unless it be by meer casualtie) he shal let them goe free from his service, and shal allow such farther recompence as the Court shal adjudge him.

---

35. pinnaces—small vessels.

9. And all servants that have served diligently and faithfully to the benefit of their Masters seven years shal not be sent away emptie: and if any have been unfaithfull, negligent, or unprofitable in their service, notwithstanding the good usage of their Masters, they shal not be dismissed till they have made satisfaction according to the judgement of Authoritie. [1630, 1633, 1635, 1636, 1641]. . . .

## MONOPOLIES

*no one should get wealthyer at the Community*

It is ordered, decreed and by this Court declared; that there shal be no Monopolies graunted or allowed amongst us, but of such new inventions that are profitable for the Countrie, and that for a short time. [1641]

*Publie well being Comes first*

## PROFANE SWEARING

It is ordered, and by this Court decreed, that if any person within this Jurisdiction shal swear rashly and vainly either by the holy Name of God, or any other oath, he shal forfeit to the common Treasurie for everie such severall offence ten shillings. And it shal be in the power of any Magistrate by Warrant to the Constable to call such person before him, and upon sufficient proof to passe sentence, and levie the said penaltie according to the usuall order of Justice. And if such person be not able, or shal utterly refuse to pay the aforesaid Fine, he shal be committed to the Stocks there to continue, not exceeding three hours, and not lesse then one hour [1646]. . . .

## SCHOOLS

1. It being one chief project of that old deluder, Satan, to keep men from the knowledge of the Scriptures, as in former times keeping them in an unknown tongue, so in these later times by perswading from the use of Tongues,[36] that so at least the true sense and meaning of the Originall might be clowded with false glosses[37] of Saint-seeming-deceivers; and that Learning may not be buried in the graves of our fore-fathers in Church and Common-wealth, the Lord assisting our indeavours: it is therfor ordered by this Court and Authoritie therof;

   That everie Township in this Jurisdiction, after the Lord hath increased them to the number of fifty Housholders shal then forthwith appoint one within their Town to teach all such children as shal resort to him to write and read, whose wages shal be paid either by the Parents or Masters of such children, or by the Inhabitants in general . . . as the major part of those that order the *prudentials*[38] of the Town shal appoint. Provided that those which

---

36. Tongues—modern languages as opposed to Latin.
37. glosses—words of explanation or translation.
38. prudentials—local government, daily affairs.

send their children be not oppressed by paying much more then they can have them taught for in other Towns.

2.  And it is farther ordered, that where any Town shal increase to the number of one hundred Families or Housholders they shal set upon a Grammar-School, the Masters therof being able to instruct youth so far as they may be fitted for the Universitie. And if any Town neglect the performance heerof above one year then everie such town shal pay five pounds *per annum* to the next such School, till they shal perform this Order. [1647]

## STRANGERS

It is ordered by this Court and the Authoritie therof; that no Town or person shal receive any stranger resorting hither with intent to reside in this Jurisdiction, nor shal allow any Lot or Habitation to any, or entertain any such above three weeks, except such person shal have allowance under the hand of some one Magistrate, upon pain of everie Town that shal give, or sell any Lot or Habitation to any not so licenced such Fine to the Countrie as that County Court shal impose, not exceeding fifty pounds, nor lesse then ten pounds. And of everie person receiving any such for longer time then is heer expressed or allowed, in some special cases as before, or in case of entertainment of friends resorting from other parts of this Country . . . shal forfeit as aforesaid, not exceeding twenty pounds, nor lesse then four pounds: and for everie month after so offending, shal forfeit as aforesaid not exceeding ten pounds, nor lesse then fourty shillings. Also, that all Constables shal inform the Courts of new commers which they know to be admitted without licence, from time to time. [1637, 1638, 1647]. . . .

## TOWNSHIPS

1.  It is ordered, decreed, and by this Court declared, that if any man shal behave himselfe offensively at any Town-meeting, the rest then present shal have power to sentence him for such offence, so be it the *mulct*[39] or penalty exceed not twenty shillings.

2.  And that the Freemen of everie *Township*, and others authorized by law, shal have power to make such Laws and Constitutuions as may concern the welfare of their Town. Provided they be not of a criminal but only of a prudential[40] nature, and that their penalties exceed not twenty shillings (as aforesaid) for one offence, and that they be not repugnant to the publick Laws and Orders of the Countrie. And if any Inhabitant shal neglect or refuse to observe them, they shal have power to levie the appointed penalties by *distresse*.

---

39. mulct—fine.
40. prudential—local government, daily affairs.

3.  Also that the Freemen of everie town or *Township*, with such other of the Inhabitants as have taken the Oath of fidelitie shal have full power to choose yearly, or for lesse time, within each Township a convenient number of fit men to order the planting and *prudential* occasions of that Town, according to instructions given them in writing.

    Provided, nothing be done by them contrary to the publick Laws and Orders of the Countrie. Provided also that the number of such Select persons be not aboue nine.

4.  Farther, it is ordered by the Authoritie aforesayd, that all Towns shal take care from time to time to order and dispose of all single persons, and In-mates[41] within their Towns to service, or otherwise. And if any be grieved at such order or dispose, they have libertie to appeal to the next County Court.

5.  This Court taking into considerattion the usefull Parts and abilities of divers Inhabitants amongst us, which are not Freemen, which if improved to publick use, the affairs of this Common-wealth may be the easier caried an end in the severall Towns of this Jurisdiction doth order, and heerby declare;

    That henceforth it shal and may be lawfull for the Freemen within any of the said Towns, to make choice of such Inhabitants (though non-Freemen) who have taken, or shal take the Oath of fidelitie to this Government to be Jurie-men, and to have their Vote in the choice of the Select-men for the town Affairs, *Assessments* of Rates, and other *Prudentials* proper to the Select-men of the several Towns. Provided still that the major part of all companyes of Select-men be Free-men from time to time that shal make any valid Act. As also, where no Select-men are, to have their Vote in ordering of Schools, hearding of cattle, laying out of High-wayes and distributing of Lands; any Law, Use or Custom to the contrary notwithstanding. Provided also that no non-Freeman shal have his Vote, untill he have attained the age of twenty one years. [1636, 1641, 1647]. . . .

**USURIE**

*interest rate*

It is ordered, decreed & by this Court declared, that no man shal be adjudged for the meer forbearance[42] of any debt, above eight pounds in the hundred for one    year,    and    not    above    that    rate    proportionably    for    all    sums whatsoever . . . neither shal this be a colour[43] or countenance to allow any *usurie* amongst us contrary to the Law of God [1641, 1643]. . . .

---

41.  In-mates—those residing in a house owned or rented by another; lodgers, subtenents.
42.  forbearance—extention of time for payment of a debt.
43.  colour—reason, pretext.

# INTRODUCTION & QUESTIONS

## THE STRUCTURE OF SOCIETY

Now read the following sections of *The Lauues and Libertyes* which bear the headings which appear below:

**Bond-Slavery**

1. What legality does slavery have in Massachusetts? What, if any, exemptions are there? What guidelines help to define the legal and proper treatment of a slave?

**Cattel, Corn-fields, Fences**

1. What do the provisions of this section suggest about the method of agricultural organization in Massachusetts?

2. What shared responsibility do farmers have under this system? How are disputes resolved?

3. What attitudes toward property rights and responsibilities are revealed in the section relating to brands?

**Charges publick**

1. What do the provisions for salaried officials, required public service and taxation indicate about the Puritan's attitude toward community?

2. To what public agencies does an inhabitant have obligations? On what basis are taxes assessed?

**Freemen, Non-Freemen**

1. What particular tasks are considered the responsibility of freemen? What presumption underlies such legislation?

**Fugitives, Strangers**

1. Under what circumstances are fugitives and strangers welcome in Massachusetts? In the present context, what would "the true Christian Religion" mean here? Does such legislation suggest anything about the Puritan's attitude toward geographical mobility?

## Indians

1. Under what arrangements are Puritans to obtain land from the Indians? What role does the state play in this process?

2. What restraints are placed on Europeans selling firearms to the Indians? What further extension of these regulations was passed in 1642? Why was such an extension necessary?

3. What do the regulations regarding Indian corn suggest as to possible changes in the Indians' economic patterns?

4. What regulations here were designed to aid in the proselytizing of the Indians? What agencies were expressly assigned this function? What degree of continuity would exist in such a scheme?

5. What prohibitions are placed on the Indians' practice of their native religion? On their general life style?

## Master, Servants, Labourers

1. What aspects of the relationships among "masters, servants and labourers" are legally defined here? What procedure is prescribed for in the case of runaways? Under what circumstances might the law protect a runaway from being returned? Under what circumstances might a servant be set free before his scheduled term of service was to end? Do these provisions suggest anything concerning the expected roles of the participants?

## Strangers

1. What does this provision indicate about the nature of the Puritan community? Who is charged with enforcement? What means do they employ to restrict the community's limits?

## Townships

1. How is order maintained at town meetings and what does such a procedure suggest about the fundamental method of decision making? What form of government is employed in Puritan towns? What limits are placed on town authority? What qualifications must an individual meet in order to participate in political decision making?

2. Who has responsibility for the daily operations of townships and how are they "selected?"

3. What rights are extended to non-freemen in Puritan towns? From what activities are they barred? How critical are these issues?

# INTRODUCTION & QUESTIONS

## THE ETHICS OF ECONOMICS

For this third assignment on *The Lauues and Libertyes of Massachusetts*, read the sections under the following headings:

### BAKERS

    1. What are the objectives of this legislation? By what means are they to be enforced? How are such officials selected and compensated? What punishment is prescribed for violators?

### IDLENES

    1. What does this particular section indicate regarding the extent of social control over individual behavior? How is such control exercised in this instance? What officials are involved in enforcement? What are the specific criteria used to determine idleness?

### GAMING

    1. What is the basic argument for this legislation? What are assumed as the predictable consequences of shuffleboard? What arrangement insures that offenses will be reported in this case?

### MASTERS, SERVANTS, LABOURERS

    1. What specific aspects of labor contracts are regulated by the state? Note, in particular, the primary agencies responsible for defining and enforcing these arrangements.

    2. What are acceptable media of exchange? What rights has the servant *vis a vis* the master in assessing their value?

### MONOPOLY

    1. What are the only circumstances under which a monopoly may be legal? Given the other legislation defining the social dimensions of economic life, what could be the basic rationale for this position?

**USURIE**

1. What is the definition of usury maintained in Puritan law? What legal basis is cited for this legislation?

# INTRODUCTION & QUESTIONS

## THE WELL-ORDERING OF FAMILIES AND CHILDREN

Read the following headings in *The Lauues and Libertyes of Massachusetts*

### CHILDREN

1. What considerations led to the development of these provisions? What responsibilities do heads of families have toward their children? How is it determined whether these responsibilities have been met?

2. What is meant by "calling"? What appears to be the criteria for valid callings? Are there distinctions among callings? What phenomena suggest non-compliance with these regulations? What legal action is prescribed in such cases?

### COLLEDGE

1. What relationship exists between the state and higher education in Massachusetts? How is this relationship exercised? How autonomous is the college under this arrangement?

2. What are the primary means of financial support for the college? What does this indicate regarding the successful individual's responsibility to the community?

### MARRIAGE

1. What legal preliminary must precede a marriage? What purposes could this serve?

2. What is assumed to be the proper role for parents in the question of their children's marriage? Of the state?

### SCHOOLS

1. What is given as the primary justification for formal elementary education?

2. What conditions require a township to appoint a teacher? What is his function? By whom is he paid and how is his salary determined? To whom are his services available?

3. What circumstances require establishment of specialized schools? For what purpose? How are they financed?

# INTRODUCTION & QUESTIONS

## SCIENCE AND THE NATURAL WORLD

Cotton Mather, this selection's author, was one of New England Puritanism's leading intellects. Born in Boston in 1663, Mather was a child prodigy. At twelve, as he could read, write and speak Latin, he was admitted to Harvard. The university's youngest graduate at the age of eighteen, he left in 1681 to become co-minister with his father at Boston's Second Church.

His personal life was dogged by tragedy. His last and third wife went insane, his favorite son became a prodigal and only two of his fifteen children outlived him. His diary, still preserved, recounts these personal experiences and reveals Mather's constant concern with religious introspection.

Overshadowing his entire career was the fact of his parentage. His name recalls a descent from both John Cotton and Increase Mather, two of New England's foremost ministers. His father Increase, in addition to being a leading ecclesiastical and literary figure, was a political power in the Bay colony and president of Harvard from 1685 to 1701. He died in 1723, leaving his son Cotton only five short years of independence before the son followed his illustrious parent to the grave.

Parentage helps account for Cotton's general conservatism. In political controversy his was a voice urging a return to the ideals and faith of Massachusetts' founders. He helped, too, to establish Yale College in opposition to the "liberalism" of his native Harvard.

Cotton Mather's literary output was truly phenomenal. Over 444 books are known to have been authorized by him. Included are sermons, histories, biographies, elegies, poetry and translations, together with a goodly number of theological treatises and moral essays, all characterized by vast scholarship verging sometimes on pedantry.

In his literary interests and achievements there is real attention given to science. His library, one of the largest in the American colonies, contained many scientific works. In 1721, he very dangerously advocated innoculation for small pox against powerful critics, including the young Benjamin Franklin. One of the few colonial Americans to be elected to the Royal Society, an honorary fraternity of Britain's finest scientific minds, Cotton Mather was in continuous contact with the latest scientific developments through correspondence with some of Europe's leading men of science.

Published in 1720, *The Christian Philosopher* was an encyclopedic work designed to acquaint New England with the latest scientific discoveries being made in Europe. Its pages attempt to cover all scientific concerns, each in a form similar to this excerpt. One of the work's many chapters is presented here preceded by the volume's general introduction. As you read this selection remember you are studying a representative example of a Puritan scientific work. Its function was not unlike today's college textbook.

## The Introduction

1. What, in Mather's view, is the relationship between "philosophy" (i.e. natural philosophy or science) and religion? What role does a man (or the scientist) perform in such work?

2. How does Mather explain the frequent need for quotation in this work? What does this suggest about his own scientific experience?

3. What, according to Mather, caused the scientific discoveries he will describe? With such an explanation, what role does the scientist assume?

4. What does he announce will be his own personal contribution to "these Essays"? Would the presumptions and ideas expressed so far tend to encourage others to active scientific experimentation?

## Essay XXIV—Of Magnetism

1. Where, in general, did Mather obtain his data about the magnet? Did he observe at first hand the discoveries he reports? How much attention does he give to the experimental approaches and techniques used to make these discoveries? What appears to be the basic organizing principle used to report the facts about the magnet he has collected?

2. What speculation does Mather make regarding terrestial magnetism? What is the extent of Mather's knowledge of geography as evidenced by his summary of Mr. Halley's proposals? What conclusions does he draw from this hypothesis? Does he suggest any experiment to validate it or any further possibilities for investigation?

3. What are the substance and implications of his address to "Gentleman Philosophers"? What caused the human characteristic of which he speaks?

4. What are the uses of magnetism for him? To what ends have its practical functions led?

5. For him, what is the "true" meaning of magnetism which he describes in the final paragraph? Who is his primary authority here? What is the specific source and date for this concluding speculation?

# THE CHRISTIAN PHILOSOPHER

*Cotton Mather*

## THE INTRODUCTION

The Essays now before us will demonstrate, that Philosophy is no Enemy, but a might and wondrous Incentive to Religion. . . .

In the Dispositions and Resolutions of PIETY thus enkindled, a Man most effectually shews himself a MAN, and with unutterable Satisfaction answers the grand END of his Being, which is, To glorify GOD. . . . The whole World is indeed a Temple of GOD, built and fitted by that Almighty Architect; and in this Temple, every such one, affecting himself with the Occasions for it, will Speak of His Glory. . . . Behold, a Religion, which will be found without Controversy; a Religion, which will challenge all possible Regards from the High, as well as the Low, among the People; I will resume the Term, a PHILOSOPHICAL RELIGION: And yet how Evangelical!

In prosecuting this Intention, and in introducing almost every Article of it, the Reader will continually find some Author or other quoted. This constant Method of Quoting, 'tis to be hoped, will not be censured, as proceeding from an Ambition to intimate and boast a Learning. . . . Nor will there be discernible any Spice of impertinent Vanity. . . . But in these Quotations, there has been proposed, first, a due Gratitude unto those, who have been my Instructors. . . . It appears also but a piece of Justice, that the Names of those whom the Great GOD has distinguished, by employing them to make those Discoveries, which are here collected, should live and shine in every such Collection. . . .

'Tis true, some Scores of other Philosophers have been consulted on this Occasion; but an Industry so applied, has in it very little to bespeak any Praises for him that has used it: He earnestly renounces them, and sollicits, that not only he, but the Greater Men, who have been his Teachers, may disappear before the Glorious GOD, whom these Essays are all written to represent as worthy to be praised, and by whose Grace we are what we are; nor have we any thing but what we have received from Him. . . .

Most certainly there can be very little Pretence to an I, or ME, for what is done in these Essays. 'Tis done, and entirely, by the Help of God; This is all that can be pretended to.

There is very little, that may be said, really to be performed by the Hand that is now writing; but only the Devotionary Part of these Essays. . . .

# ESSAY XXIV

## OF MAGNETISM

Such an unaccountable thing there is as the Magnetism of the Earth. A Principle very different from that of Gravity.

The Operations of this amazing Principle, are principally discovered in the communion that Iron has with the Loadstone; a rough, coarse, unsightly Stone, but of more Value than all the Diamonds and Jewels in the Universe.

It is observed . . . That the attractive Quality of the Magnet was known to the Antients, even beyond all History. . . .

It was Roger Bacon who first of all discovered the Verticity of the Magnet, or its Property of pointing towards the Pole, about four hundred Years ago.

The Communication of its Vertue to Iron was first of all discovered by the Italians. One Goia first lit upon the Use of the Mariner's Compass, about A.C. 1300. After this, the various Declination of the Needle under different Meridians, was discovered by Cabot and Norman. And then the Variation of the Declination, so as to be not always the same in one and the same place, by Hevelius, Auzot, Volckamer, and others.

The inquisitive Mr. Derham[1] says, The Variation of the Variation was first found out by our Gellibrand, A.C. 1634. . . .

In every Magnet there are two Poles, the one pointing to the North, and the other to the South.

The Poles, in divers Parts of the Globe, are diversly inclined towards the Center of the Earth.

These Poles, tho contrary to one another, do mutually help towards the Magnet's Attraction, and Suspension of Iron.

If a Stone be cut or broke into ever so many pieces, there are these two Poles in each of the pieces.

If two Magnets are spherical, one will conform itself to the other, so as either of them would do to the Earth; and after they have so turned themselves, they will endeavor to approach each other: but placed in a contrary Position, they avoid each other.

If a Magnet be cut thro the Axis, the Segments of the Stone, which before were joined, will now avoid and fly each other.

If the Magnet be cut by a Section perpendicular to its Axis, the two Points, which before were conjoined, will become contrary Poles. . . .

---

1. William Derham (1657–1735)—English author of *Physico-Theology or a Demonstration of the Being and Attributes of God from His Works of Creation* (1713).

Iron receives Vertue from the Magnet, by application to it, or barely from an approach near it, tho it do not touch it; and the Iron receives this Vertue variously, according to the Parts of the Stone it is made to approach to.

The magnet loses none of its own Vertue by communicating any to the Iron. This Vertue it also communicates very speedily; tho the longer the Iron joins the Stone, the longer its communicated Vertue will hold. And the better the Magnet, the sooner and stronger the communicated Vertue.

Steel receives Vertue from the Magnet better than Iron.

A Needle touch'd by a Magnet, will turn its Ends the same way towards the Poles of the World as the Magnet will do it. But neither of them conform their Poles exactly to those of the World; They have usually some Variation, and this Variation too in the same place is not always the same.

A Magnet will take up much more Iron when arm'd or cap'd than it can alone. And if the Iron Ring be suspended by the Stone, yet the magnetical Particles do not hinder the Ring from turning round any way, to the Right or Left. . . .

In our Northern Parts of the World, the South Pole of a Loadstone will raise more Iron than the North Pole.

A Plate of Iron only, but no other Body interposed, can impede the Operation of the Loadstone, either as to its attractive or directive Quality.

The Power and Vertue of the Loadstone may be impair'd by lying long in a wrong posture, as also by Rust, and Wet, and the like.

A Magnet heated red-hot, will be speedily deprived of its attractive Quality; then cooled, either with the South Pole to the North, in an horizontal position, or with the South Pole to the Earth in a perpendicular, it will change its Polarity; the Southern Pole becoming the Northern, and vise versa. . . .

Well temper'd and harden'd Iron Tools, heated by Attrition, will attract Filings of Iron and Steel.

The Iron Bars of Windows, which have stood long in an erect position, do grow permanently magnetical; the lower ends of such Bars being the Northern Poles, and the upper the Southern.

Mr. Boyle[2] found English Oker, heated red-hot, and cooled in a proper posture, plainly to gain a magnetick Power.

The illustrious Mr. Boyle, and the inquisitive Mr. Derham, have carried on their Experiments, till we are overwhelmed with the Wonders, as well as with the Numbers of them.

That of Mr. Derham, and Grimaldi, That a piece of well-touch Iron Wire, upon being bent round in a Ring, or coiled round upon a Stick, loses its Verticity; is very admirable.

The Strength of some Loadstones is very surprizing.

---

2. Mr. Boyle—Robert Boyle (1627–1691)—natural philosopher, chemist, member of the Royal Society and theologian.

Dr. Lister saw a Collection of Loadstones, one of them weighed naked not above a Dram, yet it would raise a Dram and a half of Iron; but being shod, it would raise one hundred and forty and four Drams. A smooth Loadstone, weighting 65 Grains, drew up 14 Ounces; that is, 144 times its own weight. A Loadstone that was no bigger than an Hazel-nut, fetch'd up an huge bunch of Keys.

The Effluvia of a Loadstone seem to work in a Circle. What flows from the North Pole, comes round, and enters the South Pole; and what flows from the South Pole, enters the North Pole. . . .

On that astonishing Subject, The Variation of the Compass, what if we should hear the acute Mr. Halley's Proposals?

He proposes, That our whole Globe should be looked upon as a great Magnet, having four magnetical Poles, or Points of Attraction, two near each Pole of the Equator. In those Parts of the World which lie near adjacent unto any one of these magnetical Poles, the Needle is governed by it; the nearer Pole being always predominant over the remoter. The Pole which at present is nearest unto Britain, lies in our near the Meridian of the Lands-end of England, and not above seven Degrees from the Artick Pole. By this Pole the Variations in all Europe, and in Tartary, and in the North Sea, are principally governed, tho' with some regard to the other Northern Pole, which is in a Meridian passing about the middle of Calefornia, and about fifteen Degrees from the North Pole of the World. To this the Needle pays its chief respect in all the North America, and in the two Oceans on either side, even from the Azores Westward, unto Japan, and further. The two Southern Poles are distant rather further from the South Pole of the World; the one is about sixteen Degrees therefrom, and is under a Meridian about twenty Degrees to the Westward of the Magellanick Streights; this commands the Needle in all the South America, in the Pacifick Sea, and in the greatest part of the Ethiopick Ocean. The fourth and last Pole seems to have the greatest Power and the largest Dominions of all, as it is the most remote from the Pole of the World; for 'tis near twenty Degrees from it, in the Meridian which passes thro Hollandia Nova, and the Island Celebes. This Pole has the mastery in the South part of Africa, in Arabia, and the Red Sea, in Persian, in India, and its Islands, and all over the Indian Sea, from the Cape of Good Hope Eastwards, to the middle of the great South Sea, which divides Asia from America.

Behold, the Disposition of the magnetical Vertue, as it is throughout the whole Globe of the Earth at this day!

But now to solve the Phoenomena!

We may reckon the external Parts of our Globe as a Shell, the internal as a Nucleus, or an inner Globe included within ours; and between these a fluid Medium, which having the same common Center and Axis of diurnal Rotation, may turn about with our Earth every four and twenty Hours: only this outer Sphere having its turbinating Motion some small matter either swifter or slower than the internal Ball, and a very small difference becoming in length of Time sensible by many Repetitions; the internal Parts will by degrees recede from the external, and not keeping pace with one another, will appear gradually to move, either Eastwards or Westwards, by the difference of their Motions. Now if the exterior Shell of our Globe should be a Magnet, having its Poles at a distance from the Poles of diurnal Rotation; and if the internal Nucleus be likewise a Magnet, having its Poles in two other places, distant also from the Axis, and these latter, by a slow and gradual Motion, change their place in respect of the external, we may then give a reasonable account of the four magnetical Poles, and of the Changes of the Needle's Variations. . . . Sir Isaac Newton has demonstrated the Moon to be more solid than our Earth, as nine to five; why may we not then suppose four Ninths of our Globe to be Cavity? Mr. Halley allows there may be Inhabitants of the lower Story, and many ways of producing Light for them. The Medium itself may be always luminous; or the concave Arch may shine with such a Substance as does invest the Surface of the Sun. . . .

The Diameter of the Earth being about eight thousand English Miles, how easy 'tis to allow five hundred Miles for the Thickness of the Shell! And another five hundred Miles for a Medium capable of a vast Atmosphere, for the Globe contained within it!—But it's time to stop, we are got beyond Human Penetration; we have dug as far as 'tis fit any Conjecture should carry us!

[A Digression, if worthy to be called so!]

But is it possible for me to go any further without making an Observation, which indeed would ever now and then break in upon us as we go along?

Once for all; Gentlemen Philosophers, the MAGNET has quite puzzled you. It shall then be no indecent Anticipation of what should have been observed at the Conclusion of this Collection, here to demand it of you, that you glorify the infinite Creator of this, and of all things, as incomprehensible. You must acknowledge that Human Reason is too feeble, too narrow a thing to comprehend the infinite God. The Words of our excellent Boyle deserve to be recited on this Occasion: 'Such is the natural Imbecillity of the Human Intellect, that the most piercing Wits and excellent Mathematicians are forced to confess, that not only their own Reason, but that of Mankind, may be puzzled and nonplus'd about QUANTITY, which is an Object of Contemplation natural, nay, mathematical. Wherefore why should we think it unfit to be believed, and to be acknowledged, that in the Attributes of God [it may be added, and in His Dispensations towards the Children of Men] there should be some things which our finite Understandings cannot clearly comprehend? . . . .'

Go on my learned Grew,[3] and maintain [who more fit than one of thy recondite Learning?] that there is hardly any one thing in the World, the Essence whereof we can perfectly comprehend. But then to the natural Imbecillity of REASON, and the moral Depravations of it, by our Fall from God, and the Ascendant which a corrupt and vicious Will has obtain'd over it, how much

---

3. Nehemiah Grew (1641–1712)—English minister and botanist, author of *Cosmologian Sacra, or a Discourse of the Universe as it is the Creation and Kingdom of God* (1701).

ought this Consideration to warn us against the Conduct of an unhumbled Understanding in things relating to the Kingdom of God? I am not out of my way, I have had a Magnet all this while steering of this Digression: I am now returning to that. . . .

. . . .They have done well to call it the Loadstone, that is to say, the *Lead-stone*: May it lead me unto Thee, O my God and my Saviour! Magnetism is in this like to Gravity, that it leads us to GOD, and brings us very near to Him. When we see Magnetism in its Operation, we must say, This is the Work of GOD! And of the Stone, which has proved of such vast use in the Affairs of the Waters that cover the Sea, and will e'er long do its part in bringing it about that the Glory of the Lord Shall cover the Earth, we must say, Great God, this is a wonderful Gift of Thine unto the World! . . . .

However, to animate the Devotion of my Christian Philosopher, I will here make a Report to him. The ingenious Ward[4] wrote a pious Book, as long ago as the Year 1639, entitled, *Magnetis Reductorium Theologicum*. The Design of his Essay, is, to lead us from the Consideration of the Loadstone, to the Consideration of our Saviour, and of his incomparable Glories. . . . For what is now before us, if our Ward may be our Adviser; Christian, in the Loadstone drawing and lifting up the Iron, behold thy Saviour drawing us to himself, and raising us above the secular Cares and Snares that ruin us. In its ready communication of its Vertues, behold a shadow of thy Saviour communicating his holy Spirit to his chosen People; and his Ministers more particularly made Partakers of his attractive Powers. When Silver and Gold are neglected by the Loadstone, but coarse Iron preferred, behold thy Saviour passing over the Angelical World, and chusing to take our Nature upon him. The Iron is also undistinguished, whether it be lodged in a fine Covering, or whether it be lying in the most squalid and wretched Circumstances; which invites us to think how little respect of Persons there is with our Saviour. However, the Iron should be cleansed, it should not be rusty; nor will our Saviour embrace those who are not so far cleansed, that they are at least willing to be made clean, and have his Files pass upon them. The Iron is at first merely passive, then it moves more feebly towards the Stone; anon upon contact it will fly to it, and express a marvellous Affection and Adherence. Is not here a Picture of the Dispositions in our Souls towards our Saviour? It is the Pleasure of our Saviour to work by Instruments, as the Loadstone will do most when the Mediation of a Steel Cap is used about it. After all, whatever is done, the whole Praise is due to the Loadstone alone. But there would be no end, and indeed there should be none, of these Meditations!

---

4. Samuel Ward (d. 1643)—English Puritan scholar and theologian.

# INTRODUCTION & QUESTIONS

## THE REALITY OF THE INVISIBLE WORLD

Included in Cotton Mather's *Magnalia Christi America*, published in 1702, is this section dealing with witchcraft or "the wonders of the invisible world." The *Magnalia*, "the great achievements of Christ in America," was Mather's mammoth history of the Puritans in New England. Through an all encompassing survey of the sum total of Puritan ideals and concerns in the seventeenth century, along with biographies of all the leading personalities, Mather intended to demonstrate the manner by which God "hath Irradiated an Indian Wilderness."

Part of his evidence included "Memorable Occurrences" of a "preternatural" order, instances of which are given here. On the subject of witchcraft, Mather was indeed something of a New England authority, having written the "official" history of the Salem outbreak of 1692, which ended with the death of twenty pronounced witches.

This excerpt consists of case histories of activities that Mather argues are evidence of witchcraft. Using examples four through seven in particular, see if you can develop alternative hypotheses to account for these events. Using as much of the reported evidence as possible, try to construct possible explanations that do not assume the involvement of supernatural forces, but instead rely wholly on natural phenomena. Remember that these incidents were not observed by Mather at first hand and the data is far from trustworthy. Assume, however, that there is some objective reporting. Attempt to formulate tentative explanations for each case that will explain the greatest amount of data by the simplest means. For the sake of the exercise, you may not, like Cotton Mather, blame witches or the like, even though these may provide the easiest solutions.

# MAGNALIA CHRISTI AMERICANA

*Cotton Mather*

## BOOK VI—CHAPTER VII—THAUMATOGRAPHIA PNEUMATICA.

### RELATING THE WONDERS OF THE INVISIBLE WORLD IN PRETERNATURAL OCCURRENCES

Miranda cano, sed sunt credenda.[1]

. . . .When our Lord Jesus Christ underwent his humiliation for us, this point was very considerable in it; he was carried into the wilderness, and there he was exposed unto the the buffetings and outrages of Azazel.[2] The assaults that Satan then and afterwards made on our Lord Jesus Christ, producing a most horrible anguish in his mind, made such a figure in his conflicts for us, that they were well worthy of a most particular prefiguration. And one thing in the prefiguration must be, that . . . Azazel must be sent into the desart. In the days of Moses, it seems, desarts were counted very much an habitation of devils . . . when the Scriptures foretel desolations to such and such places, they still make the Devils to be their inhabitants.

Who can tell whether the envy of the Devils at the favour of God unto men, may not provoke them to affect retirement from the sight of populous and prosperous regions, except so far as they reckon their work of tempting mankind necessary to be carry'd on? Or, perhaps, it is not every countrey before which the Devils prefer the desarts. Regions in which the Devils are much serv'd by those usages, either in worship or manners, which are pleasing to them, are by those doleful creatures enough resorted unto. Yea, if sin much abound any where, some Devils entreat that they may not be sent from thence into the wilderness. But regions, like the land of Israel, where the true God is continually pray'd unto, and where the word of God is continually sounding, are filled with such things as are very uneasie unto the devils: The devils often recede much from thence into the wilderness. . . .

---

1. *Miranda cano, sed sunt credenda*—Latin for: "What I sing is marvelous, but true."
2. Azazel—the demon mentioned in *Lev.* 16.1–28.

Whatever becomes of the observation which we have hitherto been making, there has been too much cause to observe, that the christians who were driven into the American desart, which is now call'd New-England, have to their sorrow seen Azazel dwelling and raging there in very tragical instances. The devils have doubtless felt a more than ordinary vexation, from the arrival of those christians with their sacred exercises of christianity in this wilderness: But the sovereignty of heaven has permitted them still to remain in the wilderness, for our vexation, as well as their own.

Molestations from evil spirits, in more sensible and surprising operations, than those finer methods, wherein they commonly work upon the minds of all men, but especially of ill men, have so abounded in this countrey, that I question whether any one town has been free from sad examples of them. The neighbours have not been careful enough to record and attest the prodigious occurrences of this importance, which have been among us. Many true and strange occurrences from the invisible world, in these parts of the world, are faultily buried in oblivion. But some of these very stupendous things, have had their memory preserv'd in the written memorials of honest, prudent, and faithful men; whose veracity in the relations cannot without great injury be question'd.

Of these I will now offer the publick some remarkable histories; for every one which we have had such a sufficient evidence, that no reasonable man in this whole countrey ever did question them; and it will be unreasonable to do it in any other. For my part, I would be as exceedingly afraid of writing a false thing, as of doing an ill thing: but have my pen always move in the fear of God. . . .

## THE FOURTH EXAMPLE

IN THE YEAR 1683. the house of Nicholas Desborough, at Hartford, was very strangely molested by stones, by pieces of earth, by cobs of indian corn, and other such things, from an invisible hand, thrown at him, sometimes thro' the door, sometimes thro' the window, sometimes down the chimney, and sometimes from the floor of the room (tho' very close) over his head; and sometimes he met with them in the shop, the yard, the barn, and in the field.

There was no violence in the motion of the things thus thrown by the invisible hand; and tho' others besides the man happen'd sometimes to be hit, they were never hurt with them; only the man himself once had pain given to his arm, and once blood fetch'd from his leg, by these annoyances; and a fire in an unknown way kindled, consum'd no little part of his estate.

This trouble began upon a controversie between Desborough and another person about a chest of cloaths, which the man apprehended to be unrighteously detain'd by Desborough; and it endur'd for divers months: but upon the restoring of the cloaths thus detain'd, the trouble ceased. . . .

## THE FIFTH EXAMPLE

ON JUNE 11, 1682. Showers of stones were thrown by an invisible hand upon the house of George Walton at Portsmouth. Whereupon the people going out,

found the gate wrung off the hinges, and stones flying and falling thick about them, and striking of them seemingly with a great force; but really affecting 'em no more than if a soft touch were given them. The glass windows were broken to pieces by stones that came not from without, but from within; and other instruments were in like manner hurl'd about. Nine of the stones they took up, whereof some were as hot as if they came out of the fire; and marking them, they laid them on the table; but in a little while they found some of them again flying about. The spit was carry'd up the chimney; and coming down with the point forward, stuck in the back-log; from whence one of the company removing it, it was by an invisible hand thrown out at the window. This disturbance continu'd from day to day; and sometimes a dismal hollow whistling would be heard, and sometimes the trotting and snorting of a horse, but nothing to be seen. The man went up the great bay in a boat unto a farm he had there: but there the stones found him out; and carrying from the house to the boat a stirrup-iron, the iron came jingling after him through the woods as far as his house; and at last went away, and was heard of no more. The anchor leap'd overboard several times and stopt the boat. A cheese was taken out of the press, and crumbl'd all over the floor: a piece of iron stuck into the wall, and a kettle hung thereupon. Several cocks of hay, mow'd near the house, were taken up and hung upon trees, and others made into small whisps, and scattered about the house. The man was much hurt by some of the stones: he was a Quaker, and suspected that a woman, who charg'd him with injustice in detaining some land from her, did by witchcraft occasion these preternatural occurrences. However, at last, they came unto an end.

## THE SIXTH EXAMPLE

IN JUNE, 1682. Mary the wife of Antonio Hortado, dwelling near the Salmon-falls, heard a voice at the door of her house, calling *What do you here?* and about an hour after had a blow on her eye, that almost spoil'd her. Two or three days after a great stone was thrown along the house; which the people going to take up, was unaccountably gone. A frying pan then in the chimney rang so loud, that the people at an hundred rods distance heard it; and the said Mary with her husband, going over the river in a canoo, they saw the head of a man, and about three foot off, the tail of a cat, swimming before the canoo, but no body to join them; and the same apparition again follow'd the canoo when they return'd: but at their landing it first disappear'd. A stone thrown by an invisible hand after this, caus'd a swelling and a soreness in her head; and she was bitten on both arms black and blue, and her breast scratch'd; the impression of the teeth, which were like a man's teeth, being seen by many.

They deserted their house on these occasions, and tho' at a neighbour's house, they were at first haunted with apparitions, the satanical molestations quickly ceas'd. When Antonio return'd unto his own house, at his entrance there, he heard one walking in his chamber, and saw the boards buckle under the feet of the walker; and yet there was no body there. For this cause he went back to dwell on the other side of the river; but thinking he might plant his ground, tho' he left his house, he had five rods of good log-fence thrown down at once and the footing of neat[3] cattle plainly to be seen almost between every row of corn in the field; yet no cattle seen there, nor any damage done to his corn, or so much as a leave of it cropt.

## THE SEVENTH EXAMPLE

Mr. Philip Smith, aged about fifty years, a son of eminently vertuous parents, a deacon of a church in Hadley, a member of the General Court, a justice in the countrey Court, a select man for the affairs of the town, a lieutenant of the troop and which crowns all, a man for devotion, sanctity, gravity, and all that was honest, exceeding exemplary. Such a man was in the winter of the year 1684, murder'd with an hideous witchcraft, that fill'd all those parts of New-England, with astonishment. He was, by his office, concern'd about relieving the indigences of a wretched woman in the town; who being dissatisfy'd at some of his just cares about her, express'd her self unto him in such a manner, that he declar'd himself thenceforward apprehensive of receiving mischief at her hands.

About the beginning of January he began to be very valetudinarious,[4] labouring under pains that seem'd Ischiatick.[5] The standers by could now see in him one ripening apace for another world, and fill'd with grace and joy to a high degree. He shew'd such weanedness from and weariness of the world, that he knew not (he said) whether he might pray for his continuance here: and such assurance he had of the Divine love unto him, that in raptures he would cry out, *Lord, stay thy hand! it is enough, it is more than thy frail servant can bear!* But in the midst of these things he still utter'd an hard suspicion that the ill woman who had threatned him, had made impressions with inchantments upon him. While he remain'd yet of sound mind, he very sedately, but very solemnly charg'd his brother to look well after him. Tho', he said, he now understood himself, yet he knew not how he might be. *But be sure,* (said he), *to have a care of me; for you shall see strange things. There shall be a wonder in Hadley! I shall not be dead, when 'tis thought I am!* He press'd this charge over and over; and afterwards became delirious; upon which he had a speech incessant and voluble, and (as was judg'd) in various languages. He cry'd out not only of pains, but also of pins, tormenting him in several parts of his body; and the attendants found one of them.

In his distresses he exclaim'd much upon the woman aforesaid, and others, as being seen by him in the room; and there was divers times, both in that room and over the whole house, a strong smell of something like musk, which once particularly so scented an apple roasting at the fire, that it forc'd them to throw it away. Some of the young men in the town being out of their wits at the strange

---

3. neat—heifer.
4. valetudinarous—weakness of health.
5. Ischiatick—sciatic, i.e., hip or buttock pains.

calamities thus upon one of their most belov'd neighbours, went three or four times to give disturbance unto the woman thus complain'd of: and all the while they were disturbing of her, he was at ease, and slept as a weary man: yea, these were the only times that they perceiv'd him to take any sleep in all his illness. Gally pots[6] of medicines provided for the sick man, were unaccountably empty'd: audible scratchings were made about the bed, when his hands and feet lay wholly still, and were held by others. They beheld fire sometimes on the bed; and when the beholders began to discourse of it, it vanish'd away. Divers people actually felt something often stir in the bed, at a considerable distance from the man; it seem'd as big as a cat, but they could never grasp it. Several trying to lean on the bed's head, tho' the sick man lay wholly still, the bed would shake so as to knock their heads uncomfortably. A very strong man could not lift the sick man to make him lie more easily, tho' he apply'd his utmost strength unto it; and yet he could go presently and lift a bed-sted and a bed, and a man lying on it, without any strain to himself at all. Mr. Smith dies; the jury that view'd his corpse found a swelling on one breast, his privities wounded or burn'd, his back full of bruises, and several holes that seem'd made with awls. After the opinion of all had pronounc'd him dead, his countenance continued as lively as if he had been alive; his eyes closed as in a slumber, and his nether jaw not falling down.

Thus he remain'd from Saturday morning about sun rise, till Sabbath day in the afternoon; when those who took him out of the bed, found him still warm, tho' the season was as cold as had almost be known in any age: and a New-English winter does not want for cold. On the night following his countenance was yet fresh as before; but on Monday morning they found the face extreamly tumify'd and discolour'd. It was black and blue, and fresh blood seem'd running down his cheek upon the hairs. Divers noises were also heard in the room where the corpse lay; as the clattering of chairs and stools, whereof no account could be given.

This was the end of so good a man.

And I could with unquestionable evidence relate the tragical deaths of several good men in this land, attended with such praeternatural circumstances which have loudly called upon us all to *work out our own salvation with fear and trembling.* . . . .

---

6. Gally pots—small earthenware pots used for medicines.

# INTRODUCTION & QUESTIONS

## THE INDIVIDUAL PURITAN AND HIS WORLD

Samuel Sewall, the author of this diary excerpt, was born in England in 1652 of an Englishman who settled in Massachusetts in 1661. He graduated from Harvard in 1671, married the daughter of the colony's mintmaster, was made a member of Boston's South Church in 1677, a freeman in 1679 and a deputy in the General Court in 1683. He occupied a number of judicial positions, among them chief justice of the colony from 1718 to 1728. He served also as a member of the governor's council from 1684 until five years before his death in 1730.

During his lifetime, he was an acute observer of and central actor in a train of events of momentous importance for the future of Massachusetts Bay. These began with the Restoration of the English monarchy in 1660, a development which ushered in a period of extreme political turbulence in New England. The Restoration saw the end of the English Commonwealth, that eleven year period when a Puritan Parliament had, as the sole national political authority, ruled England and her colonies. With the return of the Stuarts came vigorous efforts to reassert royal authority, both at home and abroad. The issue of Massachusetts' rebelliousness received the special attention of a series of royal commissions sent to investigate accusations made against the Puritan colony.

These royal agents needed little time to confirm their suspicions and send their indictment home. They charged Massachusetts' magistrates with passing laws contrary to English precedent, prohibiting the practice of orthodox Anglicanism and ignoring or circumventing English attempts to bring colonial commerce under imperial control. Equally damning was the colony's minting of coin and negotiating with foreign countries in the capacity of an independent power, totally denying British sovereignty.

After a series of confrontations and specious compromises between equally adament colony and crown, King Charles II, in total exasperation, annulled Massachusetts' charter in 1684. In its stead, his successor, James II, installed a royal dictatorship in the person of Sir Edmund Andros. Andros governed the newly created Dominion of New England, a political union of all of New England, New York and East and West Jersey. Lacking a representative assembly, the regime of Sir Edmund was much hated by both Puritan and non-Puritan alike. It was, however, short, as he was summarily expelled from both his post and Massachusetts by the people of Boston in 1689. This rebellion in New England corresponded to the deposing of Andros' Catholic patron, James II, in England, a part of the so-called Glorious Revolution of 1688–9. This bloodless coup inaugurated a constitutional monarchy for England and a new ruling dynasty with the coronation of the joint-sovereigns, William and Mary from the Protestant house of Orange.

Sewall not only critically observed these developments but was quite prominent in a number of actions stemming from them. He was, for example, a member of the party of New Englanders who journeyed back to the mother country to request another charter from the new sovereigns. Granted in 1691, the colony's new legal base was a compromise between imperial demands and Puritan desires. Henceforth, a royally appointed governor, not an elected one, would preside in Boston armed with the veto and assisted by a council chosen from and by the General Court. No longer would this General Court be representative only of the colony's church members, for a measure of property, not a certification of religious orthodoxy, would henceforth be the prerequisite for the franchise.

Sewall not only held on to high office during these years but recorded his reactions to these developments in his personal diary. Note those specific reactions included in this selection. The diary which contains them extends from 1674 to 1729 and was not designed for publication. Reproduced here are representative selections from that work. Included are all the entries for the months of January, March, May, June and November of 1700. (Under the Julian, or "Old Style," calendar in use until 1752, a New Year did not begin until March 25. All dates between January 1 and March 24 were in the old year and frequently are followed by both the old and new years combined, for example, Jan. 14, 1699/1700)

This selection should reveal the everyday operation of the cultural system in the life of an individual. Your primary attention should focus therefore, on the *repeated* or *patterned* aspects of Sewall's behavior and notation of events as he selects and editorializes on those items which have significance for him. Attempt to make your definition of his perspective as precise as possible. To do so, define the categories of experience he reports on by determining:

1. What particular aspects of community life merit Sewall's notice? What kinds of political activities is he involved in or does he record? What are his special concerns at these political functions?

2. In the notations of deaths and funerals, what kinds of data does he record? Are there certain characteristics of the deceased that are more important than others? Three members of his family die during this period. What characterizes his response to these events?

3. What activities take place on his travels? What are the purposes of these visits?

4. What is his attitude toward and interest in Negro slavery in Massachusetts? From his references, what is the position of the slave in Massachusetts? I.e., what legal rights and restrictions apply to him?

5. What are the characteristics of Sewall's social life? With whom does he associate? What social activities are indulged in by him and his associates?

6. What is the nature of his references to members of his family? About which of their activities does he display interest?

7. Of what does his religious life consist? Take note of its private as well as its public dimensions. What is his relationship with the ministry?

8. What phenomena in the natural enviroment are noticed by Sewall? How systematic is he in making these observations? What is the most unusual natural event he observes? What meaning does he give it?

9. What occasions appear to represent basic change to him? How is it symbolized? With which individuals or groups is it associated?

# DIARY OF SAMUEL SEWALL

JAN. 14, 1669/1700. Elder Jonas Clark, of Cambridge, dies, a good man in a good old Age, and one of my first and best Cambridge friends. He quickly follows the great Patron of Ruling Elders, Tho. Danforth, Esqr.

15. This day fortnight Lawrence Copeland of Braintry was buried; 'tis counted that he liv'd to be at least one hundred and ten years old. *Teste Arnoldo octogenario olim ejusdem vicino.*[1]

JAN. 17. A great fire brake out at Charlestown last night though very rainy. Three Houses burnt; viz. the widow Cutlers and two more: on the left hand of the way as one goes to Cambridge, upon the side of the hill. Other Houses on the opposite side of the Ally very narrowly escaped. Elder Clark is buried this day. Snowy all day long.

Gave Mr. Willard two volums of Rivets[2] works.

JAN. 17, ABOUT 5 P.M. Dame Hanah Townsend dies in the 93rd year of her Age. Cook, Hutchinson, Sewall, Addington, Chiever, Maryon *pater*, Bearers. . . .

FEBR. 12. A considerable snow falls. Jan. 11th was a storm of snow; which occasiond Mr. C. Mather to take for his Text, White as the snow of Salmon: Quickly melted away. Have not as yet had any path to make upon the Lords Day.

FEBR. 12. Justices met with the Selectmen at the Stone-House, Davis's, to take away some misunderstandings between us; and to agree to take Lists of each quarter of the Town to reform and prevent disorders.

TUESDAY, FEBR. 13. I got up pretty early, being forc'd to it by a laxness. Had sweet communion with God in Prayer, and in reading the two last Sermons I heard in London, about Assurance &c. This came to my hand by accident, the book being fallen upon my wood in the closet. Had read before, my own Notes upon Ephes. 5, 15, 16, 7 16. 1679. at Mrs. Oliver's. The Lord inlighten my Understanding, and incline my Will.

FEBR. 14. I visit Mr. Tho. Thornton in the Afternoon between 3 and 4. He made a shift to say he was willing to dy, but wanted Patience. Hop'd should dy next night. I spake to him what I could. Holp him up while he drank something comfortable.

---

1. *Teste Arnoldo octogenario olim ejusdem vicino*—In accordance with the testimony of an eighty year old Arnold, formerly of his neighborhood.
2. Rivet—Andrew Rivet (1572–1647)—a British theologian.

At three past midnight he alter'd much.

FEBR. 15, 3 P.M. Mr. Tho. Thornton dyes very quietly; which Mr. Gee acquaints me with. Is very near 93 years old. . . .

MARCH 4, 1699. Capt. Gullock is sent to Prison for his contempt of the Government in giving in to the Governor and Council an Insolent writing under his hand, and justifying it.

MARCH 5, TUESDAY, 1699/1700. Mr. Sergeant, Capt. Frary, Capt. Hill, Capt. Checkly and my self goe to Cambridge over the Ferry, and acquaint Mr. Pemberton with the Church's Call, and their desire of his Acceptance. He makes a very sensible Answer as to the Weight of the Work, his own inability; hop'd God would hear his earnest Prayer, and help him to make a right Answer. Din'd at Remington's, Mr. Flint, Fitch, and Blower din'd with us: visited Mr. Brattle, came home round: Saw a man plowing at Muddy River; breaking up a Pasture with two oxen and a horse.

MARCH 7TH. Mrs. Williams dies.

MARCH 11TH 1699/1700. Town-Meeting, chose Seven Select-men; Mr. Daniel Oliver, Mr. Isa Tay, Mr. Joseph Prout, Mr. Jn Maryon junior. Capt. Timothy Clark, Mr. Elizur Holyoke, Mr. Obadia Gill, Mr. James Taylor Treasurer, William Griggs Town-Clerk. 5 overseers of the Poor; Elisha Hutchinson esqr. 38, Mr. Samuel Lynde, 33, Mr. Jn Eyre 31, Mr. Nathanial Oliver 30. Capt. Nathaniel Byfield, 23. Constables, Benja Fitch, 90. Henry Hill, 83. William Man 63. William Welsteed 61. Joseph Billing, 57. William Clark Jr. 45. James Gooch, 40. Joseph Dowden 67. Jose Winthrop constable of Rumney-Marsh.

Surveyors of High Ways. Tho Walker, Stephen Minott, Jacob Melyen, Jn Goodwin Sr.

Voted to raise Money;

```
Stock to set poor on work . . . . . . . . . . . . . . . . . . . . . . . . . . . . . £500
To maintain impotent poor . . . . . . . . . . . . . . . . . . . . . . . . . . . . 400
Schools, Bells, etc. . . . . . . . . . . . . . . . . . . . . . . . . . . . . . . . . . . . . . 300
To mend the Way over the Neck. . . . . . . . . . . . . . . . . . . . . . . . 200
                                                                                       ─────
                                                                                       £1400.0.0
```

Capt. Byfield was Moderator; had Candles, broke up at 8. Began at 10 m. Mr. Colman began with Prayer. Capt. Byfield dismiss'd the Assembly with Prayer.

TUESDAY, MARCH, 19. 1699/1700. Three young men: viz. Robert Cunable, William Salter, and Tho Comer, went in a Canoo a Gunning before day-light, and were drowned. Wind high, and wether cold. Only James Tileston was saved.

MARCH 21. Mrs. Martha Collins dieth.

MARCH 23. She is buried between 5 and 6 P.M. Bearers Lt. Governor Stoughton, Mr. Russel, Sewall, Lynde, Byfield, Hayman. Mr. Cooke was at the funeral. Col. Phillips not well. Had Gloves and Rings. The under-bearers were honest men. I took my cousin Moodey, minister of York, over with me. Mr. Leverett there. Mr. Bradstreet the minister. Snow'd hard as we came home.

MONDAY, MARCH 25, 1700. Set out with Mr. Cooke for Plimouth, visited Mr. Torrey, staid near 3 hours, then to Mr. Norton's where Major Gen Winthrop came to us late, so got late to Sittiate to Mr. Cushings, lodg'd there just by the ruins of Mr. Chauncey's house. Major Gen. had appointed to visit said Cushing. Were so belated that fail'd Major Thomas, who with some other Gentlemen waited for us at the old Ferry on Marshfield side.

TUESDAY, MARCH 26. The wind is very bleak that it was ready to put me into an Ague, having rid late the night before. Had a noble Treat at Major Thomas's. Mr. Sheriff and his Gentlemen were so wearied that they were afraid of some Miscarriage at the Ferry. Began the Court about five. Wednesday and Thorsday were extravagantly stormy. On Friday Mr. Cooke comes home but the wind was strong in my face, and cold that I durst not venture. Satterday was also very cold and chose rather to keep the Sabbath at Plimouth than by the way. Staid at Plimouth. At noon was a Contribution for one that had his house burnt. Mr. Little invited me to sup with him, which I did.

MONDAY, APRIL 1. I was in a great quandary whether I had best, to avoid the wind, come home by water and leave my Horse, or no. At last I went on board Elisha Hedge's decked sloop laden with Oyle. He put in there in the storm from Yarmouth and lay till now for a wind. Came aboard about 2 hours by Sun, and landed at Mrs. Butlers Wharf before 3 P.M.Having had a very speedy and pleasant Passage, wherein I have experienced much of God's parental pity towards me, and care over me. I could not have got home to day by Land: and I fear my health would have been much impair'd, if I had come but part of the way. Jonathan Wheeler ridd in the Rain from Milton. I have now kept one Sabbath with those who first kept Sabbaths in New England. . . .

MONDAY, APR. 29, 1700. Sam. Sewall, Josiah Willard Jn Bayly, Sam. Gaskill, and _____ Mountfort goe into the Harbour a fishing in a small Boat. Seeing Richard Fifield coming in, some would needs meet the ship and see who it was: Ship had fresh way with a fair wind; when came neare, Capt. call'd to them to beware, order'd what they should doe. But they did the clear contrary, fell foul on the ship, which broke their Mast short off, fill'd the Boat with water, threw Willard and Gaskill into the River. Both which were very near drown'd; especially Gaskill, who could not swim. It pleas'd God Fifield's Boat was out, so he presently man'd it and took them in. Gaskill was under water, but discover'd by his Hat that swam atop as a Buoy. Sam, Jn Bayly and Mountfort caught hold of the Ship and climbed on board in a miserable fright as having stared death in the face. This is the second time Sam has been near drown'd with Josiah Willard. Mother was against his going, and prevented Joseph, who pleaded earnestly to go. He sensibly acknowledged the Good Providence in his staying at home, when he saw the issue.

1. *A Narrative of the Portsmouth Disputation between Presbyterians and Baptists at Mr. Williams's Meetinghouse.*

2. *Bp. of Norwich's Sermon of Religious Melancholy.*

3. *Amintor, a defence of Milton with Reasons for abolishing the 30th Jan.*

4. *An Account of the first Voyages into America by don Barthol de las Casas.*

5. *Account of a Jew lately converted and baptis'd at the Meeting near Ave Mary-Lane.*

The President desires me to send for the above mentioned Books.

MONDAY, MAY 13. 1700. Mr. Wheelwright dies. This day P.M. I set out towards Kittery, Lodge at Salem.

MAY 14. Get to Newbury a little before sunset, visit my sick Father in bed, call in the Major General whom Father salutes. Kiss'd my hand, and I his again. Mr. Tappan came in and pray'd with him and us.

MAY 15. Walks into the west end of the house with his staff, breakfasts there. I read the 17th Luke, and went to Prayer. My father would have stood up but I persuaded him to sit still in his chair. Took leave and went on to Portsmouth. Major General and I lodge at Col. Parkers. Most Gentlemen out of Town, some at Mr. Wheelrights funeral and som about Business. Mr. Hirst and Geoffries welcom'd us to Town. May 16th goe to Spruce-Crick and hold Court at Mr. Curtis's. Cousin Moodey comes thither and tells me of his son born that morn when sun about 2 hours high. Return in the night to Portsmouth.

MAY 17. Benj Moss junr is sent to me to acquaint me that my dear Father died the evening before. It rains hard. Holds up about 5 P.M. I ride to Hampton, lodge at Mr. Cottons, where am very kindly entertained.

MAY 18TH. ride to Newbury in the Rain; when breaks up, Brother and Sister come from Salem. Bury my Father, Bearers, Col. Peirce, Mr. Nich. Noyes, Mr. Sam. Plummer, Mr. Tristam Coffin, Major Dan Davison, Major Thomas Noyes, had 8 Underbearers.

SABBATH, MAY. 19. Mr. Tappan in the afternoon preach'd a funeral Sermon from Prov. 19. 20. Said my Father was a true Nathanael: Mention'd 3 or four other deaths which occasion'd his discourse: gave a good character of most of them. May, 20. Rains hard, holds up in the afternoon. Major Gen and Mr. Cooke come to Newbury in the night.

MAY 21. ride to Ipswich: Sheriff, Mr. Harris, and Major Epes meet us at Rowley. Give no Action to the Jury till after dinner. Lodge at Mr. Rodgers's where am very kindly entertain'd.

MAY 23. Mr. Rogers preaches very well of the Divine Efficiency in Mans Conversion, from Philip. 2. 13. Invite the Ministers to dinner, There are Mr. Hubbard, Rogers, Mr. Gerrish, Mr. Payson, Mr. Capen, Mr. Green, Mr. Rolf; last did not dine.

MAY 24TH. Set out for Salem about an hour by sun, Mr. Joseph Woodbridge with me, Got to Brothers a little before Nine, met there Mrs. Anne Woodbridge. Proved my Fathers Will. May 25. 1700 went homeward in company Mrs. Anne as far as Col. Paiges. Got home about 3 o'clock, found all well, Blessed by God. My

Wife provided Mourning upon my Letter by Severs, all went in mourning save Joseph, who staid at home because his Mother lik'd not his cloaths. Sister Short here, came from newbury the morn father died, and so miss'd being at the funeral. It seems about a 14night before, upon discourse of going to Meeting, my Father said, He could not goe, but hop'd to go shortly to a Greater Assembly. The Lord pardon all my sin of omission and commission towards him, and help me to prepare to Dye. Accept of any little Labour of Love towards my dear Parents. I had just sent four pounds of Raisins, which with the Canary[3] were very refreshing to him.

Worthy Mr. Hale of Beverly was buried the day before my father. So was Mr. John Wadsworth of Duxbury, who died May, 15th 1700. I used to be much refreshed with his company when I went to Plimouth; and was so this last time. He gave me an account of the beginning of their Town, and of his Fathers going over to fetch Mr. Partridge.

FRIDAY, JUNE, 7TH, 1700. mane, the Gov nominates Major Jn Walley for a Judge of the Super court, gives time of consideration till after dinner, Then give in Yes and No in papers. Said Walley had all present save his own and one No. Col. Hathorne was absent. I think had 25 Papers written YES. Chose Mr. John Clark a Justice Peace in Boston and many other; Justices of Inferior Courts, Coroners &c. Mr. Jn Wheelwright chosen Justice of Peace at Wells. Things were carried with Peace and comfortable unanimity.

LORDS-DAY, JUNE 16, 1700. Mr. Daniel Oliver has his son Daniel baptised.

JUNE 17. Mr. John Eyre makes his Will in the morning, and dies in the Afternoon, an hour or 2. before Sunset. Born Febr. 19th 1653/4 I visited him on Satterday in the Afternoon: He was sitting up in his little Room, Took me by the hand at first coming in, Desired me to pray for him when took leave.

FOURTH-DAY, JUNE, 19, 1700. Mr. Jn Eyre is entomed in the new burying place. Nine of his children are laid there to handsel the new Tomb: Bearers, Sewall, Addington, Townsend, Byfield, Dummer, Davis: Scarvs and Rings. Lt. Govr and many of the Council there. Mr. Thomas Brattle led his mourning widowed Sister. When I parted, I pray'd God to be favourably present with her, and comfort her in the absence of so near and dear a Relation. Having been long and much dissatisfied with the Trade of fetching Negros from Guinea; at last I had a strong Inclincation to Write something about it; but it wore off. At last reading Bayne, Ephes. about servants, who mentions Blackamoors; I began to be uneasy that I had so long neglected doing any thing. When I was thus thinking, in came Brother Belknap to shew me a Petition he intended to present to the Gen Court for the freeing a Negro and his wife, who were unjustly held in Bondage. And there is a Motion by a Boston Committee to get a Law that all Importers of Negros shall pay 40 *per* head, to discourage the bringing of them. And Mr. C. Mather resolves to publish a sheet to exhort Masters to labour their Conversion. Which makes me

---

3. canary—a kind of wine.

hope that I was call'd of God to Write this Apology for them; Let his Blessing accompany the same. . . .

THORSDAY, SEPT 26TH, 1700. Mr. John Wait and Eunice his wife, and Mrs. Debora Thair come to Speak to me about the Marriage of Sebastian, Negro servant of said Wait, with Jane, Negro servant of said Thair. Mr. Wait desired they might be published in order to marriage Mrs. Thair insisted that Sebastian might have one day in six allow'd him for the support of Jane, his intended wife and her children, if it should please God to give her any. Mr. Wait now wholly declin'd that, but freely offer'd to allow Bastian Five pounds, in Money per annum towards the support of his children per said Jane (besides Sebastians cloathing and Diet). I persuaded Jane and Mrs. Thair to agree to it, and so it was concluded; and Mrs. Thair gave up the Note of Publication to Mr. Wait for him to carry it to Wm Griggs, the Town Clerk, and to Williams in order to have them published according to Law. . . .

OCT. 18. Mr. Pemberton and Mr. Colman and his wife dine with us. Sent and Spent 21. Cakes.

OCT. 20, 1700. In the Afternoon I and my wife, Mr. Hirst and his Bride, Sam. and Eliza Hirst, Will. Hirst and Hannah Sewall, James Taylor and Esther Wyllie, Joseph and Mary Sewall, walk to Meeting together.

OCT. 30. Mr. Hirst comes and carries his daughter Betty to Salem. Mr. Grove Hirst and his wife accompany them.

NOVEMBER 4TH, 1700. A Council was called at the Town-House. Present, The honorable William Stoughton Esqr. Lt. Gov, Elisha Cooke, Elisha Hutchinson, Sam Sewall, Isaac Addington, Jn Foster, Peter Sergeant, John Walley, Eliakim Hutchinson, Penn Townsend, Nathanael Byfield, esqrs. Lt. Gov ask'd Advice whether Benjamin Bedwell should be tryed by Commissioners of Oyer and Terminer; or at the Court of Assize and Gen Goal Delivery, to be held at Plimouth next March. Twas carried for the latter. A Proclamation was ordered to prevent endangering the Town by Fire-Works.

Francis Hudson, Ferry-man, dyed last Lords-Day, Nov. 3. Was one of the first who set foot on this Peninsula.

NOV. 10, 1700. Lords-day Madam Elizabeth Sergeant died in the Afternoon, half an hour past three. Was taken last Thorsday Sennight[4] at night. Hath been delirious a great part of the Time, and hardly sensible since Friday.

NOV. 11TH. Salem Court is adjourned by reason of Mr. Cooks Indisposition of Body.

NOV. 12. Last night a considerable Snow fell which covers the Ground several Inches thick. This morn Mr. Thomas Broughton expires about 87 years old: once a very noted Merchant in Boston, Select-man &c. About 3 years agoe he join'd to the North church. On Satterday- night I was with him when the President pray'd with him.

---

4. Sennight—a week ago.

NOV. 14. Madam Eliza. Sergeant is entombed, Bearers, Cooke, Hutchinson Elisha, Sewall, Addington, Foster, Walley. She was born Apr. 11. 1660. Maj Gen Winthrop was at the Funeral. He came last night from New-London.

NOV. 14, 1700. about ¹/₂ hour past one in the Afternoon, Mr. Joseph Eliot dieth. He was abroad on the Lords day at Meeting. I saw him in the street near his own house, about 8 in the morning. The Lord fit us for his good pleasure.

NOV. 15, 1700. Mr. Tho. Broughton buried in the old burying place. Bearers, Sewall, Foster, Em Hutchinson, Byfield, Howard, Fayerwether. No scarf. No Gloves. Went back again to the house.

NOV. 16. Mr. Joseph Eliot was buried. Bearers, Capt. Alford, Capt. Checkley, Mr. Dan Oliver, Mr. Bennet, Mr. Cutler, Mr. Gibbs. 38. years old.

This day John Soams, the Quaker, dies. Was well this day sennight.

NOV. 20. Mrs. [Mary] Lynde (formerly Richardson) was buried: Bearers, Cook, Sewall, Addington, Bennet, Dering, Gibbs. Scarf and Ring.

NOV. 21, 1700. Day of publick Thanksgiving. At 3. *post merid* Mr. Willard comes abroad and Prays to the great Refreshment of the Congregation. This the first time since his sickness. In the evening I made these verses on it, viz,

> *As Joseph let his brethren see*
> *Simeon both alive, and free:*
> *So JESUS brings forth Samuel,*
> *To tune our hearts to praise Him well.*
> *Thus He with beams of cheerfull light,*
> *Corrects the darkness of our night.*
> *His Grace assists us in this wise.*
> *To seise, and bind the Sacrifice.*

MONDAY, NOV. 25TH. 1700. Prime brot me a horse to Winnisimmet, and I ridd with him to Salem.

NOV. 26. Sup'd at Mr. Hirst's in company of said Hirst, his wife, Mrs. Betty Hirst, Mr. Noyes and my Brother. Nov 28. Court rose. Mr. Higginson was not at Lecture nor abroad this Court; so miss'd the pleasure of dining with Him. Visited him at his house and his sick wife. Madam Bradstreet, Mrs. Batter in Bed. Mrs. Jn Higginson the 2nd Set out to come home about ¹/₂ hour past two in the Afternoon: came by Charlestown. Very cold going, abiding there, and Returning. Yet hope have taken very little hurt through the Goodness of God.

Major Walley has a swell'd face that keeps him from Meeting on the Sabbath xr. 1. 1700.

NOV. 30TH. My Aunt Quinsey dieth of the Jaundice befor break of day.

THORSDAY, XR. 5TH 1700. Sam. and I ride to the Funeral of Aunt Eli. Quinsey. Because of the Porrige of snow, Bearers—Mr. Torrey, Fisk, Thacher, J., Danforth, Wilson, Belchar—rid to the Grave, alighting a little before they came there. Mourners, Cous. Edward and his Sister rid first, then Mrs. Ana Quinsey, widow, behind Mr. Allen; and cous. Ruth Hunt behind her Husband; then Sam. and I.

None of the Gookins there. Mr. Torrey prayed. Bearers had Rings and Wash-Lether Gloves. I had Gloves and a Ring. Cous. Edmund invited us; for I lodg'd there all night, with Mr. Torrey, Sam. with his Cousin. All else went home. Cousin Savil was at Weymouth and came not. Funeral about 4. P.M.

DEC. 6TH. Mr. Torrey and I and Sam. about 12 set forward and ride home; Find all pretty well, about 2 or 3 aclock, and good satisfaction as to our Lodging there. It Rain'd quickly after our getting home. Very foggy thawing wether.

Justice [Daniel] Cushing of Hingham died on Tuesday and, as is said, was buried this Thorsday. . .

JAN 1, 1700/1701. Just about Break-a-day Jacob Amsden and 3 other Trumpeters gave a Blast with the Trumpets on the common near Mr. Alford's. Then went to the Green Chamber, and sounded there till about sunrise. Bell-man said these verses a little before Break-a-day, which I printed and gave them.

> Once more! our God vouchsafe to shine:
> Correct the Coldness of our Clime.
> Make haste with thy Impartial Light,
> And terminate this long dark night.
> Give the poor Indians Eyes to see
> The Light of Life: and set them free.
> So Men shall God in Christ adore,
> And worship Idols vain, no more.
> So Asia, and Africa,
> Europa, with America;
> All Four, in Consort join'd, shall Sing
> New Songs of Praise to Christ our King.

The Trumpeters cost me five pieces 8/8. Gave to the College-Library Dr. Owens two last Volumes on the Hebrews. Sent them by Amsden. When was about to part with Dr. Owen, I look'd, to read some difficult place; pitch'd on v. 11th of the 8th Chapter—Know the Lord—I read it over and over one time and another and could not be satisfied: At last this came in my mind Know the Lord, i.e. Know the Messiah, to whom the word Lord is very much appropriated &c. vide locum. Now my mind was at quiet, and all seem'd to run smooth. As I hope this is Truth, so I bless God for this New-years Gift; which I also writt in a spare place, and gave it with the Book to the College.

JAN. 1, 1700/1701. Went afoot to Dorchester, carried Mr. Willard's Fountain open'd. Eat Yokeheg in Milk. Lt Gov orders me to wait on him next Tuesday morn.

SATTERDAY, JAN. 4, 1700/1701. Mrs. [Deborah] Thair is this morn taken with an Apoplexy after she had been up and employ'd a while; was at our pump for water. Dies about six in the Evening. . . .

JAN. 7TH. Mrs. Thair is buried: By reason of the Court, Stars were seen before we went; but comfortably Light by remains of the Day. Moon-shine and Snow.

Bearers, Cook, Sewall, Addington, Oakes, Melyen, Maryon, Jn Buried in the new burying place, close to the Alms-house [Granary] Ground. . . .

JAN. 14TH. Having been certified last night about 10. oclock of the death of my dear Mother at Newbury, Sam. and I set out with John Sewall, the Messenger, for that place. Hired Horses at Charlestown: set out about 10. aclock in a great Fogg. Din'd at Lewis's with Mr. Cushing of Salisbury. Sam. and I kept on in Ipswich Rode, John went to accompany from Salem. About Mr. Hubbard's in Ipswich farms, they overtook us. Sam. and I lodg'd at Cromptons in Ipswich. Brother and John stood on for Newbury by Moon-shine. Jan. 15th Sam. and I set forward. Brother Northend meets us. Visit Aunt Northend, Mr. Payson. With Brother and sister we set forward for Newbury: Where we find that day apointed for the Funeral: twas a very pleasant Comfortable day.

Bearers, Jn Kent of the Island, Lt. Cutting Noyes, Deacon William Noyes, Mr. Peter Tappan, Capt. Henry Somersby, Mr. Joseph Woodbridge. I follow'd the Bier single. Then Brother Sewall and sister Jane, Brother Short and his wife, Brother Moodey and his wife, Brother Northend and his wife, Brother Tappan and sister Sewall, Sam. and cous. Hanah Tappan. Mr. Payson of Rowley, Mr. Clark, Minister of Excester, were there. Col. Pierce, Major Noyes &c. Cous. John, Richard and Betty Dummer. Went abt. 4. P.M.Nathan Bricket taking in hand to fill the Grave, I said, Forbear a little, and suffer me to say That amidst our bereaving sorrows We have the Comfort of beholding this Saint put into the rightfull possession of that Happiness of Living desir'd and dying Lamented. She liv'd commendably Four and Fifty years with her dear Husband, and my dear Father: And she could not well brook the being divided from him at her death; which is the cause of our taking leave of her in this place. She was a true and constant Lover of Gods Word, Worship, and Saints: And she always, with a patient cheerfullness, submitted to the divine Decree of providing Bread for her self and others in the sweat of her Brows. And now her infinitely Gracious and Bountiful Master has promoted her to the Honor of higher Employments, fully and absolutely discharged from all manner of Toil, and Sweat. My honoured and beloved Friends and Neighbours! My dear Mother never thought much of doing the most frequent and homely offices of Love for me; and lavish'd away many Thousands of Words upon me, before I could return one word in Answer: And therefore I ask and hope that none will be offended that I have now ventured to speak one word in her behalf; when shee her self is become speechless. Made a Motion with my hand for the filling of the Grave. Note, I could hardly speak for passion and Tears. Mr. Tappan pray'd with us in the evening. I lodg'd at sister Gerrishes with Joseph. Brother and Sam. at Br. Tappans.

JAN. 16TH. The two Brothers and four sisters being together, we took Leave by singing of the 90th Psalm, from the 8th to the 15th verse inclusively. Mr. Brown, the Scholar, was present. Set out abt. 11. for Ipswich, got time enough to hear Mr. Rogers preach the Lecture from Luke 1. 76. about ministerial preparation for Christ. Sung the nine first verses of the 132. Psalm. Mr. Rogers prai'd for the prisoner of death, the Newbury woman who was there in her chains. This is the last Sermon preached in the old Meeting-house. Eat Roast Fowl at Crompton's. Delivered a Letter to the Widow Hale; got very comfortably over the Ferry to Brothers, whether Mr. Hirst quickly came to welcome us and invite us to dine or breakfast next day, which we did, the morning being cold: Visited Madam Bradstreet and Major Brown, and told them of the death of their fellow-passenger. Rec'd me very courteously. Took horse about one P.M. Baited at Lewis's; Stop'd at Govr. Usher's to pay him a visit. He and his Lady being from home, we pass'd on, and got to Charlestown about Sun-set, very comfortably. Found all well at home through the Goodness of God.

LORDS-DAY, JAN. 19TH, 1700/01. Ipswich people Meet the first time in their New- Meeting-House, Deacon Knowlton informs me at Cousin Savages Meeting Jan. 22th.

JAN. 29TH, 1700/01. Sam. and I went to Dedham Lecture, and heard Mr. Belchar preach excellently from Mat. 9. 12. Dined at said Belchars. Gave him and some young men with him my New-years verses: He read them and said Amen. Said twas a good Morning's Work.

JAN. 30. Mr. Willard preaches from Eccles. 9. 2—he that sweareth and he that feareth an Oath. Spake very closely against the many ways of Swearing amiss. Great Storm.

FEBR. 1, 1700/1701. Waited on the Lt Gov and presented him with a Ring in Remembrance of my dear Mother, saying, Please to accept of the Name of one of the Company your Honor is preparing to go to. Mr. Baily, Oliver, and Chip were there when I came in.

FEB. 3. 1700/01. Little Richd Fifield, a child of ½ a year old, died very suddenly last Friday, and was buried this day. Mr. Simon Willard, and S. Sewall [the son] Bearers. Very windy and cold after the Rain. . . .

TUESDAY, JUNE 10TH. Having last night heard that Josiah Willard had cut off his hair (a very full head of hair) and put on a Wigg, I went to him this morning. Told his Mother what I came about, and she call'd him. I enquired of him what Extremity had forced him to put off his own hair, and put on a Wigg? He answered, none at all. But said that his Hair was streight, and that it parted behinde. Seem'd to argue that men might as well shave their hair off their head, as off their face. I answered men were men before they had hair on their faces, (half of mankind have never any). God seems to have ordain'd our Hair as a Test, to see whether we can bring our minds to be content to be at his finding: or whether we would be our own Carvers, Lords, and come no more at Him. If disliked our Skin, or Nails; 'tis no Thanks to us, that for all that, we cut them not off: Pain and danger restrain us. Your Calling is to teach men self Denial. Twill be displeasing and burdensom to good men: And they that care not what men think of them care not what God thinks of them. Father, Brother Simon, Mr. Pemberton, Mr. Wigglesworth, Oakes, Noyes (Oliver), Brattle of Cambridge their example. Allow me to be so far a *Censor Morum* for this end of the Town. Pray'd him to read the Tenth Chapter of the Third book of Calvins Institutions. I read it this morning in course, not of choice. Told him that it was condemn'd by a Meeting of Ministers at Northampton in Mr. Stoddards house, when the said Josiah was there. Told him of the Solemnity of the Covenant which he and I had lately enterd into, which put me upon discoursing to him. He seem'd to say would leave off his Wigg when his hair was grown. I spake to his Father of it a day or two after: He thank'd me that had discoursed his Son, and told me that when his hair was grown to cover his ears, he promis'd to leave off his Wigg. If he had known of it, would have forbidden him. His Mother heard him talk of it; but was afraid positively to forbid him; lest he should do it, and so be more faulty.

JUNE 12. Mr. Willard marries Mr. Pemberton and Mrs. Mary Clark. All Mr. Willard's family there, as I am informed, and many others. Come to our Meeting the next Sabbath. . . .

MONDAY, OCT. 6, 1701. Very pleasant fair Wether; Artillery trains in the Afternoon [Sewall in command]. March with the Company to the Elms; Go to prayer, March down and Shoot at a Mark. Mr. Cushing I think was the first that hit it, Mr. Gerrish twice, Mr. Fitch, Chauncy, and the Ensign of the Officers. By far the most missed, as I did for the first. Were much contented with the exercise. Led them to the Trees agen, perform'd some facings and Doublings. Drew them together; propounded the question about the Colours; twas voted very freely and fully. I inform'd the Company I was told the Company's Halberds &c. were borrowed; I understood the Leading-staff was so, and therefore ask'd their Acceptance of a Half-Pike,[5] which they very kindly did; I deliver'd it to Mr. Gibbs for their Use.

They would needs give me a Volley, in token of their Respect on this occasion. The Pike will, I suppose, stand me in fourty shillings, being headed and shod with Silver: Has this Motto fairly engraven:

Agmen Massachusettense
est in tutelam Sponsoe
AGNI Uxoris.
1701.[6]

The Lord help us to answer the Profession. Were treated by the Ensign in a fair chamber. Gave a very handsome Volley at Lodging the Colours. The Training in Sept was a very fair day, so was this. . . .

THURSDAY, OCT. 23. Mr. Increase Mather said at Mr. Wilkins's, If I am a Servant of Jesus Christ, some great Judgment will fall on Capt. Sewall, or his family.

---

5. Half-Pike—This, as well as the Halberds and Leading-staff, are weapons.
6. *Agmen Massachusettense est in tutelam Sponsoe AGNI Uxoris. 1701*—For the Massachusetts Artillery Company, for the defense of the Bride, Spouse of the Lamb (Christ). 1701.

OCT. 24. Rainy Day, yet Judge Atwood comes from Rehoboth to Boston. 25. Visits several, and me among the rest. This day in the morn. I got Mr. Moody to copy out my Speech, and gave it to Mr. Wilkins that all might see what was the ground of Mr. Mather's Anger.

Writ out another and gave it to Joshua Gee. I perceive Mr. Wilkins carried his to Mr. Mathers; They seem to grow calm. (On Friday received Mr. Fitch's Letter and Blessing.) Receive the News of Sister Sewall's being brought to Bed of a Son, which is the Sixth; and the fifteenth Child. Messenger came in when Judge Atwood here. Son Hirst comes to Town. Was in danger to be cast away coming over the Ferry, the wind was so very high. Mr. Chiever visits me this Afternoon.

OCT. 28, 1701. Mr. William Atwood Takes the Oaths and subscribes the Declaration and Association, to qualify himself to exercise his Authority here as Judge of the Admiralty. He ask'd for a Bible: but Mr. Cooke said our Custom was to Lift up the hand; then he said no more, but used that Ceremony. His Commission was first read before the Council. At going away, he thanked me for, The Selling of Joseph,[7] saying twas an ingenious Discourse.

Thus a considerable part of Executive Authority is now gon out of the hands of New England men. . . .

NOV 23, 1701. John Joyliffe Esqr. dies. He had been blind, and laboured under many Infirmities for a long time. Mr. Brunsdon died the night before: and one Birds-eye a few days before; 3 men. Jn Arnolds wife is also dead. I wish it do not prove a sickly time after long Health.

Mr. Nicholas Noyes of Newbury, aged about 86 years, died on the Lords-Day 9 23. 1701. Mr. Oliver Purchas, late of Lin, now of Concord, is to be buried this week. Bearers of Mr. Joyliffe; Mr. Cooke, Addington, Sergeant, Anth. Checkly, El Hutchinson, Mr. Saffin.

SABBATH, NOV 30. I went to the Manifesto church to hear Mr. Adams; Mr. Coleman was praying when I went in, so that I thought my self disappointed. But his Prayer was short; When ended, he read distinctly the 137, and 138th Psalms, and the seventh of Joshua, concerning the conviction, sentence, and execution of Achan. Then sung the second part of the Sixty ninth Psalm. Mr. Brattle set it to Windsor Tune. Then Mr. Adams pray'd very well, and more largely: And gave us a very good Sermon from Gal. 4. 18. Doct. It is just and commendable &c. Mr. Adams gave the Blessing.

In the Afternoon Mr. Adams made a short Prayer, read the 139th Psalm, and the six and twentieth chapter of the Acts; Then Agrippon said—Sung. Mr. Coleman made a very good Sermon from Jer. 31. 33.—and will be their God, and they shall be my people.

---

7. The Selling of Joseph—Sewall's anti-slavery tract, referred to also on June 17, 1700. In *The Selling of Joseph*, Sewall, using Biblical references, refuted a series of arguments justifying slavery.

Pray'd sung—Contribution. Gave the Blessing. I spent this Sabbath at Mr. Colman's, partly out of dislike to Mr. Josiah Willard's cutting off his Hair, and wearing a Wigg: He preach'd for Mr. Pemberton in the morning; He that contemns the Law of Nature, is not fit to be a publisher of the Law of Grace: Partly to give an Example of my holding Communion with that Church who renounce the Cross in Baptisme, Humane Holydays &c. as other New-English Churches doe. And I had spent a Sabbath at the Old Church, and at Mr. Mathers. And I thought if I should have absented my self in the *forenoon* only, it might have been more gravaminous to Mr. Willards friends than keeping there *all day.* I perceive by several, that Mr. Coleman's people were much gratified by my giving them my Company, Several considerable persons express'd themselves so. The Lord cleanse me from all my Iniquity &c. Jer. 33. 8. and 16. which chapter read in course xr. 5th 1701.

DEC. 24, 1701. Sam sets out for Newbury with Capt. Somersby; went away about 1/2 hour past 12.

JAN. 2.,1701/1702. My Wife had some thoughts the Time of her Travail might be come, before she went to bed: But it went over. Between 4 and 5 m. I go to prayer, Rise, make a Fire, call Mrs. Ellis, Hawkins, Mary Hawkins calls Midwife Greenlef. I go to Mr. Willard and desire him to call God. The Women call me into chamber, and I pray there. Jn Barnard comes to me for Money: I desire him to acquaint Mr. Cotton Mather, and Father.

JAN 2. 1701/2. My Wife is well brought to Bed of a Daughter just about two p.m., a very cold day: Was got into Bed without a fainting Fit.

Sabbath-day night my wife is very ill and something delirious. Pulse swift and high. I call Mr. Oakes about Two aclock or before. Grows a little better.

JAN. 6, 1701/2. Nurse Hill watch'd last night. Wife had a comfortable night.

MEMORANDUM.

Sarah Sewall was born Nov. 21 1694. Baptised per Mr. Willard Nov 25. Died Dec 23. Was buried xr. 25. 1696.

A dear amiable Son of Samuel Sewall and Hanah his wife, was Still-born May, 21. 1696.

Judith Sewall was born upon Friday, Jan 2. at two in the Afternoon, Hannah Greenlef Midwife, Judd Nurse. Lords-Day, Jan 4. p.m., Was baptised by the Reverend Mr. Ebenezer Pemberton. It being his Turn: because The Rev. Mr. Willard administered the Lord's supper just before. So is a New Midwife, and a New Baptiser. What through my wives many Illnesses, more than ordinary, her fall upon the stairs about 5 weeks before; from which time she kept her chamber; her thoughtfullness between whiles whether she were with child or no; her Fears what the issue would be, and the misgiving of our Unbelieving hearts, GOD hath beem wonderfully merciful to us in her comfortable Delivery; which I desire to have Recorded.

Note. This is the Thirteenth Child that I have offered up to God in Baptisme; my wife having born me Seven Sons and Seven Daughters. I have named this little Daughter Judith, in Remembrance of her honoured and beloved Grandmother Mrs. *Judith Hull*. And it may be my dear wife may now leave off bearing.

JAN 8, 1701/2. Mr. Incr. Mather preaches the Lecture from Gen. 18. 24. Doct[rine] The Wicked many times fare the better for the sake of the Godly, Hopes for England and N. E. because many Righteous ones in both. About 4. Alice Macdonnel is buried. Mr. Lynde and I were there as Overseers of the poor. This day agreed with Nurse Randal to suckle Judith.

FRIDAY JAN 9, 1701/2. Buy a Wicker Cradle for Judith of Tho. Hunt; which Cost Sixteen Shillings.

My wife puts on her Cloaths, and sits up in the Bed.

JAN 10. My Wife gets on to the Pallat Bed in her Cloaths, and there keeps, while Linen Curtains are put up within the Serge; and is refresh'd by it.

JAN 12,1701/2. The Harbour is open again, and pretty well freed from the Ice. Jan 13. m. I pray'd earnestly by my self and in the family for a Nurse; Went and expostulated with Mr. Hill about his daughters failing me; in the chamber: In the mean time, one of his family went and call'd the Nurse and I brought her home with me; which was beyond my expectation. For Mr. Jesse huff'd and ding'd, and said he would lock her up, and she should not come. I sent not for her. So I hope twas an Answer of Prayer.

FRIDAY, JAN. 16. My Wife Treats her Midwife and Women: Had a good Dinner, Boil'd Pork, Beef, Fowls; very good Rost-Beef, Turkey-Pye, Tarts. Madam Usher carv'd, Mrs. Hannah Greenlef; Ellis, Cowell, Wheeler, Johnson, and her daughter Cole, Mrs. Hill our Nurses Mother, Nurse Johnson, Hill, Hawkins, Mrs. Goose, Deming, Green, Smith, Hatch, Blin. Comfortable, moderat wether: and with a good fire in the Stove warm'd the Room.

JAN 17. We hear that Mrs. Sam. Brown of Salem is dead, and the first child she had. She earnestly desired a child, having been a pretty while married. Col. Turner's sister.

JAN 18. Storm of snow: but not very cold.

JAN 20. between 11 and 12. Farnum the Father, was pecking Ice off the Mill-wheel, slipt in and was carried and crush'd, and kill'd, with the wheel. Elder Copp and Mr. Walley came to call Cousin Savage at my house.

Note. Last night were under awfull apprehensions, lest the House was on fire, there was such a smoke and smell in the cellar like as of a Colepit. Got Joseph Clark to view it and neibour Cole. Could find nothing. Cole suppos'd twas a Steem by reason of the cold. Many watch'd but found nothing. And blessed be God, the House is still standing. . . .

THURSDAY, FEBR. 19. Mr. I. Mather preached from Rev. 22. 16—bright and morning Star. Mention'd Sign in the Heaven, and in the Evening following I saw a large Cometical Blaze, something fine and dim, pointing from the Westward, a little below Orion.

FEBR. 21. Capt. Tim. Clark tells me that a Line drawn to the Comet strikes just upon Mexico, spake of a Revolution there, how great a Thing it would be. Said one Whitehead told him of the magnificence of the City, that there were in it 1500 Coaches drawn with Mules. This Blaze had much put me in mind of Mexico; because we must look toward Mexico to view it. Capt. Clark drew a Line on his Globe. Our Thoughts being thus confer'd, and found to jump, makes it to me remarkable. I have long pray'd for Mexico, and of late in those Words, that God would open the Mexican Fountain.

FEBR. 21. This day Goodw[ife] Pope, and John Wait dye.

FEBR. 22. My Wife goes to Meeting in the Afternoon, after long Restraint.

FEBR. 23. Goodw. Pope is buried. Capt Byfield and I and the Select-Men, and about 12 women there; Cowel, Wheeler, Calef &c. One or two Bacons, her Grand-sons, followed next.

FEBR. 25. Archibald Macquerry has a son born at Charlestown without Arms.

Jn Wait is buried; Gen Court Sat, and I think none of the Council at the Funeral.

FEBR. 26. Sixteen of the Council sign an order for making Dracot a Town. . . .

March 11, 1701/2 In the Afternoon, there are great Southerly Gusts and Showers; Considerable Thunder and Lightening. Last night between 10 and 11, A great Fire brake out in Mr. Thomson's Warehouse upon the Dock: Seven or Eight of the chief Warehouses were burnt and blown up. 'Tis said the Fire began in that part which Monsr. Bushee hires. About half a Ship's Loading was lately taken into it.

SATTERDAY, MARCH 14. AT 5 P.M.Capt. John Alden expired; Going to visit him, I happened to be there at the time. . . .

JUNE, 11. Thorsday, before I was dress'd, Sam. Gave the Word the Gov [Joseph Dudley] was come. Quickly after I got down, Maxwell summoned me to Council, told me the Secretary had a Letter of the Governours Arrival yesterday, at Marblehead. Mr. Addington, Eliakim Hutchinson, Byfield and Sewall, sent per the Council, go with Capt Crofts in his Pinace to meet the Governour, and Congratulat his Arrival. We get aboard a little before got within Point Alderton; Capt Heron introduced us; After had all saluted the Gov I said,

Her Majesty's Council of this Province have commanded us to meet your Excellency, and congratulate your safe Arrival in the Massachusetts Bay, in quality of our Governour: Which we do very heartily; not only out of Obedi-ence to our Masters who sent us; but also of our own accord. The Cloaths your Excellency sees us wear, are a true Indication of our inward Grief for the Depar-ture of K. William. Yet we desire to remember with Thankfullness the Goodness of God, who has at this time peacably placed Queen Anne upon the Throne. And as Her Majestys Name imports Grace, so we trust God will shew Her Majesty Favour; and Her Majesty us. And we look upon your Excellency's being sent to us, as a very fair First-Fruit of it, for which we bless God and Queen Anne.

I was startled at 2 or 3 things; viz. The Lt Governour [Thomas Povey] a stranger, sent, whom we knew nor heard anything of before: When the Gov first mention'd it, I understood him of Mr. Addington. I saw an ancient Minister, enquiring who it was, Governour said, twas G[eorge] Keith, had converted many in England, and now Bp. London had sent him hether with Salery of 200. Guineys per annum. I look'd on him as Helena aboard. This man crav'd a Blessing and return'd Thanks, though there was the chaplain of the Ship, and another Minister on board. Governour has a very large Wigg. Drink Healths, About one and Twenty Guns fired at our leaving the Centurion; and Cheers, then Capt Scot and another Ship fired. Castle fired many Guns; Landed at Scarlet's Wharf, where the Council and Regiment waited for us; just before came at the North-Meetinghouse Clock struck five. Was the Troop of Guards, and Col. Paige's Troop. March'd to the Townhouse. There before the Court; Ministers, and as many else as could crowd in, the Governour's and Lt Gov Commissions were published; they took their Oaths laying their hands on the Bible, and after Kissing it. Had a large Treat. Just about dark Troops Guarded the Gov. to Roxbury. He rode in Major Hobby's Coach Drawn with six Horses richly harnessed. By mistake, my coachman stayed in the yard, and so Joseph and I went alone. Foot gave 3 very good Volleys after the publication of the Commissions, and were dismiss'd. Mr. Mather crav'd a Blessing and Mr. Cotton Mather Return'd Thanks.

# INTRODUCTION & QUESTIONS

## THE ARTIFACTS OF THE PURITANS

The materials for study in this topic consist of a collection of photographic reproductions of Puritan objects on the "Artifacts of the Puritans."

As you view, or review, this program, consider the following questions:

1. On what basis did the Puritans deny the worth of most traditional art forms? Do any of their reasons include a strong condemnation of any established religious institutions?

2. By Puritan criteria, what functions was a painting supposed to fulfill? What basic Puritan ideas are apparent here?

3. The portrait of Richard Mather is not signed by the artist. Why? In what ways might the concept of "calling" be involved here?

4. What were the primary functions of the Richard Mather portrait if it was not expected to be a visually realistic reproduction of the individual?

5. Given the fact that the personal or individual characteristics of Cotton Mather were largely excluded from his portrait, what does this suggest about the relative weight Puritans assigned to personal as opposed to social worth?

6. What social purposes could be served by the distribution of pictorial representations of Puritan divines? How have the artist's major preoccupations and procedures assisted such objectives?

7. What circumstances would make the portrait of a layman acceptable to the Puritan? How were such requirements present in the case of Samuel Sewall?

8. What were the artist's major concerns in his portrayal of William Stoughton? What Puritan values are thus apparent?

9. Women are also captured in Puritan portraiture. How could this be a consequence of the basic functions of Puritan portraiture?

10. Why were portraits of Puritan children so rare? What necessary prerequisites for portraiture would normally be lacking here?

11. Why would the Puritans reject the newer artistic innovations of contemporaneous England and instead choose the older and archaic modes of painting represented in the portrait of Margaret Gibbs?

12. What considerations underlie the arrangement, placement and poses for each child in the Mason portrait? What similarities with adult portraiture exist here?

13. In what role does the Puritan artist depict children in portraiture? Why do you think he conceptualizes children in this way?

14. Why should Cotton Mather's map of New England exclude any areas beyond the Atlantic coastline? What social ideals are present here and in the map maker's concentration on the region's waterways?

15. Mather's map also devotes much attention to the careful notation of towns or communities. What does this suggest about the importance of the local community in this culture?

16. What kind of relationship between town and church is suggested by the fact that each town is identified by the symbol of a meeting house?

17. What could explain the haphazard street arrangement of Boston? What assumptions regarding the natural world might be present here?

18. What can you ascertain from the layout of Boston about the significance of economic concerns among the Puritans of New England? Of the relative importance of religious institutions?

19. What kind of social order is suggested by the house lots of Boston?

20. What kind of relationship between man and the natural world is indicated by the absence of trees, shrubs and other vegetation near these Puritan dwellings?

21. What does the lack of symmetry, balance and mathematical correctness in Puritan architecture suggest about his evaluation of man's capabilities to control his environment?

22. What is the function of the "porch?" Why is there so little attention given to purely decorative elements in such interior spaces?

23. What kind of social organization was required to build private houses with this type of construction? What Puritan cultural characteristics are therefore apparent?

24. Why would individual innovation and variation be subordinated in Puritan architecture? Can you cite any other areas, besides architecture, where personal innovation is restricted? What does this indicate about Puritan cultural priorities?

25. What is suggested about the nature of social relations by the variations in house plans used by the Puritans?

26. Why should it be that so few architects and builders from New England are known from this period?

27. What basic architectural tradition did the Puritans follow? What basic attitudes are reflected here?

28. Why would the Puritans find it impossible to use an Anglican church building as a model for their own religious housings?

29. What is revealed about the church's role by the size, shape and location of the meeting house? What social ideals and values are revealed in its interior, especially in the seating arrangement?

30. In most areas of Puritan manufacture, ornamentation is very reserved. However, their gravestones are highly elaborate. How can this be explained?

31. What significant information about the deceased is provided on the face of the gravestone? What cultural values are thereby revealed?

32. What were the major functions of the Puritan gravestone? Which of these, given Puritan priorities, would be the most important?

33. What can you determine, from the gravestone examples shown, about the Puritans' attitude toward death?

34. What is significant about the shape of the Puritan gravestone? How would this contribute to the viewers' religious instruction? What other features of the object contribute to this end?

35. How is the individual identified on the Rebecca Row stone? What does this indicate about Puritan cultural priorities?

36. To what degree was the Puritan stone cutter free to introduce personal innovation? Why? What does such suggest about personal identity as opposed to group or community importance in New England?

# INTRODUCTION & QUESTIONS

## THE SOUTHERN EXPERIENCE—
## A SELECTIVE CULTURAL
## RECONSTRUCTION

From the outset, the colony of Virginia was designed to follow the basic English ideal and method for the "planting" of Britain's New World possessions. Undertaken in earnest in 1606, this process began when King James I gave a joint-stock company the right to own and develop the area centering around Chesapeake Bay. By the terms of this royal charter, the Virginia Company was to remain in London while sending out and supervising English colonists in Virginia. The venture was considered, first of all, as a private business operation designed to realize continuing dividends for the Company's stockholders. While the endeavor would ultimately benefit the whole kingdom, the government's role in the enterprise was generally restricted to secondary supervision and offering encouragement.

In 1607, with the founding of Jamestown, the colony entered its first difficult years, complicated by disease, starvation, conflicts with the Indians, and rampant insubordination among the first comers. Thinking in terms of military beachheads from which to explore and exploit the surrounding country, Virginia's conquerors included many gentlemen-adventurers expecting to plunder a developed native civilization as had the Spaniards earlier in South America. Only after they abandoned the attempts to discover a "northwest passage," mineral deposits or a rich Indian civilization did the colonists begrudgingly move toward permanent settlement and intensive economic development of the region. To promote these ends, women were sent, lands distributed to individuals and the settlers granted a measure of self-government by the Company.

Central to both the Company's and the colonists' planning in these years was the ideal of developing a diversified economy, one based not only on agriculture, but with attention given also to the profitable manufacturing of such products as silk, glass, wines, and naval stores. Essentially a British tradesmen's scheme, Virginia was, at the outset, an attempt to reproduce a broad cross section of English life, one including a rural gentry along with a thriving mercantile community centered in the future cities of the colony.

Yet the Company's direction was marked by generally ineffectual leadership, which, with continuing factional disputes both at home and in the colony and the severe political instability of England in these years, seriously affected the venture. Subject also to other, equally devastating factors, the Company was bankrupt in 1624 and Virginia reverted to the Crown to become the first royal colony in British North America.

Despite this new development, the King made few fundamental changes in the arrangements developed during the colony's initial years. For instance, the scheme of land allotment and tenure remained intact. Under that arrangement, known as the "head right" system, each settler was given a 50 acre plot for each colonist he brought into the developing area. Granted as a contiguous area, these lands, within three years, had to be "seated" (improved), before the settler could acquire final title. Envisioned as a device for creating relatively limited, self-sustaining agricultural units, the "head right" system also sought to encourage rapid and extensive settlement of the potentially rich wilderness of Virginia, an ideal shared by both Company and Crown.

Nor did royal direction significantly change the political mechanisms developed under the Company's auspices. True, Virginia's governor was now appointed by the King, but his duties as the colony's chief executive, administrative and judicial officer remained intact. Coupled with his power to grant land patents and to appoint most of Virginia's minor political functionaries, his was the voice of Crown and Empire in the New World.

Advising the governor was a council of less than a dozen men selected from among Virginia's settlers and holding life-time royal appointments. Beyond their advisory and administrative role, they, with the governor, made up the General Court, Virginia's highest judicial body. Their assent was also necessary before any legislation passed by the House of Burgesses might become law.

The role and responsibilities of the last of the major colonial political institutions, the House of Burgesses, was given special consideration by Hugh Jones, one of its chaplains. In the selection which follows, part of Jones' *The Present State of Virginia*, he describes the functioning of Virginia's original legislature. Jones' account appeared in 1724, one of a number of works designed to acquaint intrigued Englishmen with the characteristics of this richest of England's American colonies.

Born in 1692, Jones arrived in Virginia at the age of 25, an Anglican minister hired as professor of math at Williamsburgh's College of William and Mary. Although perhaps overly concerned with what he regarded as a lack of colonial support for the college and clergy, his account is a complete survey of those elements of the Virginia experience considered most relevant to his contemporaries. Part I was devoted to the curious customs of the colony's Indians. The remainder of the book outlined the English inhabitants' "Religion, Manners, Government, Trade, Way of Living, etc., with a description of the Country." In analysing this selection, pay special attention to Jones' unspoken criteria for selecting the particular matters he discusses as well as to his structuring of this material. Both selection and structure reveal much of the cultural dynamics of colonial Virginia.

## PART II—CHAPTER I

1.  Whom does Jones credit with promoting early exploration and settlement in Virginia? How does this contrast with the beginnings in Massachusetts?

2.  What events does Jones consider of most significance in the early years of the colony's history? Do they share any common characteristics?

3. How does Jones explain the intervention of Charles I into the colony's operations? What affect upon Virginia does he ascribe to the King's actions? Does this suggest anything about his own sentiments?

4. What factors does Jones cite to explain migrations from England to Virginia? How might they compare with those prompting migration from England to Massachusetts Bay?

5. What is the nature of religious commitments in Virginia? With what social characteristics is the prevailing religious institution associated?

## CHAPTER III

1. What is, for Jones, the most significant geological feature of Virginia? What uses does this feature have? How does it affect settlement patterns?

2. What has retarded the development of towns? What has characterized the attempts to create them?

3. What materials and distinctive features are employed in domestic building? What does this indicate about Virginia's social system?

## CHAPTER IV

1. How does Jones define the overseer's role? How is he compensated?

2. What characteristics does slavery in Virginia have, according to Jones? What data does he use to substantiate this?

3. How does Jones assess a slave's various abilities? What comparison does he make between the Negro and the Indian? What are the behavioral characteristics of a "good" slave? What experience best prepares one for servitude?

## CHAPTER V

1. What are the most noticeable character traits of the English in Virginia? What are the most notable defects Jones finds in them?

2. What attitudes toward education prevail among the Virginians? How are the young men among them educated? What "singular service" does Jones indicate is served by the college at Williamsburgh? How does Jones view the other American colonies with respect to Virginia? What factors might shape such assessments on his part?

3. What particular leisure activities are practiced in Virginia? What elements of the Virginia character are apparent in them?

4. What are the principal features of the economic system of the colony? Of what significance is credit in this system? What consequences might such a system have for the relationship between Virginia and England?

**CHAPTER VI**

1. For what purposes does the militia exist? How is it officered? What does this suggest about Virginia's social structure?

2. What forms of taxation are levied? By whom? On what basis? In what form? For what purposes?

3. How are Burgesses selected? What precedents are followed by Virginia's government, both in its structure and operations?

**PART III**

1. What relation does the church in Virginia have to the ecclesiastical hierarchy of the Church of England? Who and how significant is the commissary?

2. What is the governing body of a parish? How might a parish's size affect its functioning?

# THE PRESENT STATE OF VIRGINIA

*Hugh Jones*

## Part II

### CHAPTER I—OF THE ENGLISH SETTLEMENTS IN VIRGINIA

The first Discovery made for the English in North-America, was in the Year 1584. . . .

They anchored at Roenoak Inlet, now belonging to the government of North Carolina, and from the Virgin Queen, and the apparent purity of the Indians, and primitive plenty of the place, that new discovered part of the world was named Virginia.

After that, Sir Richard Greenvile, Sir Francis Drake, and Sir Walter Raleigh carried on the project, and made advancements in it, with the leave of the government; which were promoted and continued by the merchants of London, Bristol, Exeter and Plymouth; with variety of accidents, successes and disappointments in respect of their trade and possessions; and war and peace with the Indians; especially under the conduct of Captain Smith, who was employed by the company of merchants incorporated by King James I in 1606; and has written a large history of his particular transactions.

They then fixed chiefly at, and near James Town, on a small island in James River, till the year 1609, when they sent out settlements to Nansemond, Powhatan, and the year after to Kiquotan.

After that the plantations of Virginia were formed into a government, managed first by three, and afterwards by one governor, to whose assistance in a small time they added counsellors; and in 1620, they called an Assembly of Burgesses, who being elected by the people, met the governor and council at James Town, and debated matters for the improvement and good government of the country.

About this time the Dutch brought over some Negroes for sale, who are now wonderfully encreased; besides the constant supplies of them imported yearly.

At this time, they made new settlements, laid out and apportioned lands, some to the governor, some for a college and Indian school, some to the church and glebes,[1] and some to particular persons; and carried on salt works and iron works, besides tobacco.

This prosperity of the colony so encouraged its increase, that one thousand three hundred people have gone over in one year to settle there; upon which they made country courts for the tryal of some causes and criminals under the General Court and assembly; but private interest and quarrels by [p]assing the governors and other persons concerned, often introduced ill success, faction and Indian wars.

The fatal consequences of this male-administration cryed so loud, that King Charles I coming to the crown of England, had a tender concern for the poor people, that had been betrayed thither and almost lost: upon which he dissolved the company in 1626, reducing the country and government into his own immediate direction, appointing the governor and council himself, and ordering all patents and processes to issue in his own name, reserving to himself a quit-rent of two shillings for every hundred acres of land.

In this happy constitution, the Colony of Virginia has prosperously encreased gradually and wonderfully, to its present most flourishing condition. . . .

The assured good report of this vast tract of land and happy climate encouraged several gentlemen of condition and good descent, to transport themselves and families, and settle in this new paradise; some for the sake of wealth, some for religion, and others because they could not well live elsewhere; and others because they dared not, or cared not to stay at home.

But one particular occasion that sent several families of good birth and fortune to settle there, was the civil wars in England; for Sir William Barkley the governor being strong for the King, held out the last of all the King's dominions against the usurper;[2] and likewise proclaimed King Charles II before the Restoration.

This safe receptacle enticed over several Cavalier[3] families, where they made many laws against Puritans, though they were free from them; which had this good success, that to this day, the people are as it were quite free from them, being all of the Church of England, without the odious distinguishing characters of high or low among themselves. Indeed, there are a few Quakers in some of the worst counties, where clergymen are unwilling to settle, such as the lower parts of Nansemond County; but these might easily be brought over to the church; and

---

1. glebes—lands assigned to ministers.
2. The Puritan forces in Parliament who executed Charles I in 1649, and ruled during the Commonwealth until the Restoration of the Stuarts.
3. Cavaliers—Englishmen who remained loyal to the crown during the Commonwealth.

I am fully persuaded that the growth of their doctrine might be easily nipped in the bud, by very plain methods. . . .

## CHAPTER III—OF THE SITUATION AND NATURE OF THE COUNTRY OF VIRGINIA, AND ITS COASTS, ETC.

There are belonging to Virginia four principal rivers (neither of them inferior upon many accounts to the Thames or Severn) that empty themselves into the [Chesapeake] Bay after they have glided some hundreds of miles fromwards the mountains, the western bounds of Virginia.

The most southerly of these rivers is called James River, and the next York River, the land in the latitude between these rivers seeming most nicely adapted for sweet scented, or the finest tobacco; for 'tis observed that the goodness decreaseth the farther you go to the northward of the one, and the southward of the other; but this may be (I believe) attributed in some measure to the seed and management, as well as to the land and latitude: for on York River in a small tract of land called Digges's Neck, which is poorer than a great deal of other land in the same latitude, by a particular seed and management, is made the famous crop known by the name of the E Dees, remarkable for its mild taste and fine smell.

The next great river is Rappahonnock, and the fourth is Potowmack, which divides Virginia from the Province of Maryland.

These are supplied by several lesser rivers, such as Chickahommony and others, navigable for vessels of great burthen.

Into these rivers run abundance of great creeks or short rivers, navigable for sloops, shallops, long-boats, flats, canoes and periaguas.

These creeks are supplied with the tide, (which indeed does not rise so high as in Europe, so prevents their making good docks) and also with fresh-water-runs, replenished with branches issuing from the springs, and soaking through the swamps; so that no country is better watered, for the conveniency of which most houses are built near some landing-place; so that any thing may be delivered to a gentleman there from London, Bristol, etc with less trouble and cost, than to one living five miles in the country in England. . . .

Because of this convenience, and for the goodness of the land, and for the sake of fish, fowl, etc. gentlemen and planters love to build near the water; though it be not altogether so healthy as the uplands and barrens, which serve for ranges for stock.

In the uplands near the ridge generally run the main roads, in a pleasant, dry, sandy soil, free from stones and dirt, and shaded and sheltered chiefly by trees; in some places being not unlike the walks in Greenwich Park.

Thus neither the interest nor inclinations of the Virginians induce them to cohabit in towns; so that they are not forward in contributing their assistance towards the making of particular places, every plantation affording the owner the provision of a little market; wherefore they most commonly build upon some convenient spot or neck of land in their own plantations, though towns are laid out and established in each county; the best of which (next Williamsburgh) are York, Glocester, Hampton, Elizabeth Town, and Urbanna.

The Colony now is encreased to twenty-nine counties, naturally bounded (near as much as may be) one with another about as big as Kent; but the frontier counties are of vast extent, though not thick seated[4] as yet.

The whole country is a perfect forest, except where the woods are cleared for plantations, and old fields, and where have been formerly Indian towns, and poisoned fields and meadows, where the timber has been burnt down in fire-hunting or otherwise; and about the creeks and rivers are large rank morasses or marshes, and up the country are poor savannahs.[5]

The gentlemen's seats[6] are of late built for the most part of good brick, and many of timber very handsom, commodious, and capacious; and likewise the common planters live in pretty timber houses, neater than the farm houses are generally in England: With timber also are built houses for the overseers and out-houses; among which is the kitchen apart from the dwelling house, because of the smell of hot victuals, offensive in hot weather.

## CHAPTER IV—OF THE NEGROES, WITH THE PLANTING AND MANAGEMENT OF INDIAN CORN, TOBACCO, ETC. AND OF THEIR TIMBER, STOCK, FRUITS, PROVISION, AND HABITATIONS, ETC.

The Negroes live in small cottages called quarters, in about six in a gang, under the direction of an overseer or bailiff; who takes care that they tend such land as the owner allots and orders, upon which they raise hogs and cattle, and plant Indian corn (or maize) and tobacco for the use of their master; out of which the overseer has a dividend (or share) in proportion to the number of hands including himself; this with several privileges is his salary, and is an ample recompence for his pains, and encouragement of his industrious care, as to the labour, health, and provision of the Negroes.

The Negroes are very numerous, some gentlemen having hundreds of them of all sorts, to whom they bring great profit; for the sake of which they are obliged to keep them well, and not over-work, starve, or famish them, besides other inducements to favour them; which is done in a great degree, to such especially that are laborious, careful, and honest; though indeed some masters, careless of their own interest or reputation, are too cruel and negligent.

The Negroes are not only encreased by fresh supplies from Africa and the West India Islands, but also are very prolifick among themselves; and they that are born there talk good English, and affect our language, habits, and customs; and though they be naturally of a barbarous and cruel Temper, yet are they kept

---

4. seated—settled, populated.
5. Savannahs—treeless, grassy plains.
6. Seats—manor houses.

under by severe discipline upon occasion, and by good laws are prevented from running away, injuring the English, or neglecting their business.

Their work (or chimerical hard slavery) is not very laborious; their greatest hardship consisting in that they and their posterity are not at their own liberty or disposal, but are the property of their owners; and when they are free, they know not how to provide so well for themselves generally; neither did they live so plentifully nor (many of them) so easily in their own country, where they are made slaves to one another, or taken captive by their enemies.

The children belong to the master of the woman that bears them; and such as are born of a Negroe and an European are called Molattoes; but such as are born of an Indian and Negroe are called Mustees.

Their work is to take care of the stock, and plant corn, tobacco, fruits, etc. which is not harder than thrashing, hedging, or ditching; besides, though they are out in the violent heat, wherein they delight, yet in wet or cold weather there is little occasion for their working in the fields, in which few will let them be abroad, lest by this means they might get sick or die, which would prove a great loss to their owners, a good negroe being sometimes worth three (nay four) score pounds sterling, if he be a tradesman; so that upon this (if upon no other account) they are obliged not to overwork them, but to cloath and feed them sufficiently, and take care of their health.

Several of them are taught to be sawyers, carpenters, smiths, coopers, etc. and though for the most part they be none of the aptest or nicest; yet they are by nature cut out for hard labour and fatigue, and will perform tolerably well; though they fall much short of an indian, that has learned and seen the same things; and those negroes make the best servants, that have been slaves in their own country; for they that have been kings and great men there are generally lazy, haughty, and obstinate; whereas the others are sharper, better humoured, and more laborious. . . .

## CHAPTER V—OF THE HABITS, CUSTOMS, PARTS, IMPLOYMENTS, TRADE, ETC., OF THE VIRGINIANS . . .

The habits, life, customs, computations, etc. of the virginians are much the same as about london, which they esteem their home . . . for the most part they are much civilized, and wear the best of cloaths according to their station; nay, sometimes too good for their circumstances, being for the generality comely handsom persons, of good features and fine complexions (if they take care) of good manners and address. the climate makes them bright, and of excellent sense, and sharp in trade, an ideot, or deformed native being almost a miracle. . . .

They are not very easily persuaded to the improvement of useful inventions (except a few, such as sawing mills) neither are they great encouragers of manufacturers, because of the trouble and certain expence in attempts of this kind, with uncertain prospect of gain; whereas by their staple commodity, tobacco, they are in hopes to get a plentiful provision; nay, often very great estates.

Upon this account they think it folly to take off their hands (or Negroes) and employ their care and time about any thing, that may make them lessen their crop of tobacco. . . .

As for education several are sent to England for it; though the Virginians being naturally of good parts, (as I have already hinted) neither require nor admire as much learning, as we do in britain; yet more would be sent over, were they not afraid of the small-pox, which most commonly proves fatal to them. . . .

[T]he youth might as well be instructed there as here by proper methods, without the expence and danger of coming hither; especially if they make use of the great advantage of the college at Williamsburgh, where they may (and many do) imbibe the principles of all human and divine literature, both in English and in the learned languages.

By the happy opportunity of this college may they be advanced to religious and learned education, according to the discipline and doctrine of the established Church of England; in which respect this college may prove of singular service, and be an advantageous and laudable nursery and strong bulwark against the contagious dissentions in Virginia, which is the most antient and loyal, the most plentiful and flourishing, the most extensive and beneficial colony belonging to the crown of Great Britain. . . .

If New England be called a receptacle of dissenters, and an Amsterdam of religion, Pensylvania the nursery of Quakers, Maryland the retirement of Roman Catholicks, North Carolina the refuge of run-aways, and South Carolina the delight of buccaneers and pyrates, Virginia may be justly esteemed the happy retreat of true Britons and true churchmen for the most part; neither soaring too high nor drooping too low, consequently should merit the greater esteem and encouragement.

The common planters leading easy lives don't much admire labour, or any manly exercise, except horse-racing, nor diversion, except cock-fighting, in which some greatly delight. this easy way of living, and the heat of the summer makes some very lazy, who are then said to be climate-struck.

The saddle-horses, though not very large, are hardy, strong, and fleet; and will pace naturally and pleasantly at a prodigious rate.

They are such lovers of riding, that almost every ordinary person keeps a horse; and I have known some spending the morning in ranging several miles in the woods to find and catch their horses only to ride two or three miles to church, to the court-house, or to a horse-race, where they generally appoint to meet upon business; and are more certain of finding those that they want to speak or deal with, than at their home.

No people can entertain their friends with better cheer and welcome; and strangers and travellers are here treated in the most free, plentiful, and hospitable manner; so that a few inns or ordinaries on the road are sufficient. . . .

In all convenient places are kept stores or ware-houses of all sorts of goods managed by store-keepers or factors, either for themselves or others in the country, or in Great Britain.

This trade is carried on in the fairest and genteelest way of merchandize, by a great number of gentlemen of worth and fortune; who with the commanders of their ships, and several Virginians (who come over through business or curiosity, or often to take possession of estates, which every year fall here to some or other of them) make as considerable and handsom a figure, and drive as great and advantageous a trade for the advancement of the publick good, as most merchants upon the Royal-Exchange.[7]

At the stores in Virginia, the planters, etc. may be supplied with what English commodities they want.

The merchants, factors, or store-keepers in virginia buy up the tobacco of the planters, either for goods or current spanish money, or with sterling bills payable in Great Britain.

The tobacco is rolled, drawn by horses, or carted to convenient rolling houses, whence it is conveyed on board the ships in flats or sloops, etc. . . .

The tobacco purchased by the factors or store-keepers, is sent home to their employers, or consigned to their correspondent merchants in Great Britain.

But most gentlemen, and such as are beforehand in the world, lodge money in their merchant's hands here, to whom they send their crop of tobacco, or the greatest part of it.

This money is employed according to the planter's orders; chiefly in sending over yearly such goods, apparel, liquors, etc. as they write for, for the use of themselves, their families, slaves and plantations; by which means they have every thing at the best hand, and the best of its kind.

Besides English goods, several merchants in virginia import from the West-Indies great quantities of rum, sugar, molossus, etc. and salt very cheap from the Salt Islands; which things they purchase with money, or generally with pork, beef, wheat, indian-corn, and the like. . . .

## CHAPTER VI— . . . THE MILITIA, . . . TITLES, LEVIES, BURGESSES, LAWS, AND GENERAL ASSEMBLY

In each country is a great number of disciplined and armed militia, ready in case of any sudden irruption of Indians or insurrection of Negroes, from whom they are under but small apprehension of danger. . . .

The gentlemen of the country have no other distinguishing titles of honour, but colonels and majors and captains of the militia, except the honourable the Council, and some commissioned in posts by HIS Majesty or his orders, who are nominated esquires; but there is one baronet's family there, viz. Sir William Skipwith's.

---

7. Royal-Exchange—a famous merchants' exchange in London.

The taxes or levies are either publick, county, or parish; which are levied by the justices or vestries, apportioning an equal share to be paid by all persons in every family above sixteen; except the white women, and some antiquated persons, who are exempt.

The payment is tobacco, which is sold or applied in specie to the use intended.

The publick levy is for the service of the colony in general, the county levy is for the use of the county, collected by the sheriffs and their offices and receivers; and the parish levy is for its own particular use, collected by the church-wardens for payment of the minister, the church, and poor.

There are two burgesses elected by the freeholders, and sent from every county; and one for James Town, and another for the College; these meet, choose a speaker, etc. and proceed in most respects as the House of Commons in England, who with the upper house, consisting of the governor and council, make laws exactly as the king and parliament do; the laws being passed there by the governor, as by the king here.

All the laws and statutes of England before Queen Elizabeth are there in force, but none made since; except those that mention the plantations, which are always specified in English laws, when occasion requires.

The General Assembly has power to make laws, or repeal such others, as they shall think most proper for the security and good of the country, provided they be not contradictory to the laws of England, nor interfering with the interest of Great Britain; these laws are immediately in force there, and are transmitted hither to the Lords of the Plantations and Trade for the royal assent; after which they are as obligatory as any laws can possibly be. . . .

All laws that the king dislikes upon the first perusal, are immediately abrogated.

Thus, in state affairs liberty is granted, and care is taken to make such laws from time to time, as are different from the laws in England, whenever the interest or necessity of the country, or the nature of the climate, and other circumstances shall require it.

# Part III

## CHAPTER I—OF THE STATE OF THE CHURCH AND CLERGY OF VIRGINIA.

Though provision is made, and proper measures are taken to make allowances and alterations in matters of government, state and trade; yet in matters of religion, there has not been the care and provision that might be wished and expected. . . .

This, with all the other plantations, is under the care of the Bishop of London, who supplies them with what clergymen he can get from England, Scotland, Ireland, and France. The late bishop appointed the Reverend Mr. James Blair to be his Commissary, who is likewise president of the College, and one of the Council. He by the bishop's order summoned the clergy to conventions, where he sate as chairman; but the power of conventions[8] is very little, as is that of the commissary at present. . . .

The vestries consist of the minister, and twelve of the most substantial and intelligent persons in each parish. These at first were elected by the parish by pole, and upon vacancies are supplied by vote of the vestry . . . By the vestry are all parochial affairs managed, such as the church, poor, and the minister's salary. . . .

The parishes being of great extent (some sixty miles long and upwards) many dead corpses cannot be conveyed to the church to be buried: so that it is customary to bury in gardens or orchards, where whole families lye interred together, in a spot generally handsomly enclosed, planted with evergreens, and the graves kept decently: hence likewise arises the occasion of preaching funeral sermons in houses, where at funerals are assembled a great congregation of neighbors and friends; and if you insist upon having the sermon and ceremony at church, they'll say they will be without it, unless performed after their usual custom. in houses also there is occasion, from humour, custom sometimes, from necessity most frequently, to baptize children and church women,[9] otherwise some would go without it. In houses also they most commonly marry, without regard to the time of the day or season of the year. . . .

---

8. conventions—meetings of the clergy.

9. church women—to conduct a religious service for a woman for her recovery from childbirth.

# INTRODUCTION & QUESTIONS

## THE SOUTHERN INDIVIDUAL AND HIS WORLD

*The Secret Diary of William Byrd of Westover* was written by William Byrd II, a Southern aristocrat whose grandfather was a London goldsmith. The first William Byrd inherited some 1800 acres in Virginia from a relative in 1670, came to the colony, married well, amassed a fortune in the fur and slave trade and became a member of the House of Burgesses and later the Council.

His son, William Byrd II, was born in Virginia in 1674. At seven he was sent to England for schooling and at sixteen to Holland to study business methods. He later received formal legal training in London and made extensive contacts with the British aristocracy and literary community. In 1696, at the age of twenty-two, he secured election to the Royal Society.

In the same year he returned to Virginia and was elected to the House of Burgesses. Soon after, he returned to England to serve as the colony's agent in London, a position that placed him in the thick of political battles.

In 1704, at thirty, he fell heir to some 26,231 acres in Virginia. Now one of the wealthiest men in the colony, he returned to his main plantation of Westover and married Lucy Parke, a member of the aristocracy. Unfortunately for Byrd she was a woman of some temperament. In 1709 he was appointed to the Council and began a diary which he maintained until his death. The diary was maintained in a special code not "broken" until the twentieth century.

Except for one year, the period 1715 to 1726 was spent in England on public and personal business. Part of the latter entailed courting the daughters of wealthy Londoners after Lucy's death in 1716. Byrd's London life, both socially and sexually, was extraordinarily full. During this period he found his second wife, Maria Taylor, a placid, homeloving woman who, during their marriage, presented him with four children.

After 1726, Byrd remained in Virginia, improving his estate, speculating in western lands, actively participating in public affairs, authoring a number of literary pieces and indulging his interests in natural history, medicine and mining. Much energy went into collecting an extensive library and corresponding with influential Britishers. He was made president of the Council one year before his death in 1744. His estate included nearly 180,000 acres.

Reproduced here are two representative months in Byrd's life. Parentheses indicate that the transcriber of the diary was unsure of Byrd's reference. In analysing this selection, it may be valuable to draw comparisons between this individual and Samuel Sewall.

1. What data does Byrd present that describes his occupation of planter? What responsibilities are his? What needs does he meet as the owner of large plantations and what skills does he display?

2. What kinds of activities does he note that pertain to his private or personal life? Of what does his reading consist? What references does he make regarding it?

3. What constitute his religious activities? What concern does he display regarding this aspect of his life?

4. What notice does the diary take of members of his family? Considering the diary references, what appears to be the role of the woman in colonial Virginia?

5. What social contacts does Byrd have apart from those on his plantation? What kinds of social occasions does he mention? What are the limits of the community for him?

6. What natural phenomena does he observe? How does he conceptually treat this data?

# THE SECRET DIARY OF
# WILLIAM BYRD OF WESTOVER

## APRIL, 1709

1. I rose before 6 o'clock and read a chapter in Hebrew and 250 verses in Homer's *Odyssey*. I said my prayers and ate [...] for breakfast. John [West] made an end of the two little houses and I settled the account with him. I ate some cold beef and then I waited on the ladies to Mr. Anderson's,[1] where we got about 12 o'clock. About 3 o'clock we ate, and I ate nothing but dry beef, notwithstanding there were several other dishes. We returned home about sunset, and found the Doctor[2] just come from Williamsburg. He brought a good deal of news from Europe and particularly that our last fleet was arrived in England. He told me likewise there was a report that my father Parke[3] was killed by the [l-v-n-t] of a man-of-war in the West Indies, which God grant may not be true. I said my prayers and had a small headache but good thoughts and good humor this day, thanks be to God Almighty.

2. I rose at 6 o'clock and read a chapter in Hebrew and 250 verses in Homer's *Odyssey*. I said my prayers devoutly, and ate milk for breakfast. I danced my dance. I settled my accounts and read Italian. It rained all day. I ate nothing but roast beef for dinner. In the afternoon we played at billiards. In the evening we took a walk. I said my prayers. I had good thoughts, good health, and good humor, thanks be to God Almighty.

3. I rose at 6 o'clock and read a chapter in Hebrew and four chapters in the Greek Testament. I said my prayers devoutly and ate hominy for breakfast. I danced my dance. We prepared to go to church, but the parson did not come, notwithstanding good weather, so I read a sermon in Dr. Tillotson[4] at home. I ate nothing but boiled beef for dinner but a great deal of that. In the evening we took a walk about the plantation. I read again in Dr. Tillotson. I had good health, good

---

1. Mr. Anderson—the minister of Westover Parish.
2. the Doctor—one of Byrd's neighbors.
3. Parke—Byrd's father-in-law, governor of the Leeward Islands.
4. Dr. Tillotson—John Tillotson (1630–94), Anglican Archbishop of Canterbury.

thoughts, and good humor all day, thanks be to God Almighty. The river sloop arrived before dinner with 24 hogsheads of tobacco.

4. I rose before 6 o'clock and read a chapter in Hebrew and 230 verses in Homer's *Odyssey*. I said my prayers devoutly and ate milk for breakfast. I danced my dance. The sloop was unloaded this morning. Captain Thomson and Captain Littlepage of New Kent came to buy quitrents and dined with me. So did Mr. Parker. While we were at dinner Mr. Bland[5] came and told us abundance of news and particularly that our fleet was arrived safe home. Mr. Harrison, Captain Stith, and Will Randolph came likewise to see me. After dinner we played at billiards. My people set Mr. Bland home and all the company went away. We put everything on board the sloop in order to go to Williamsburg. In the evening we took a walk and I wrote a letter to Mr. Bland about the sloop. I neglected to say my prayers, for which God forgive me. I had good health, good thoughts, and good humor all day, thanks be to God Almighty.

5. I rose at 6 o'clock this morning and read a chapter in Hebrew and 250 verses in Homer's *Odyssey*. I said my prayers and ate milk for breakfast. The sloop sailed away this morning. I danced my dance. I was griped this morning a little and had a loose stool. I settled my accounts and read Italian. I ate hashed beef for dinner only. The Doctor had a fever and ague. We played at billiards. I read more Italian. In the evening we took a walk about the plantation. The brick-maker came this evening. I scolded with John about [managing] the tobacco. I read to the ladies Dr. Lister's *Journey to Paris*. I was ill treated by my wife, at whom I was out of humor. I said my prayers and had good health, good thoughts, and good humor, thanks be to God Almighty.

6. I rose before 6 o'clock and read two chapters in Hebrew and 200 verses in Homer's *Odyssey*. I said my prayers devoutly. My wife and I disagreed about employing a gardener. I ate milk for breakfast. John made an end of [trimming]the boat, which he performed very well. I settled my accounts and read Italian. I ate nothing but fish for dinner and a little asparagus. We played at billiards. I read more Italian. In the evening we walked about the plantation after I read in Dr. Lister's book to the ladies. My wife and I continued very cool. I said my prayers, and had good health, good thoughts and good humor, thanks be to God Almighty.

7. I rose before 6 o'clock and read two chapters in Hebrew and 250 verses in Homer's *Odyssey* and made an end of it. I said my prayers devoutly. I ate milk for breakfast. I danced my dance. The men began to work this day to dig for brick. I settled my accounts and read Italian. I reproached my wife with ordering the old beef to be kept and the fresh beef used first, contrary to good management, on which she was pleased to be very angry and this put me out of humor. I ate nothing but boiled beef for dinner. I went away presently after dinner to look after my people. When I returned I read more Italian and then

5. Mr. Bland—a neighbor from across the river.

my wife came and begged my pardon and we were friends again. I read in Dr. Lister again very late. I said my prayers. I had good health, good thoughts, and bad humor, unlike a philosopher.

8. I rose after 6 o'clock this morning and read a chapter in Hebrew and 150 verses in Homer's last work. I said my prayers and ate milk for breakfast. I danced my dance. My wife and I had another foolish quarrel about my saying she listened on the top of the stairs, which I suspected, in jest. However, I bore it with patience and she came soon after and begged my pardon. I settled my accounts and read some Dutch. Just before dinner Mr. Custis[6] came and dined with us. He told us that my father Parke instead of being killed was married to his housekeeper which is more improbable. He told us that the distemper continued to rage extremely on the other side the Bay and had destroyed abundance of people. I did not keep to my rule of eating but the one dish. We played at billiards and walked about the plantation. I said my prayers and had good humor, good health, and good thoughts, thanks be to God Almighty. The Indian woman died this evening, according to a dream I had last night about her.

9. I rose at 5 o'clock and read a chapter in Hebrew and 150 verses in Homer. I said my prayers devoutly and ate milk for breakfast. My wife and I had another scold about mending my shoes but it was soon over by her submission. I settled my accounts and read Dutch. I ate nothing but cold roast beef and asparagus for dinner. In the afternoon Mr. Custis complained of a pain in his side for which he took a sweat of snakeroot. I read more Dutch and took a little nap. In the evening we took a walk about the plantation. My people made an end of planting the corn field. I had an account from Rappahannock that the same distemper began to rage there that had been so fatal on the Eastern Shore. I had good health, good thoughts and good humor, thanks be to God Almighty. I said my prayers.

10. I rose at 6 o'clock and read two chapters in Hebrew and four chapters in the Greek Testament. I said my prayers with great devoutness and ate milk for breakfast. Our maid Jane began to cry out. I danced my dance. Jane was brought to bed of a boy. About 12 o'clock we went to my Cousin Harrison's, where we dined. I ate fowl and bacon for dinner only. Here I heard that Colonel Harrison had been very sick but was now something better and that Colonel Basset had likewise been sick and Mr. Burwell, but that they were all very well again. Here we stayed till almost sunset when we walked home where we found all things well, thanks be to God. I ate some milk for supper. I said my prayers and had good thoughts, good health, and good humor all day, thanks be to God Almighty.

11. I rose at 5 o'clock and read a chapter in Hebrew and 300 verses in Homer. I said my prayers and ate milk for breakfast. I danced my dance. My brother Custis took a vomit this morning which worked very well. I settled my accounts and read Dutch. I ate nothing but hashed beef for dinner. In the afternoon Ned

---

6. Mr. Custis—Byrd's brother-in-law.

Randolph came over in order to go to school at Mr. Harrison's. I proffered Colonel Randolph that he might be here for that purpose. This day my neighbor Harrison was taken with the gout in his leg. I packed up my things to send to Williamsburg by Mr. Harrison's boat. In the evening we took a walk about the plantation. I ate some milk. It rained a little this evening. I had good health, good thoughts, and good humor, thanks be to God Almighty.

12. I rose at 5 o'clock and read a chapter in Hebrew and 200 verses in Homer. I said my prayers and ate milk for breakfast. Mr. Harrison's boat called here for my things which I sent to Williamsburg. I danced my dance. I settled my accounts. Before noon Mr. Anderson and his wife and Mistress B-k-r came and dined with us. I ate fish for dinner only. In the afternoon we played at billiards. In the evening they went away and Mr. Bland came on his way to Williamsburg and told us that Colonel Basset was very ill again. Mr. Bland and I played at piquet.[7] I said my prayers shortly. We went to bed about 10 o'clock. I had good health, good thoughts, and indifferent humor, thanks be to God Almighty.

13. I rose at 5 o'clock this morning and read a chapter in Hebrew and no Greek. I said my prayers and ate milk for breakfast. Mr. M-r-s-l came from Williamsburg, where he had been purchasing the leather. We walked out and saw Mr. Will Randolph calling the ferry. Mr. Bland and I played at piquet before dinner. I ate nothing but boiled beef. After dinner Mr. Tom Randolph came to see me, to inquire into what land I [or they] had. We played at billiards. In the evening Mr. Mumford came and told me the President had written to the court of Prince George not to sit until they would accept of Mr. Robin Bolling. We walked and I showed Mr. Mumford three hogsheads of bad tobacco of his receiving. I had a great hoarseness. I ate milk. I neglected to say my prayers. I had good health, good thoughts and good humor, thanks be to God Almighty.

14. I rose at 6 o'clock and read a chapter in Hebrew and 100 verses in Homer. I neglected to say my prayers. I ate milk for breakfast. About 10 o'clock my brother and sister Custis went away, and presently after Mr. Mumford likewise. Captain Llewellyn came to see me and stayed about an hour. The Doctor came home. I paid the old wire man for what work he had done at Falling Creek.[8] I ate only honey and bread for dinner and drank milk and water. Last night three moons were seen about 10 o'clock. We played at billiards. I read some Dutch. In the evening it rained very much. I ate milk for supper but in the night it made me a little feverish and my spirits were strangely disturbed. Our daughter was taken ill at night of a fever. I neglected to say my prayers. I had good thoughts, indifferent health, and good thoughts [sic], thanks be to God Almighty.

15. I rose about 6 o'clock and read a chapter in Hebrew and 150 verses in Homer. I said my prayers and ate milk for breakfast. I had a little looseness. I gave

---

7. piquet—a card game.
8. Falling Creek—another of Byrd's plantations, near the site of Richmond.

some men leave to fish at the bay. I prepared my accounts against the General Court. I read some Dutch. My hoarseness was something better. The child continued to have her fever till about noon and then she fell into a sweat which drove out red spots. At noon I ate nothing but squirrel and asparagus for dinner. We played at billiards in the afternoon. Then I mended the locks of my closet and secretary. In the evening we took a walk to the bay to see the men fishing. We had a letter from sister Custis by which we learned that Crapeau[9] is come into our cape and taken a vessel. I neglected to say my prayers. I had good health, good thoughts, and good humor, thanks be to God Almighty.

16. I rose before 6 o'clock and read a chapter in Hebrew and 150 verses in Homer. I said my prayers and ate milk for breakfast. The child was a great deal better and had no fever this day. I prepared my accounts for Williamsburg and read some Dutch. Mr. Harrison's boat brought my [chains] from Williamsburg. I ate nothing at dinner but pork and peas which were salty and made me dry all the afternoon. We played at billiards, and I won a bit of the Doctor. I read more Dutch. In the evening I walked about the plantation and showed John what work I would have done when I was gone to Williamsburg. At night I wrote a letter to Falling Creek to send by Henry, who is to go tomorrow morning. I said my prayers. I had good health, good thoughts, and good humor, thanks be to God Almighty.

17. I rose at 5 o'clock and read a chapter in Hebrew and 150 verses in Homer. I said my prayers, and ate milk for breakfast. I danced my dance. The child had her fever again last night for which I gave her a vomit this morning, which worked very well. Anaka was whipped yesterday for stealing the rum and filling the bottle up with water. I went to church, where were abundance of people, among whom was Mrs. H-m-l-n, a very handsome woman. Colonel Eppes and his wife, with Captain Worsham came to dine with me, who told me that Tom Haynes was gone out of his wits. I sent Tom and Eugene to Mr. Harvey's to meet me tomorrow morning. I took a walk about the plantation. I said my prayers. I had good health, good thoughts, and good humor, thanks be to God Almighty.

18. I rose at 3 o'clock and after committing my family to the divine protection, I went in the boat to Mr. Harvey's, where I got by break of day. Mr. Harvey's mother met me on the shore and desired me to persuade her son to be more kind to her, which I promised I would. From thence I proceeded to Williamsburg, where I got about 10 o'clock. I waited on the President, where I saw Mr. Blair and Colonel Duke. Then I went to Mr. Bland's where I ate some custard. Then I went to court where I presented a petition to the General Court for Captain Webb's land as lapsed. When the court rose I went to dinner to C-t Y-n with the Council, where I ate nothing but boiled beef. Then we went to the President's where we played at cards till 10 o'clock. I won 25 shillings. I went and lay at my new lodgings. I had good health, good thoughts, and good humor, thanks be to God Almighty.

---

9. Crapeau—a French privateer.

19. I rose at 5 o'clock and read in Homer and a chapter in Hebrew. I said my prayers and ate rice milk for breakfast. About 10 o'clock I went to court where I paid Mr. Conner 40 shillings instead of the note for £7 drawn by Daniel Wilkinson. He told me his sloop came the last of March from Barbados, and brings word that the King of France was dead and that my father Parke was well and not married. I read in Justin.[10] In the afternoon I played at piquet with Mr. W-l-s. We dined very late and I ate nothing but fowl and bacon. When that was over we went to Mr. David Bray's where we danced till midnight. I had Mrs. Mary Thomson for my partner. I recommended myself to the divine protection. I had good thoughts, good health, and good humor, thanks to God Almighty. This day I learned that one of my new negroes died of a fever. God's will be done.

20. I rose at 7 o'clock and read a chapter in Hebrew and looked over two books of Homer. I said my prayers and ate rice milk for breakfast. Mr. [Claiborne] came to my chambers and we had some words about a protested bill of exchange of his. I went to court and did a great deal of business all day. The news was confirmed of the King of France's death. We did not dine till 6 o'clock [when] I ate nothing but boiled beef. I was at a meeting of the College where we chose Colonel Randolph [rector]. We had Mr. Luke[11] before us about his accounts, who could not justify them, nor say anything in his excuse. Afterwards we played at whist[12] with the President and I lost £ . . . I said my prayers shortly, had good health, and good thoughts, and good humor, thanks be to God Almighty.

21. Rose at 6 o'clock and read three books of Homer. I said my prayers and ate milk for breakfast. I did a great deal of business this day. We dined about 3 o'clock and I ate fowl and bacon for dinner. Afterwards we went to whist £5.10 [sic] and then I played at dice and lost 50 shillings and John Bolling won £10. I wrote a letter to my wife to let her know my health. We sat up till 12 o'clock. I had good health, good thoughts, and good humor all day, thanks be to God Almighty.

22. I rose at 6 o'clock and read two books in Homer and said my prayers. I ate rice milk for breakfast and did some business. Then I went to church, it being Good Friday, where the Commissary preached. After church I went with abundance of company to dine at the Commissary's where I ate with moderation. In the evening I returned into the town and played at whist and won 8:10 of Colonel Smith. We sat up till 12 o'clock and then separated. I had good health, good thoughts, and good humor, thanks be to God Almighty. Here we saw Mistress H-l-y who is a great instance of human decay.

23. I rose at 6 o'clock and read two books in Homer. I said my prayers, and ate milk for breakfast. I went to the President's, where I learned that the Tuscarora Indians would not deliver up the men we demanded and Colonel Harrison now wrote that now it was his opinion the trade should be open, contrary to

---

10. Justin—third century Roman historian.
11. Mr. Luke—a customs collector.
12. whist—a card game.

what he thought before. I did a great deal of business and dined with the President because it was St. George his day. Then I went with Colonel Ludwell to Green Springs with Colonel Carter, where we danced and were very merry. I neglected to say my prayers. I had good thoughts, good humor, and good health, thanks be to God Almighty.

24. I rose at 6 o'clock and said my prayers very shortly. We breakfasted about 10 o'clock and I ate nothing but bread and butter and sack. We rode to Jamestown Church, where Mr. Commissary preached. When church was done I gave 10 shillings to the poor. Nothing could hinder me from sleeping at church, though I took a great deal of pains against it. We rode home to Colonel Ludwell's again where we dined and I ate fish and asparagus. In the afternoon we took a walk and saw the carcasses of 50 cows which had been burnt in a house belonging to Colonel Ludwell. Mr. W-l-s ran two races and beat John Custis and Mr. [Hawkins]. He likewise jumped over the fence which was a very great jump. Colonel Carter returned to town with Mr. Harrison and we stayed and ate syllabub for supper. I neglected to say my prayers. I had good thoughts, good humor, and good health, thanks he to God Almighty.

25. I rose at 6 o'clock and said my prayers shortly. Mr. W-l-s and I fenced and I beat him. Then we played at cricket. Mr. W-l-s and John Custis against me and Mr. [Hawkins], but we were beaten. I ate nothing but milk for breakfast and then we returned to Williamsburg, where we received the news that the Governor was returned to France, not being able to get his exchange, and that he could not be here before the fall, and that tobacco was very low and that the Lord Somers was president of the Council.[13] I did a great deal of business. About 5 o'clock we went to dinner and I ate nothing but boiled beef. In the evening I took a walk and then went to Mr. Bland's, where I examined my godson and Johnny Randolph and found the last well improved. I said my prayers shortly and went to bed in good time to recover my lost sleep. I had good health, good thoughts, and good humor all day, thanks to God Almighty.

26. I rose at 6 o'clock and read two books in Homer and two chapters in Hebrew. I said my prayers, and ate milk for breakfast. We went to the Council where it was agreed to open the Indian trade. I did a great deal of business. The sheriffs were appointed this day. They passed several accounts. About 4 o'clock we went to dinner and I ate nothing but beef. Then I took a walk and came to Mr. Bland's, from whence Mr. Will Randolph and I went to Colonel Bray's, where we found abundance of ladies and gentlemen dancing. We did not dance but got some kisses among them. About 11 o'clock we returned home. I recommended myself to the divine protection. I had good health, good thoughts, and good humor, thanks be to God Almighty.

---

13. the Council—in this case, the English Privy Council, the royal overseer of colonial affairs.

27. I rose at 6 o'clock and read two books in Homer and a chapter in Hebrew. I said my prayers and ate milk for breakfast. I wrote a letter to my wife by Will Randolph. I did abundance of business. My sister Custis came to town on her way to Major Burwell's. I went to wait on her at Mr. Bland's, where came abundance of other ladies. I stayed with them two hours. My brother and sister Custis went away. I paid several of the Council their money. I agreed with Captain C-l to give him bills for money at five guineas per cent. I went to dinner where I ate nothing but mutton hash. After dinner we played at cricket and then went to whist and I lost 30 shillings. I went home about 11 o'clock. I had good health, good thoughts, and good humor all day, thanks be to God Almighty.

28. I rose at 6 o'clock and read two books in Homer and a chapter in Hebrew. I said my prayers and ate milk for breakfast. Mr. President and Colonel Duke came to see me at my chambers where we talked about the accounts. I did abundance of business and got all the warrants ready. It was 5 o'clock before we went to dinner and I ate mutton and asparagus. After dinner I went to the President's, and then took a walk. Then I went to Mr. Bland's, where I found Mr. Harrison and Mr. Robinson. I went to bed early and committed myself to God's protection. I had good health, good thoughts, and good humor, thanks be to God Almighty. It rained much this night.

29. I rose at 6 o'clock and read a chapter in Hebrew and a book in Homer. I had not time to say my prayers in form, and ate milk for breakfast. I received £600 of Captain C-l for bills at five guineas per cent. About noon my spouse arrived and left all things well at home this morning, thanks be to God. We dined at Mr. Bland's and then rode to Mr. Commissary Blair's and were overtaken with a gust of thunder and rain. Mrs. Blair was sick and talked very [simply]. We were kindly entertained. About 10 o'clock we went to bed, where I lay in my wife's arms. I had good health, good thoughts, and good humor, thanks be to God Almighty.

30. I rose at 6 o'clock and read nothing, nor did I say my prayers, for which God forgive me. I drank two dishes of chocolate and after it some broth. About 8 o'clock we walked to the capitol, where my warrants were signed. I ate about 12 o'clock some hashed mutton with the President, and then took my leave of the Council. When the ladies had put their things in order we went into the vault and drank a glass of Rhenish wine and sugar. Then we rode to Kings Creek to Major Burnwell's. We found him at dinner with my brother and sister Custis and Mistress Betty Todd. We ate with them. I ate nothing but boiled beef. The Major had the gout in one foot, very moderately because of his temperance. We took a walk to the marsh lately drained by a dam and sluice. We went to bed about 9 o'clock. I had good health, good thoughts, and good humor, thanks be to God Almighty. I prayed shortly. . . .

## JULY, 1710

1. I rose at 6 o'clock and read a chapter in Hebrew and some Greek in Thucydides.[14] I said my prayers and ate milk for breakfast with Mr. Mumford.

Soon after he went aboard my sloop with design to go up with the goods that were put into her. I read news. Mr. C-s came a little before dinner. I ate boiled mutton for dinner. In the afternoon Colonel Eppes came over from the courthouse. About 4 o'clock they both went away. I ate so many pears that I was a little griped in the evening. I read some news and then took a walk with my wife. It was exceedingly hot. The negro woman ran away again with the [bit][15] on her mouth. I said my prayers and had indifferent health, good thoughts, and good humor, thank God Almighty.

2. I rose at 6 o'clock and read two chapters in Hebrew and some Greek in Thucydides. I said my prayers and ate milk and [m-l-y] for breakfast. It was very hot. I read a sermon in Dr. Tillotson which affected me very much. I ate boiled mutton for dinner. In the afternoon Mr. Doyley and Ben Harrison came over and stayed almost all the afternoon. They told me that Colonel Harrison was better. In the evening I took a walk about the plantation. My bum was well recovered but I had a little gripes in my belly. The negro woman ran away again with the [bit] in her mouth and my people could not find her. I said my prayers and had good health, good thoughts, and good humor, thanks be to God Almighty. Captain Harvey and Captain Burbydge came over in their boat this night.

3. I rose at 6 o'clock and read a chapter in Hebrew but had no time to read any Greek. I ate milk and apples for breakfast. About nine Captain Burbydge came with another master and after that Colonel Hill and Mr. Anderson with many others because it was court day. Some of us played at billiards. We had abundance of people dine with me and I ate some mutton hash as good as ever I ate in my life. We did not settle the freight. The company all went away in the evening, when my cousin Harrison came over to inquire if I would buy any goods, for which I thanked her and walked home with her, as did also my wife. We stayed there till 10 o'clock and then walked home where I said a short prayer and had good health, good thoughts, and good humor, thanks be to God Almighty.

4. I rose at 4 o'clock, and dressed me because I expected Colonel Hill and Captain Burbydge in his boat to carry us to Colonel Ludwell's bay, where I said a short prayer and then went about 6 o'clock. We called aboard his ship and took some bread and cheese and wine in the boat and then went to breakfast. About 11 o'clock we called at Major Tooker's where we stayed about half an hour and then proceeded to Major Harrison's, but neither he nor his lady were at home. However, we went in and had some victuals. About 5 o'clock Mrs. Harrison came home and we had just [time] to take leave of her and proceed to Green Springs, where we arrived as soon as it was dark. The Colonel was melancholy because his daughter was sick. I ate cold veal for supper. I recommended myself to heaven and had good health, good thoughts, and good humor, thank God Almighty.

---

14. Thucydides—c460–c400 B.C., Greek historian.
15. bit—part of an animal harness, used here as a disciplinary device.

5. I rose about 6 o'clock and read nothing but said a short prayer and got ready to go to Williamsburg, but it was necessary to eat milk for breakfast. About 9 o'clock we took leave of the Colonel and rode to town and when we came to Mr. Bland's he told us my chest of linen sent to his store had been plundered before it came to him. This was according to my whole fortune, which I must try to bear with patience till God shall please to better it. Then we waited on the Governor and drank coffee with him. Then the rest of the Council came and we went to Council, where the Governor's instructions were read, one of which was to suffer the people have the settlement of the habeas corpus act. Many things were debated and Major Harrison was appointed naval officer and I and Colonel Hill were his securities. About 3 o'clock we dined with the Governor where everything was very polite and well served. I ate boiled beef for dinner. In the evening we took leave and returned to my lodgings. I said my prayers and had good health, good thoughts, and good humor, thank God Almighty.

6. I rose at 4 o'clock and settled some bills of exchange. Mr. Randolph came to introduce him to the Governor and recommend him to be clerk of the House of Burgesses, which I did in the best manner and the Governor promised him. Mr. Bland and Mr. Clayton also came to my chambers. When I went to wait on the Governor I found most of the Council there. Then I drank some coffee and ate bread and butter. Then we went to Council where we stayed till about 2 o'clock in the afternoon. Then we went to dine with the Governor where everything was extremely polite and I ate fish and then we took leave of the Governor and rode to Green Springs where we found Hannah Ludwell very ill and the family melancholy. We stayed about half an hour and then went in the boat to Major Harrison's where we arrived about 8 o'clock and the Major soon after. I ate some apple pie for supper and then said my prayers and had good health, good thoughts, and good humor, thanks be to God Almighty.

7. I rose about 6 o'clock and read some of the *Tatler*.[16] I said my prayers and drank chocolate for breakfast. We had a long debate with the captains about freight and at last I generously offered them £10 per ton, which they received with negation but I believe must submit to it. We dined about 11 o'clock and I ate boiled mutton for dinner. About 2 o'clock the Major and I rode to Colonel Harrison's to make him a visit in his sickness and found him abroad in his store but very weak. I stayed there about two hours therefore and then rode home, where I found all well, thank God. My sloop was just come with tobacco. I drank some hot milk from the cow. I neglected to say my prayers but had good thoughts, good humor, and good health, thank God Almighty.

8. I rose at 6 o'clock and read a chapter in Hebrew and some Greek in Thucydides. I said my prayers and ate milk for breakfast. I settled several accounts. It rained gently all day. I sent away the sloop to Falling Creek. I was out

---

16. *Tatler*—a contemporaneous British periodical which commented upon questions of social etiquette and morality.

of humor with Bannister and G-r-l for spoiling the curtains of the bed. I ate roast pork for dinner. Messrs. C-s and Chamberlayne dined with us. In the afternoon I unpacked several things in the afternoon [*sic*] and then gave my wife a flourish and then read in the *Tatler*. Two negroes of mine brought five of the cows that strayed away from hence and told me all was well above, but that Joe Wilkinson was very often absent from his business. It rained all the afternoon, that I could not walk. The negro woman was found and tied but ran away again in the night. I said my prayers but had good health, good thoughts, and indifferent good humor, thank God Almighty.

9. I rose at 5 o'clock and read two chapters in Hebrew and some Greek in Thucydides. I [said] my prayers and ate bread and butter for breakfast. I wrote three letters to the plantations. Captain Burbydge came over before church. About 11 o'clock we went to church and had a good sermon. After church I invited nobody home because I design to break that custom that my people may go to church. I ate boiled pork for dinner. In the afternoon my wife and I had a terrible quarrel about the things she had come in but at length she submitted because she was in the wrong. For my part I kept my temper very well. In the evening Mr. C-s and I took a walk about the plantation and on our return Mr. M-r-s-l overtook us and told me all was well at Falling Creek. He told me that my two overseers above fought and that Joe Wilkinson was to blame for desiring Mr. G-r-l to bid for some things at the outcry and before anybody could bid above him Joe gave him the goods. Tom Turpin[17] told him this was not fair, which made the quarrel between them. I said my prayers and had good health, good thoughts, and indifferent good humor, thank God Almighty.

10. I rose at 5 o'clock and read a chapter in Hebrew and a little Greek in Thucydides. I ate boiled milk for breakfast, but neglected to say my prayers. More goods came up from the ship. About 10 o'clock, Mr. Anderson and his wife came to help me and my wife work. About 12 o'clock Mrs. Betty Todd and Betty Harrison came and so did Colonel Eppes and the captain of the Plymouth ship. They all dined with us, and I ate pigeon for dinner. In the afternoon we went to work again and finished about 4. Then we talked till 6 when the company went away and we walked in the garden. I said my prayers and had good health, good thoughts, and good humor, thanks be to God Almighty.

11. I rose at 6 o'clock and read two chapters in Hebrew and a little Greek in Thucydides. I said my prayers and ate boiled milk for breakfast. Mr. C-s and I worked on the [b-t-r-k] almost all day. There came a workman with an account from Falling Creek of work, which I sent away with some passion because I had ordered G-r-l to employ no workmen. I ate roast pig for dinner. In the afternoon we went to work again till the evening, when Mr. Clayton, Dr. Cocke, and Mr. Bland came over. We took a walk together about the plantation and the Doctor seemed to well pleased with the place. We gave them some supper but it was

---

17. Tom Turpin—Turpin, Wilkinson & G-r-l are all Byrd's overseers.

[late first] and I ate some roast veal with him. I neglected to say my prayers but had good health, good thoughts, and good humor, thanks be to God Almighty.

12. I rose at 5 o'clock and read a chapter in Hebrew and some Greek in Thucydides. I said a short prayer and had milk tea and bread and butter for breakfast. The Doctor, who is a man of learning, was pleased with the library. Mr. Clayton and Mr. Bland went to Prince George court, but the Doctor stayed here. About 10 o'clock Captain Broadwater came over about his freight but I could resolve nothing but advised him to take the common freight. He went likewise to court. I ate boiled beef for dinner. In the afternoon Mr. Allen and Justice [Pigeon ?] came about a protested bill of exchange but without success. Dr. Cocke and I played at piquet and I won. In the evening Major Harrison, John Bolling, and Captain Burbydge came over and went away again in half an hour. We had a hash of lamb for supper and drank a bottle of claret. I said my prayers and had good health, good thoughts, and good humor, thanks be to God Almighty.

13. I rose at 5 o'clock and read a chapter in Hebrew and a little Greek in Thucydides. I said my prayers and ate milk tea and bread and butter for breakfast. I danced my dance. It rained almost the whole day; however it did not hinder Mr. Clayton from going to Mrs. Harrison's and the Doctor and me from going to Colonel Hill's. When we came there nobody was at home but the ladies but about 2 o'clock the Colonel came home and we went to dinner and I ate sheep's head and bacon for dinner. In the afternoon we talked till about 6 o'clock and then we returned home, where we found Mr. Blair and Mr. Bland. We drank a bottle of wine and then retired to bed. I neglected to say my prayers but had good health, good thoughts, and good humor, thanks be to God Almighty.

14. I rose at 5 o'clock and read a chapter in Hebrew and some Greek in Thucydides. I neglected to say my prayers but ate bread and butter and milk tea for breakfast. Then the gentlemen took their leave and I went with them to Mrs. Harrison's where we ate again. Then they all went away and I looked into the library and bought as many books as cost £10. About 2 o'clock I returned home and found Mr. Parker there. He came to pay me interest for the money he owes me. About 4 o'clock he went away. Billy Brayne[18] and I had a quarrel because he would not learn his books and I whipped him extremely. In the evening we took a walk and I drank some milk warm from the cow. I neglected to say my prayers but had good health, good thoughts, and indifferent good humor, thank God Almighty.

15. I rose at 5 o'clock and read two chapters in Hebrew and some Greek in Thucydides. I said my prayers and ate milk and pears for breakfast. About 7 o'clock the negro boy [or Betty] that ran away was brought home. My wife against my will caused little Jenny to be burned with a hot iron, for which I quarreled with her. It was so hot today that I did not intend to go to the launching of Colonel Hill's ship but about 9 o'clock the Colonel was so kind as to

---

18. Billy Brayne—a nephew.

come and call us. My wife would not go at first but with much entreaty she at last consented. About 12 o'clock we went and found abundance of company at the ship and about one she was launched and went off very well, notwithstanding several had believed the contrary. When this was over we went to Mr. Platt's to dinner and I ate boiled beef. We stayed till about 5 o'clock and then returned home, where all was well. I found an express from above with a letter from Joe Wilkinson desiring to be discharged from my service when his year was out. I neglected to say my prayers and had good health, good thoughts, and good humor, thank God Almighty.

16. I rose at 5 o'clock and read a chapter in Hebrew and some Greek in Thucydides. I said my prayers and ate milk and pears for breakfast. Mr. G-r-l came last night after we went to bed. He told me all was well above. We did not quarrel this time. I sent my sloop to Appomattox[19] for tobacco. I ate chicken for dinner. In the afternoon I took a nap for half an hour. I read some divinity. In the evening we took a walk about the plantation. It was exceedingly hot. I said my prayers and had good health, good thoughts, and good humor, thanks be to God Almighty.

17. I rose at 5 o'clock and read a chapter in Hebrew and some Greek in Thucydides. I said my prayers and ate milk and pears for breakfast. I settled my library till 11 o'clock and then Captain Burbydge came to see me but we could not settle the freight. He stayed to dinner. I ate neat's tongue for dinner. My wife went this morning to Mrs. Harrison's and stayed all day because my cousin Todd was there. About 3 o'clock the Captain went to Mrs. Harrison's and I unpacked some goods till the evening and then we took a walk about the plantation and I went to Mrs. Harrison's to fetch my wife. There I drank some syllabub and stayed till about 10 o'clock. I neglected to say my prayers but had good health, good thoughts, and good humor, thanks be to God Almighty.

18. I rose at 5 o'clock and wrote a letter to the Governor to beg him to intercede with the men-of-war to let Colonel Hill's ship have men. I read a chapter in Hebrew and some Greek in Thucydides. I said my prayers and ate milk and pears for breakfast. I settled my cases in the library till about 11 o'clock when Major Chamberlayne came to see me, who is one of the biggest men in Virginia. I ate dry beef for dinner. In the afternoon I caused some of the goods to be unpacked. About 4 o'clock Isham Randolph came to see me. I gave him a letter to the Governor in his favor and sent a squirrel to Mrs. Russell. In the evening Mr. C-s and I went into the river. Then I drank some warm milk. Several of my negroes were taken sick. I neglected to say my prayers and had good health, good thoughts, and good humor, thanks be to God Almighty.

19. I rose at 5 o'clock and read two chapters in Hebrew and some Greek in Thucydides. I said my prayers and ate milk and pears for breakfast. I danced my dance. Three of my people were sick of fever. I settled my library. My negro boy

---

19. Appomattox—another of Byrd's plantations.

[*or* Betty] ran away again but was soon caught. I was angry with John G-r-l for losing the screw of the [bit]. I ate roast pork for dinner. In the afternoon I settled my library again. Then I wrote a letter to England. Then in the evening we took a walk about the plantation. Then Mr. C-s and I went into the river and afterwards drank some syllabub. I neglected to say my prayers but had good health, good thoughts, and good humor, thanks be to God Almighty.

20. I rose at 5 o'clock and read two chapters in Hebrew and some Greek in Thucydides. I said my prayers and ate milk and pears for breakfast. I danced my dance. I spent almost all the morning in settling my books. About 12 o'clock John Blackman [came] for his money which I paid him to his content. I ate hashed pork for dinner. In the afternoon I settled my books again. Several of my negroes were sick. We [b-t] some cider. In the evening we took a walk about the plantation. I neglected to say my prayers but had good health, good thoughts, and good humor, thanks be to God Almighty.

21. I rose at 5 o'clock and read two chapters in Hebrew and some Greek in Thucydides. I said my prayers and ate milk and apples for breakfast. I danced my dance. I settled my books again till almost 12 o'clock. Then I wrote a letter to England. About eight nights ago I dreamed that several of my negroes lay sick on the floor and one Indian among the rest and now it came exactly to pass. I ate roast chicken for dinner. In the afternoon I settled my books again till the evening and then took a walk with Mr. C-s about the plantation. I drank some milk and water after I came out of the river where I had been to swim. I said my prayers and had good health, good thoughts, and good humor, thanks be to God Almighty.

22. I rose at 5 o'clock and read two chapters in Hebrew and some Greek in Thucydides. I said my prayers and ate milk and pears for breakfast. I danced my dance. The Indian continued very ill. I settled my books till about 12 o'clock, when Captain Burbydge came to see us. I gave him a bottle of cider. I ate lamb for dinner. In the afternoon while the Captain smoked his pipe I settled my books again and then came in again. About 6 o'clock he went away and I walked along with him to the Point. He and the rest of the masters agreed at last to go at £10 per ton. A negro came from Falling Creek to tell me all was well. I said my prayers and had good health, good thoughts, and good humor, thank God Almighty.

23. I rose at 5 o'clock and read two chapters in Hebrew and some Greek in Thucydides. I said my prayers and ate milk and pears for breakfast. I wrote two letters to Falling Creek. About 11 o'clock we went to church and heard Mr. Anderson preach. We invited nobody home because we would not make our people work too much of a Sunday. I ate hashed lamb for dinner but my wife was indisposed and ate but little. In the afternoon I took a little nap and then read some Latin. In the evening I took a walk. The Indian was a little better. I neglected to say my prayers but had good health, good thoughts, and good humor, thanks be to God Almighty.

24. I rose at 5 o'clock and read two chapters in Hebrew and some Greek in Thucydides. I said my prayers and ate milk and pears for breakfast. I danced my

dance. The sloop came with tobacco from Appomattox. The Indian was a little better, thank God. My wife was also better, notwithstanding the impression she had that she should die. I sent this morning 15 hogsheads of tobacco on board Captain Burbydge. I settled my books. I wrote a letter to England. I ate roast shoat for dinner. In the afternoon I settled my books again. In the evening I quarrelled with my wife for not taking care of the sick woman, which she took very ill of me and was out of humor over it. I scolded at S-k-f-r for losing his tide. Mr. C-s and I took a walk and could hardly persuade my wife to walk with us. I neglected to say my prayers and had good health, good thoughts, but indifferent good humor, thank God Almighty.

25. I rose at 5 o'clock and read a chapter in Hebrew and a little Greek in Thucydides. I wrote letters to my overseers above. I said no prayers this morning but ate milk and apples for breakfast. Then I went to the store and opened some things there. I sent 15 hogsheads more of tobacco on board Captain Burbydge. I ate dry beef for dinner. In the afternoon my sloop returned and was loaded again with 15 hogsheads to send to Captain Bradby. There happened a gust very violent but it did no damage. I settled my books again. In the evening Mr. C-s took a walk about the plantation. My wife was out of humor this evening for nothing, which I bore very well and was willing to be reconciled. I neglected to say my prayers but had good thoughts, good humor, and good health, thank God Almighty.

26. I rose at 7 o'clock and read two chapters in Hebrew and some Greek in Thucydides. It rained very much. I said my prayers and ate bread and butter for breakfast, which made me very [dull]. I settled my books in the library. The Indian was better, thank God, and so were all that were sick. I ate hashed pork for dinner. In the afternoon I settled my library again and read some Latin. In the evening my wife and I took a walk about the plantation and were good friends. Mr. C-s went to Mrs. Harrison's. I said my prayers and had good health, good thoughts, and good humor, thanks be to God Almighty. I gave my wife a flourish.

27. I rose at 5 o'clock and read a chapter in Hebrew and some Greek in Thucydides. I said my prayers and ate milk for breakfast. I danced my dance. Colonel Hill came this morning and stayed about an hour. Then came Colonel Randolph who was just recovered of a dangerous sickness. My sloop came from Sandy Point and I sent more tobacco on board Captain Bradby. I ate boiled pork for dinner. In the afternoon I received letters from Falling Creek, where all was well, thank God. Our maid Moll was taken sick and so was Tom, to both whom I gave vomits which worked very well. About 5 o'clock Colonel Randolph went away. Then I wrote several letters to my overseer above. In the evening Mr. C-s and I took a walk about the plantation. I neglected to say my prayers but had good health, good thoughts, and indifferent good humor, thank God Almighty.

28. I rose at 5 o'clock and read two chapters in Hebrew and some Greek in Thucydides. I said my prayers and ate milk for breakfast. I danced my dance. Moll continued sick but Tom was better. I wrote several letters to Barbados and sent Mr. C-s a present of bacon, cherries, and apples. Mr. Will Eppes came to see

me but went away before dinner. I ate boiled mutton for dinner. In the afternoon my wife and I had a little quarrel because she moved my letters. Captain Burbydge came to see us and told me my great sloop was come round. I sent ten hogsheads more on board him. I walked with him some part of the way toward Mrs. Harrison's. When we came home my wife was pleased to be out of humor. I neglected to say my prayers but had good health, good thoughts, and good humor, thanks be to God Almighty. Ned Chamberlayne came over this evening.

29. I rose at 5 o'clock and read a chapter in Hebrew and a little Greek in Thucydides. I said my prayers and ate milk for breakfast. It rained this morning till 10 o'clock. I went to the store to put up some things to send to Williamsburg and gave John some rope for the press. About 1 o'clock Captain Broadwater came over in my sloop and dined with us. I ate some stewed pigeon. In the afternoon the Captain agreed to depart from his charter and take £10 per ton. I persuaded him to take my sloop with him and do some necessary things to her. I loaded my small sloop with 15 hogsheads for Captain Harvey. In the evening we took a walk about the plantation. I neglected to say my prayers but had good health, good thoughts, and good humor, thank God Almighty.

30. I rose at 5 o'clock and wrote a letter to Major Burwell about his boat which Captain Broadwater's people had brought round and sent Tom with it. I read two chapters in Hebrew and some Greek in Thucydides. I said my prayers and ate boiled milk for breakfast. I danced my dance. I read a sermon in Dr. Tillotson and then took a little [nap]. I ate fish for dinner. In the afternoon my wife and I had a little quarrel which I reconciled with a flourish. Then she read a sermon in Dr. Tillotson to me. It is to be observed that the flourish was performed on the billiard table. I read a little Latin. In the evening we took a walk about the plantation. I neglected to say my prayers but had good health, good thoughts, and good humor, thanks be to God. This month there were many people sick of fever and pain in their heads; perhaps this might be caused by the cold weather which we had this month, which was indeed the coldest that ever was known in July in this country. Several of my people have been sick, but none died, thank God.

31. I rose at 5 o'clock and read two chapters in Hebrew and some Greek in Thucydides. I said my prayers and ate boiled milk for breakfast. I danced my dance. My daughter was taken sick of a fever this morning and I gave her a vomit which worked very well and brought away great curds out of her stomach and made her well again. My people were all well again, thank God. I went to the store and unpacked some things. About 12 o'clock Captain Burbydge and Captain Broadwater came over. The first went away to Colonel Randolph's; the other stayed to dine with us. I ate hashed mutton for dinner. In the afternoon Dick Randolph came from Williamsburg and brought me the bad news that much of my wine was run out. God's will be done. In the evening Mrs. Harrison and her daughter came over. However I took a little walk. I said a short prayer and had good health, good thoughts, and good humor, thanks be to God Almighty.

# INTRODUCTION & QUESTIONS

## THE PECULIAR INSTITUTION

As a cultural phenomenon, the "peculiar institution" of black slavery, at least as it developed in Virginia and the rest of the American South, was neither a European transplant nor an indigenous product. Neither the requirements of tobacco growing, climate nor racial characteristics demanded that slavery blossom and thrive in American soil. It was instead, a special hybrid, rooted in and particularly suited to the cultural environment of the colonial South.

But this institution took root very slowly. Sold by a Dutch privateer in return for supplies, the first twenty Africans who arrived in Virginia in 1619 and the few other blacks coming in the following years seem to have been regarded not as slaves, but as indentured servants, like their white counterparts gaining their freedom after a fixed and limited period.

Nor do the legal seeds of slavery appear and germinate in these initial years. Not until the 1660's did Virginians plant categories in their law codes defining slavery and fixing the features of the institution which flourished in the eighteenth and nineteenth centuries. A first seed was sown in a Virginia law of 1661 which revealed the possibility of *de facto* life-time slavery by indicating that punishment "by addition of time" did not apply to some runaway negro servants.

The remaining years of the seventeenth century saw the legal maturing of slavery as the number of blacks in the colony slowly rose. From a mere 2000 or 5% of Virginia's population in 1670, they numbered some 16,000 or 20% of the total colonists by 1700. Only in the eighteenth century did the number of Africans reach the heavy proportions which set the future racial composition of the American South. Yet well before this time, slavery was a fully developed and flowering legal institution. By 1756, some 120,000 Virginia blacks, or nearly 41% of the population, were emeshed in its binding tendrils.

The steady emergence of this cultural organism in North America, its special characteristics and manner of its cultivation are apparent in the following excerpts from Virginia's colonial law codes. After reading through these selections, try to determine the precise evolution of this species of slavery by discovering:

1. What criteria are used to legally determine whether a newly imported servant is a slave? How significant is one's religious status here? One's national background? One's sex? One's race?

2. What legal restrictions are placed on the master's authority to discipline his slave? What is assumed to be the fundamental deterrent to his inflicting too severe punishment? What does this position assume the principal determinant of human action to be?

3. A number of provisions among these arrangements can be interpreted as means of policing a slave population and guarding against insurrections. In this regard, what specific limitations are placed on a slave's movement? On his access to weapons? On his meeting with other slaves? On his capacity, both collectively and individually, to resist? If he attempts to escape, what legal protection from the state does he enjoy? What is implied in the measures concerning the harming of slaves to be the slave's relationship to society?

4. What restrictions are placed on marriages involving slaves in these laws? Are they based on one's legal status (slave or free) or on other criteria? What kind of punishment is specified? Upon what parties is it imposed? Does the form of punishment suggest the possible consequences the legislation is designed to prevent?

5. What possibilities does a slave have for attaining his freedom? Are the conditions for manumission broadened or restricted with subsequent legislation? What prerequisites must a master meet if he desires to voluntarily manumit his slave?

6. What special provisions apply if a slave is accused of a capital crime? What evidence is legally sufficient to convict him? Does a slave operate under any other restrictions in a court of law?

7. What is the consequence, in so far as the slave's legal capacities are concerned, of the legislation referring to the branding of animals? Is there any inducement for the owner's insuring that this legislation is obeyed?

8. What responsibilities are legally imposed on the master in regard to the physical well-being, religious instruction or marriage of the slave? Are these matters assumed to be the concern of the state?

# THE LAWS ON SLAVERY OF COLONIAL VIRGINIA

### 1661

In case any English servant shall run away in company with any negroes who are incapable of makeing satisfaction by addition of time, *Bee itt enacted* that the English so running away in company with them shall serve for the time of the said negroes absence as they are to do for their owne by a former act.

### 1662

Whereas some doubts have arrisen whether children got by any Englishman upon a negro women should be slave or ffree, *Be it therefore enacted and declared by this present grand assembly,* that all children borne in this country shalbe held bond or free only according to the condition of the mother, *And* that if any christian shall committ ffornication with a negro man or woman, hee or shee soe offending shall pay double the ffines imposed by the former act.

### 1667

Whereas some doubts have risen whether children that are slaves by birth, and by the charity and piety of their owners made pertakers of the blessed sacrament of baptisme, should by vertue of their baptisme be made ffree; *It is enacted and declared by this grand assembly, and the authority thereof,* that the conferring of baptisme doth not alter the condition of the person as to his bondage or ffreedome; that diverse masters, ffreed from this doubt, may more carefully endeavour the propagation of christianity by permitting children, though slaves, or those of greater growth if capable to be admitted to that sacrament.

### 1669

Whereas the only law in force for the punishment of refractory servants resisting their master, mistris or overseer cannot be inflicted upon negroes, nor the obstinacy of many of them by other then violent meanes supprest, *Be it enacted and declared by this grand assembly,* if any slave resist his master (or other by his masters order correcting him) and by the extremity of the correction should chance to die, that his death shall not be accompted[1] ffelony, but

---

1. accompted—accounted, considered.

the master (or that other person appointed by the master to punish him) be acquit from molestation, since it cannot be presumed that prepensed[2] malice (which alone makes murther ffelony) should induce any man to destroy his owne estate.

### 1672

. . . if any negroe, molatto, Indian slave, or servant for life, runaway and shalbe persued by warrant or hue and crye, it shall and may be lawfull for any person who shall endeavour to take them, upon the resistance of such negroe, molatto, Indian slave, or servant for life, to kill or wound him or them soe resisting. . . . And if it happen that such negroe, molatto, Indian slave, or servant for life doe dye of any wound in such their resistance received the master or owner of such shall receive satisfaction from the publique for his negroe, molatto, Indian slave, or servant for life, soe killed or dyeing of such wounds; and the person who shall kill or wound by virtue of any such hugh and crye any such soe resisting in manner as aforesaid shall not be questioned for the same. . . .

### 1680

Whereas the frequent meeting of considerable numbers of negroe slaves under pretence of feasts and burialls is judged of dangerous consequence; for prevention whereof for the future, *Bee it enacted by the kings most excellent majestie by and with the consent of the generall assembly, and it is hereby enacted by the authority aforesaid*, that from and after the publication of this law, it shall not be lawfull for any negroe or other slave to carry or arme himselfe with any club, staffe, gunn, sword or any other weapon of defence or offence, nor to goe or depart from of his masters ground without a certificate from his master, mistris or overseer, and such permission not to be granted but upon perticuler and necessary occasions; and every negroe or slave soe offending not haveing a certificate as aforesaid shalbe sent to the next constable, who is hereby enjoyned and required to give the said negroe twenty lashes on his bare back well layed on, and soe sent home to his said master, mistris or overseer. *And it is further enacted by the authority aforesaid* that if any negroe or other slave shall presume to lift up his hand in opposition against any christian, shall for every such offence, upon due proofe made thereof by the oath of the party before a magistrate, have and receive thirty lashes on his bare back well laid on. *And it is hereby further enacted by the authority aforesaid* that if any negroe or other slave shall absent himself from his masters service and lye hid and lurking in obscure places, committing injuries to the inhabitants, and shall resist any person or persons that shalby any lawfull authority be imployed to appre-hend and take the said negroe, that then in case of such resistence, it shalbe lawfull for such person or persons to kill the said negroe or slave soe lying out and

---

2. prepensed—premeditated, intentional.

resisting, and that this law be once every six months published at the respective county courts and parish churches within this colony.

## 1682

Whereas by the 12 act of assembly held att James Citty the 3rd day of October, Anno Domini 1670, entituled an act declareing who shall be slaves, *it is enacted* that all servants not being christians, being imported into this country by shipping shall be slaves . . . and for as much as many negroes, moores, mollatoes and others . . . have heretofore, and hereafter may be purchased, procured, or otherwise obteigned as slaves of . . . some well disposed christian, who . . . out of a pious zeale, have wrought the conversion of such slave to the christian faith . . . *Bee it therefore enacted by the governour councell and burgesses of this general assembly, and it is enacted by the authority aforesaid,* that all the said recited act of the third of October 1670 be, and is hereby repealed and. . . . that all servants . . . whether Negroes, Moors, Mollattoes or Indians, who and whose parentage and native country are not christian at the time of their first purchase of such servant by some christian, although afterwards, and before such their importation and bringing into this country, they shall be converted to the christian faith . . . are hereby adjudged, deemed and taken, and shall be adjudged, deemed and taken to be slaves. . . .

## 1691

. . . . And for prevention of that abominable mixture and spurious issue which hereafter may encrease in this dominion, as well by negroes, mulattoes, and Indians intermarrying with English, or other white women, as by their unlawfull accompanying with one another, *Be it enacted by the authoritie aforesaid, and it is hereby enacted,* that for the time to come, whatsoever English or other white man or woman being free shall intermarry with a negroe, mulatto, or Indian man or woman bond or free shall within three months after such marriage be banished and removed from this dominion forever. . . . *And be it further enacted by the authoritie aforesaid, and it is hereby enacted,* That if any English woman being free shall have a bastard child by any negro or mulatto, she pay the sume of fifteen pounds sterling, within one moneth after such bastard child shall be born, to the Church wardens of the parish where she shall be delivered of such child. . . . and that such bastard child be bound out as a servant by the said Church wardens untill he or she shall attaine the age of thirty yeares. . . .

And forasmuch as great inconveniences may happen to this country by the setting of negroes and mulattoes free . . . *Be it enacted by the authority aforesaid, and it is hereby enacted,* That no negro or mulatto be after the end of this present session of assembly set free by any person or persons whatsoever, unless such person or persons, their heires, executors or administrators pay for the transportation of such negro or negroes out of the countrey within six moneths after such setting them free. . . .

**1692**

Whereas a speedy prosecution of negroes and other slaves for capital offences is absolutely necessarie, that others being detered by the condign[3] punishment inflicted on such offenders, may vigorously proceed in their labours and be affrighted to commit the like crimes and offences, and whereas such prosecution has been hitherto obstructed by reason of the charge and delay attending the same,

*Be it therefore enacted* . . . That every negro or other slave which shall after this present session of Assembly commit or perpetrate any cappitall offence which the law of England requires to be satisfyed with the death of the offender or loss of member, after his committing of the said offence, shall be forthwith committed to the common gaol of the county within which such offence shall be committed, there to be safely continued, well laden with irons, and . . . the governour . . . is desired and impowered to . . . direct . . . such persons of the said county as he shall think fitt . . . to cause the offender to be arraigned and indicted, and to take for evidence the confession of the party or the oaths of two witnesses or of one with pregnant[4] circumstances, without the sollemnitie of jury, and the offender being found guilty as aforesaid, to pass judgment as the law of England provides in the like case, and on such judgment to award execution.

*And be it enacted by the authority aforesaid, and it is hereby enacted,* That all horses, cattle and hoggs marked of any negro or other slaves marke or by any slave kept, and which shall not by the last day of December next, be converted by the owner of such slave to the use and marke of the said owner, shall be forfeited to the use of the poore of the parish wherein such horse, beast or hogg shall be kept, seizable by the church wardens thereof.

**1705**

. . . . That . . . negroes, mulattoes and Indian servants, and others, not being christians, shall be deemed and taken to be persons incapable in law, to be witnesses in any cases whatsoever. . . .

. . . . any overseer that hath four or more slaves under his care. . . or any slave . . . [shall] be exempted from serving [in the militia] either in horse or foot.

. . . . no minister of the church of England, or other minister, or person whatsoever, within this colony and dominion, shall hereafter wittingly presume to marry a white man with a negro or mulatto woman; or to marry a white woman with a negro or mulatto man, upon pain of forfeiting and paying, for every such marriage the sum of ten thousand pounds of tobacco.

. . . . no master, mistress, or overseer of a family, shall knowingly permit any slave, not belonging to him or her, to be and remain upon his or her plantation, above four hours at any one time, without the leave of such slave's master,

---

3. condign—deserved, appropriate.
4. pregnant—convincing, obvious.

mistress, or overseer, on penalty of one hundred and fifty pounds of tobacco to the informer. . . .

## 1723

Whereas the laws now in force, for the better ordering and governing of slaves, and for the speedy trial of such of them as commit capital crimes, are found insufficient to restrain their tumultuous and unlawful meetings, or to punish the secret plots and conspiracies carried on amongst them. . . .

*Be it enacted* . . . That if any number of negroes, or other slaves, exceeding five, shall at any time hereafter consult, advise, or conspire, to rebel or make insurrection, or shall plot or conspire the murder of any person or persons whatsoever, every such consulting, plotting, or conspiring, shall be adjudged and deemed felony; and the slave or slaves convicted thereof, in manner herein after directed, shall suffer death, and be utterly excluded the benefit of clergy, and of all laws made concerning the same. . . .

And, whereas many inconveniences have arisen, by the meetings of great numbers of negros and other slaves: For prevention thereof, *Be it enacted, by the authority aforesaid, and it is hereby enacted,* That from henceforth no meetings of negros, or other slaves, be allowed. . . . And that every master, owner, or overseer of any plantation, who shall, knowingly or willingly, permit any such meetings, or suffer more than five negros or slaves, other than the negros or slaves belonging to his, her, or their plantations or quarters, to be and remain upon any plantation or quarter, at any one time, shall forfeit and pay the sum of five shillings, or fifty pounds of tobacco, for each negro or slave, over and above such number, that shall at any time hereafter so unlawfully meet or assemble, on his, her, or their plantation. . . .

*Provided always,* That nothing herein contained, shall be construed to restrain the negros, or other slaves, belonging to one and the same owner, and seated at distinct quarters or plantations, to meet, by the licence of such owner, or his or her overseer, at any of the quarters or plantations to such owner belonging . . . nor to restrain their meeting on any other lawful occasion, by the license, in writing, of their master, mistress, or overseers; nor to prohibit any slaves repairing to and meeting at church to attend divine service, on the lord's day, or at any other time set apart by lawful authority, for public worship. . . .

*And be it further enacted, by the authority aforesaid,* That no negro, mullatto, or indian slaves, shall be set free, upon any pretense whatsoever, except for some meritorious services, to be adjudged and allowed by the governor and council, for the time being, and a licence thereupon first had and obtained. . . .

*Be it further enacted,* That no negro, mulatto, or indian, either a slave or free, shall hereafter be admitted in any court of this colony, to be sworn as a witness, or give evidence in any cause whatsoever, except upon the trial of a slave, for capital offence.

# INTRODUCTION & QUESTIONS

## TO THE READING
## ON OLAUDAH EQUIANO

Recollections from the colonial period of what "the peculiar institution" meant from the African slaves' point of view are rare indeed. One such memoir is to be found in *The Interesting Narrative of Olaudah Equiano or Gustavus Vasa the African*, which originally was published in England in 1789. It is the unique product of an Ibo from what is presently Nigeria, a former self-educated slave, who managed to purchase his freedom; travel widely in America, Europe and the Middle East; plan Sierra Leone, the first free black African colony and become active in the English anti-slavery cause.

In this section of his memoirs, he follows an account of his kidnapping and enslavement in Africa and sale to English slavers with a recollection of his ocean voyage to and initial experiences in the West Indian English colony of Barbados. As you travel with him, determine:

1. What new fears did the young Equiano experience when put on the slave ship? What, with the other conditions on board, might these suggest about the psychological and cultural effects of the experience on both slaves and captors?

2. What might be Equiano's reasons, at the close of the selection, for addressing his readers as he does? What might this suggest about his task as a writer in this work? How might this effect the veracity of his account?

# THE INTERESTING NARRATIVE OF THE LIFE OF OLAUDAH EQUIANO OR GUSTAVUS VASSA THE AFRICAN

The first object which saluted my eyes when I arrived on the coast was the sea, and a slave ship which was then riding at anchor and waiting for its cargo. These filled me with astonishment, which was soon converted into terror when I was carried on board. I was immediately handled and tossed up to see if I were sound by some of the crew, and I was now persuaded that I had gotten into a world of bad spirits and that they were going to kill me. Their complexions too differing so much from ours, their long hair and the language they spoke (which was very different from any I had ever heard) united to confirm me in this belief. Indeed such were the horrors of my views and fears at the moment that, if ten thousand worlds had been my own, I would have freely parted with them all to have exchanged my condition with that of the meanest slave in my own country. When I looked round the ship too and saw a large furnace or copper boiling and a multitude of black people of every description chained together, every one of their countenances expressing dejection and sorrow, I no longer doubted of my fate; and quite overpowered with horror and anguish, I fell motionless on the deck and fainted. When I recovered a little I found some black people about me, who I believed were some of those who had brought me on board and had been receiving their pay; they talked to me in order to cheer me, but all in vain. I asked them if we were not to be eaten by those white men with horrible looks, red faces, and loose hair. They told me I was not. . . . Soon after this the blacks who brought me on board went off, and left me abandoned to despair.

I now saw myself deprived of all chance of returning to my native country or even the least glimpse of hope of gaining the shore, which I now considered as friendly; and I even wished for my former slavery in preference to my present situation, which was filled with horrors of every kind, still heightened by my ignorance of what I was to undergo. I was not long suffered to indulge my grief; I was soon put down under the decks, and there I received such a salutation in my nostrils as I had never experienced in my life: so that with the loathsomeness of the stench and crying together, I became so sick and low that I was not able to eat, nor had I the least desire to taste anything. I now wished for the last friend, death, to relieve me; but soon, to my grief, two of the white men offered me eatables, and on my refusing to eat, one of them held me fast by the hands and laid me across I think the windlass, and tied my feet while the other flogged me severely. I had never experienced anything of this kind before, and although, not being used to the water, I naturally feared that element the first time I saw it, yet nevertheless could I have got over the nettings I would have jumped over the side, but I could not; and besides, the crew used to watch us very closely who were not chained down to the decks, lest we should leap into the water: and I have seen some of these poor African prisoners most severely cut for attempting to do so, and hourly whipped for not eating. This indeed was often the case with myself. In a little time after, amongst the poor chained men I found some of my own nation, which in a small degree gave ease to my mind. I inquired of these what was to be done with us; they gave me to understand we were to be carried to these white people's country to work for them. I then was a little revived, and thought if it were no worse than working, my situation was not so desperate: but still I feared I should be put to death, the white people looked and acted, as I thought, in so savage a manner; for I had never seen among my people such instances of brutal cruelty, and this not only shewn towards us blacks but also to some of the whites themselves. One white man in particular I saw, when we were permitted to be on deck, flogged so unmercifully with a large rope near the foremast that he died in consequence of it; and they tossed him over the side as they would have done a brute. This made me fear these people the more, and I expected nothing less than to be treated in the same manner. I could not help expressing my fears and apprehensions to some of my countrymen. . . .

At last, when the ship we were in had got in all her cargo . . . we were all put under deck. . . . The closeness of the place and the heat of the climate, added to the number in the ship, which was so crowded that each had scarcely room to turn himself, almost suffocated us. This produced copious perspirations, so that the air soon became unfit for respiration from a variety of loathsome smells, and brought on a sickness among the slaves, of which many died, thus falling victims to the improvident avarice, as I may call it, of their purchasers. This wretched situation was again aggravated by the galling of the chains, now become insupportable, and the filth of the necessary tubs, into which the children often fell and were almost suffocated. The shrieks of the women and the groans of the dying rendered the whole a scene of horror almost inconceivable. Happily perhaps for myself I was soon reduced so low here that it was thought necessary to keep me almost always on deck, and from my extreme youth I was not put in fetters. In this situation I expected every hour to share the fate of my companions, some of whom were almost daily brought upon deck at the point of death, which I began to hope would soon put an end to my miseries. Often did I think many of the inhabitants of the deep much more happy than myself. I envied them the freedom they enjoyed, and as often wished I could change my condition for theirs. Every circumstance I met with served only to render my state more painful, and heighten my apprehensions and my opinion of the cruelty of the whites. . . . We were not many days . . . before we were sold after their usual manner, which is this: On a signal given, (as the beat of a drum) the buyers rush at once into the yard where the slaves are confined, and make choice of that parcel they like best. The noise and clamour with which this is attended and the eagerness visible in the countenances of the buyers serve not a little to increase the apprehensions of the terrified Africans. . . . In this manner, without scruple, are relations and friends separated, most of them never to see each other again. I remember in the vessel in which I was brought over, in the men's apartment there were several brothers who, in the sale, were sold in different lots; and it was very moving on this occasion to see and hear their cries at parting. O, ye nominal Christians! might not an African ask you, Learned you this from your God who says unto you, Do unto all men as you would men should do unto you? Is it not enough that we are torn from our country and friends to toil for your luxury and lust of gain? Must every tender feeling be likewise sacrificed to your avarice? Are the dearest friends and relations, now rendered more dear by their separation from their kindred, still to be parted from each other and thus prevented from cheering the gloom of slavery with the small comfort of being together and mingling their sufferings and sorrows? Why are parents to lose their children, brothers their sisters, or husbands their wives? Surely this is a new refinement in cruelty which, while it has no advantage to atone for it, thus aggravates distress and adds fresh horrors even to the wretchedness of slavery.

# INTRODUCTION & QUESTIONS

## CONCRETE EXPRESSIONS OF SOUTHERN CULTURE

As with "The Artifacts of the Puritans," the materials for this topic will be found in the form of an audio-visual program. On viewing this program, determine:

1. What differences do you see between Puritan and Southern domestic architecture with respect to the size of the house, the building materials used, and the general impression it makes? What Southern cultural values might be suggested by such differences?

2. What cultural assumptions are indicated by the careful planning of details characteristic of Georgian architecture? How is this different from Puritan architecture?

3. How do the windows of this home differ from those used by the Puritans? What cultural values might be implied in their use here?

4. What cultural priorities are suggested in the decoration of the main entrance? In the treatment of the building materials used?

5. What Southern ideas regarding their social order are suggested by the treatment of this entrance?

6. What kind of social attitudes are suggested by the placement and use made of the "dependencies?" Given these features, what is indicated regarding the relationship between the slaves and their owners?

7. What characteristics are shared by both the house and its surrounding landscape? What functions does this landscape have?

8. What similarities do you see between the Virginia plantation arrangement and the English country gentleman's estate shown? What do these simularities suggest about the Virginians' criteria for what is beautiful?

9. What implications are there in the fact that both sides and entrances of the mansion are virtually identical? What cultural values are suggested in the decorative elements of the side of the house which faces the land?

10. What does the repeated use of the bird motif suggest regarding William Byrd's personality traits? Why do you think that Byrd would so blatently underline his English familial heritage?

11. What does the size, location and the epitaph on his tombstone suggest about Byrd's conception of himself? What is culturally significant in his mention of his association with English aristocrats?

12. In what specific respects does the plan of Westover echo the fractionalized character of Byrd's diary?

13. How does the treatment of the stairs and the stairhall differ from those of the Puritans? What cultural ideals are suggested here?

14. Again, compare a Puritan fireplace with that in Westover's drawing room. What Virginia values are manifested here?

15. What does the existance of mills, wharves, storehouses and chapels on the property suggest about the nature of a plantation, especially when such buildings could have easily been constructed in a nearby town?

16. What basic differences do you see between the example of a Virginia portrait and those of the New England Puritans? What functions or purposes does the portrait fulfill in this society?

17. What artistic standards were followed by the painters of Virginians? How did this affect the development of a native-born artistic community?

18. What cultural significance do you see in the fact that Williamsburg was a pre-planned community as opposed to Boston, whose design evolved over time?

19. What are the major components of Williamsburg's plan? What cultural priorities are revealed in the major buildings, their relative importance in the scheme, the street plan, the extent of the market and highway system, and the nature of private real estate allotments?

20. What values would be implied in designing a city whose ultimate limits were permanently set? Are the functions of the city significant here?

21. What concerns are reflected in the location, treatment, design and plan of the capitol building?

22. What characteristics of the political agencies housed in them are physically apparent in the governor's council chamber? In the House of Burgesses? In the General Court?

23. What might the monumental nature of the governor's palace suggest about the governing system of this English colony? Of this society's ultimate cultural standards?

24. What cultural values are revealed in the calculated design and planning that underlie the entire palace complex, including its approaches?

25. What cultural presumptions are suggested in the palace garden by its best viewing point? Its treatment of vegetation? Its organization of materials and spaces? How do these features differ from the treatment of landscape in New England? What contrasting assumptions about the natural world are implied here?

26. What previously encountered characteristics of Georgian, and thus Virginian, architecture are repeated in the College of William and Mary?

27. What social ideals are reflected in the main building for the College of William and Mary? In its two wings?

28. What distinctions exist between the Anglican church seen here and the Puritan meetinghouse? Be sure to consider its site, design features, and interior arrangements, including the seating allocations in your analysis. What cultural differences are suggested by each?

29. What cultural priorities are revealed in the concept and architectural use of the "Golden Section?"

30. What differences do you note between Puritan tombstones and the grave markers seen here? What ideas regarding death, salvation and self-conception are physically manifested here? How do they differ from comparable Puritan considerations?

# INTRODUCTION & QUESTIONS

## THE PENNSYLVANIA EXPERIMENT

To a degree absent in the preceeding examples of English colonization in the New World, the fate of the colony of Pennsylvania lay in the hands of a single individual. From the experience and demands of William Penn, this colonial example received its foundation and much of its subsequent dynamics.

William Penn (1644–1718) was the first truly illustrious Englishman to subscribe to the radical tenets of Quakerism, a religious and social reform program that is a central feature of his and his colony's history. Yet another key to understanding the successes and failures of man and colony is Penn's parentage. He was the son of Admiral Sir William Penn, one of the most distinguished members of the British Navy. In 1660 the Admiral served as Parliament's messenger to the exiled Charles Stuart, son of the former English King, Charles I, who had been deposed and executed by Parliament in the 1640s. Penn not only delivered Parliament's request that Charles return and claim his throne but guaranteed the new king's safety at the head of a fleet escorting him back to London. For this service, the now Charles II made the Admiral a court favorite and rewarded him with lands in Ireland. The Stuarts thus partially compensated the Penns for their incalculable loyalty at a critical period in the Stuarts' history. The unified fate of the two families was symbolized by the presentation of the Admiral's son William to his new sovereign on the day of Charles' coronation.

This son was given an especially fine private education meant to prepare him for a military career only to become "infected" with pacifist Quakerism during his two-year stay at Oxford. The Admiral's scheme to divert his son's attention from this religious interest by sending him abroad backfired and in 1667, William Penn formally converted to the new religious heresy. The next year he was imprisoned for authoring an heretical tract. His father secured his release on this occasion but the son was often returned to prison for his Quaker views and non-conformist activities.

Penn, in his concern for the future of Quakerism, envisioned a haven in America where the Friends had already made some promising missionary inroads. Citing a £16,000 debt the crown owed his family, Penn petitioned Charles for a land grant in the area. In large part, Charles' charter of 1681 making Penn proprietor of the area between New York and Maryland was due to the Stuart family's undiminished sense of debt for the Admiral's support during the Restoration of 1660.

By the fall of 1682 when Penn arrived to visit his new possession, he had sold some 600,000 acres to some 470 First Purchasers largely from the more prosperous of English Quakers. In addition to providing his colony with a governmental framework, on this visit he negotiated the first of the famous treaties with the Indians and welcomed a steady stream of new arrivals.

During his two year stay he also authored this letter to the committee of the Free Society of Traders. The Free Society was a London based joint-stock company chartered by Penn in 1682 to promote the settlement and development of Pennsylvania. Besides the 20,000 acre land grant which Penn describes in his letter, the Quaker dominated company was given special privileges in the colony. Philadelphia's Society Hill neighborhood continues to bear its name.

The letter, while addressed to the Society, was also published in England along with European editions in Dutch, German and French. As you read the selection, be aware not only of the data Penn describes but the process by which he selects and interprets what he sees.

1. What features of the natural landscape merit Penn's attention? What does he use as a basis of comparison? What are his general conclusions regarding the natural environment of Pennsylvania? Note particularly his observations on the characteristics of the soils of the province.

2. What economic possibilities does he foresee for the region? What knowledge does Penn display of agriculture?

3. What uses does he envision for the animal life of the country? For the plant forms? Are there any natural features that do not have such utilitarian features in his eyes?

4. What aspects of Indian life does he report on? How sympathetic does he appear to be to their culture? What features of their existence receive the most extensive treatment?

5. What aspects of their character does he find most commendable? What changes in them have occurred as a result of European contact?

6. What is the nature of their religious ideas as distinct from their religious practices? To what is this attributed?

7. What characterizes their political institutions and activities? What does he consider most impressive about their political life? Their judicial arrangements?

8. What does he speculate is the origin of the Indian? What evidence does he present that suggests such a possibility?

9. What European groups have previously settled in the region? What characteristics do they display?

10. What natural feature does he discuss separately? Why should this be considered apart from the previous section?

11. What features of Philadelphia does he report on? How successful has this settlement been so far? What seems to be the city's chief attributes in his mind?

12 What acreage has the Society purchased in the colony? Where is this real estate located? What projects is the society contemplating?

# LETTER TO THE COMMITTEE
# OF THE FREE SOCIETY OF TRADERS

*William Penn*

My Kind Friends;

    The Kindness of yours by the Ship *Thomas* and *Anne,*doth much oblige me; for by it I perceive the Interest you take in my Health and Reputation, and the prosperous Beginnings of this Province, which you are so kind as to think may much depend upon them. In return of which, I have sent you a long Letter, and yet containing as brief an Account of My self, and the Affairs of this Province, as I have been able to make. . . .

*For the Province, the general Condition of it take as followeth.*

    I. The Country it self in its Soyl, Air, Water, Seasons and Produce both Natural and Artificial is not to be despised. The Land containeth divers sorts of Earth, as Sand Yellow and Black, Poor and Rich: also Gravel both Loomy and Dusty; and in some places a fast fat Earth,[1] like to our best Vales in England, especially by Inland Brooks and Rivers, God in his Wisdom having ordered it so, that the Advantages of the Country are divided, the Back-Lands being generally three to one Richer than those that lie by Navigable Waters. We have much of another Soyl, and that is a black Hasel Mould, upon a Stony or Rocky bottom.

    II. The Air is sweet and clear, the Heavens serene, like the South-parts of France, rarely Overcast; and as the Woods come by numbers of People to be more clear'd, that it self will Refine.

    III. The Waters are generally good, for the Rivers and Brooks have mostly Gravel and Stony Bottoms, and in Number hardly credible. We have also Mineral Waters, . . . not two Miles from Philadelphia.

    IV. For the Seasons of the Year, having by God's goodness now lived over the Coldest and Hottest, that the Oldest Liver in the Province can remember, I can say something to an English Understanding.

    1st, Of the Fall, for then I came in: I found it from the 24th of October, to the beginning of December, as we have it usually in England in September, or rather like an English mild Spring. From December to the beginning of the Moneth

---

1. fast, fat Earth—close packed, sticky soil.

called March[2] we had sharp Frosty Weather; not foul, thick, black Weather, as our North-East Winds bring with them in England; but a Skie as clear as in Summer, and the Air dry, cold, piercing and hungry; yet I remember not, that I wore more Clothes than in England. The reason of this Cold is given from the great Lakes that are fed by the Fountains of Canada. The Winter before was as mild, scarce any Ice at all; while this for a few dayes Froze up our great River Delaware. From that Moneth to the Moneth called June, we enjoy'd a sweet Spring, no Gusts, but gentle Showers, and a fine Skie. Yet this I observe, that the Winds here as there, are more Inconstant Spring and Fall, upon that turn of Nature, than in Summer or Winter. From thence to this present Moneth, which endeth the Summer (commonly speaking) we have had extraordinary Heats, yet mitigated sometimes by Cool Breezese. The Wind that ruleth the Summer-season, is the South-West; but Spring, Fall and Winter, 'tis rare to want the wholesome North Wester seven dayes together: And whatever Mists, Fogs or Vapours foul the Heavens by Easterly or Southerly Winds, in two Hours time are blown away; the one is always followed by the other: A Remedy that seems to have a peculiar Providence in it to the Inhabitants; the multitude of Trees, yet standing, being liable to retain Mists and Vapours, and yet not one quarter so thick as I expected.

V. The Natural Produce of the Country, of Vegetables, is Trees, Fruits, Plants, Flowers. The Trees of most note are, the black Walnut, Cedar, Cyprus, Chestnut, Poplar, Gumwood, Hickery, Sassafrax, Ash, Beech and Oak of divers sorts, as Red, White and Black; Spanish Chestnut and Swamp, the most durable of all: of All which there is plenty for the use of man.

The Fruits that I find in the Woods, are the White and Black Mulbery, Chestnut, Wallnut, Plumbs, Strawberries, Cranberries, Hurtleberries and Grapes of divers sorts. The great Red Grape (now ripe) called by Ignorance, the Fox-Grape (because of the Relish it hath with unskilful Palates) is in it self an extraordinary Grape, and by Art doubtless may be Cultivated to an excellent Wine . . . There is a white kind of Muskadel, and a little black Grape, like the cluster-Grape of England, not yet so ripe as the other; but they tell me, when Ripe, sweeter, and that they only want skilful Vinerons[3] to make good use of them: I intend to venture on it with my French man[4] this season, who shews some knowledge in those things. Here are also Peaches, and very good, and in great quantities, not an Indian Plantation without them; but whether naturally here at first, I know not, however one may have them by Bushels for little; they make a pleasant Drink and I think not inferior to any Peach you have in England, except the true Newington. 'Tis disputable with me, whether it be best to fall to

2. the moneth called March—the Quakers rejected the common names for the days of the week and the months of the year as being pagan in origin and substituted numbers in their places.

3. Vinerons—i.e., vignerons, wine growers.

4. my French man—Penn brought over a French vigneron who supervised a 200 acre vineyard located in what is now Fairmount Park.

Fining[5] the Fruits of the Country, especially the Grape, by the care and skill of Art, or send for forreign Stems and Sets, already good and approved. It seems most reasonable to believe, that not only a thing groweth best, where it naturally grows; but will hardly be equalled by another Species of the same kind that doth not naturally grow there. But to solve the doubt, I intend, if God give me Life, to try both, and hope the consequence will be as good Wine as any European Countries of the same Latitude do yield.

VI. The Artificial Produce of the Country, is Wheat, Barley, Oats, Rye, Pease, Beans, Squashes, Pumkins, Water-Melons, Mus-Melons, and all Herbs and Roots that our Gardens in England usually bring forth.

VII. Of living Creatures; Fish, Fowl, and the Beasts of the Woods, here are divers sorts, some for Food and Profit, and some for Profit only: For Food as well as Profit, the Elk, as big as a small Ox, Deer bigger than ours, Beaver, Racoon, Rabbits, Squirrels, and some eat young Bear, and commend it. Of Fowl of the Land, there is the Turkey (Forty and Fifty Pound weight) which is very great; Phesants, Heath-Birds, Pidgeons and Partridges in abundance. Of The Water, the Swan, Goose, white and gray, Brands, Ducks, Teal, also the Snipe and Curloe, and that in great Numbers; but the Duck and Teal excel, nor so good have I ever eat in other Countries. Of Fish, there is the Sturgeon, Herring, Rock, Shad, Catshead, Sheepshead, Ele, Smelt, Pearch, Roach; and in Inland Rivers, Trout, some say Salmon, above the Falls. Of Shelfish, we have Oysters, Crabbs, Cockles, Concks, and Mushels; some Oysters six Inches long, and one sort of Cockles as big as the Stewing Oysters, they make a rich Broth. The Creatures for Profit only by Skin or Fur, and that are natural to these parts, are the Wild Cat, Panther, Otter, Wolf, Fox, Fisher, Minx, MuskRat; and of the Water, the Whale for Oyl, of which we have good store, and two Companies of Whalers, whose Boats are built, will soon begin their Work, which hath the appearance of a considerable Improvement. To say nothing of our reasonable Hopes of good Cod in the Bay.

VIII. We have no want of Horses, and some are very good and shapely enough; two Ships have been freighted to Barbadoes with Horses and Pipe-Staves, since my coming in. Here is also Plenty of Cow-Cattle, and some Sheep; the People Plow mostly with Oxen.

IX. There are divers Plants that not only the Indians tell us, but we have had occasion to prove by Swellings, Burnings, Cuts, etc., that they are of great Virtue, Suddenly curing the Patient: and for Smell, I have observed several, especially one, the wild Mirtle; the other I know not what to call, but are most fragrant.

X. The Woods are adorned with lovely Flowers, for colour, greatness, figure and variety: I have seen the Gardens of London best stored with that sort of Beauty, but think they may be improved by our Woods: I have sent a few to a Person of Quality this Year for a tryal.

Thus much of the Country, next of the Natives or Aborigines.

---

5. Fining—improving the quality.

XI. The *Natives* I shall consider in their Persons, Language, Manners, Religion and Government, with my sence of their Original. For their Persons, they are generally tall, streight, well-built, and of singular Proportion; they tread strong and clever,[6] and mostly walk with a lofty Chin: Of Complexion, Black, but by design, as the Gypsies in England: They grease themselves with Bears-fat clarified, and using no defence against Sun or Weather, their skins must needs be swarthy; Their Eye is little and black, not unlike a straight-look't Jew: The thick Lip and flat Nose, so frequent with East-Indians and Blacks, are not common to them; for I have seen as comely European-like faces among them of both, as on your side the Sea; and truly an Italian Complexion hath not much more of the White, and the Noses of several of them have as much of the Roman.

XII. Their Language is lofty, yet narrow, but like the Hebrew; in Signification full, like Short-hand in writing; one word serveth in the place of three, and the rest are supplied by the Understanding of the Hearer: Imperfect in their Tenses, wanting in their Moods, Participles, Adverbs, Conjunctions, Interjections: I have made it my business to understand it, that I might not want an Interpreter on any occasion: And I must say, that I know not a Language spoken in Europe, that hath words of more sweetness or greatness, in Accent and Emphasis, than theirs; for Instance, *Octorockon, Rancocas, Ozicton, Shakamacon, Poquerim,* all of which are names of Places, and have Grandeur in them: Of words of Sweetness, *Anna,* is Mother, *Issimus,* a Brother, *Netap,* Friend, *usque ozet,* very good; *pone,* Bread, *metse,* eat, *matta,* no, *hatta,* to have, *payo,* to come; *Sepassen, Passijon,* the Names of Places; *Tamane, Secane, Menanse, Secatereus,* are the names of Persons. If one ask them for anything they have not, they will answer, *mattá ne hattá,* which to translate is, not I have, instead of I have not.

XIII. Of their Customs and Manners there is much to be said; I will begin with Children. So soon as they are born, they wash them in Water, and while very young, and in cold Weather to chuse,[7] they Plunge them in the Rivers to harden and embolden them. Having wrapt them in a Clout, they lay them on a straight thin Board, a little more than the length and breadth of the Child, and swadle it fast upon the Board to make it straight; wherefore all Indians have flat Heads; and thus they carry them at their Backs. The Children will go very young, at nine Moneths commonly; they wear only a small Clout round their Waste, till they are big; if Boys, they go a Fishing till ripe for the Woods, which is about Fifteen; then they Hunt, and after having given some Proofs of their Manhood, by a good return of Skins, they may Marry, else it is a shame to think of a Wife. The Girls stay with their Mothers, and help to hoe the Ground, plant Corn and carry Burthens; and they do well to use them to that Young, they must do when they are Old; for the Wives are the true Servants of their Husbands: otherwise the Men are very affectionate to them.

---

6. clever—nimble.
7. chuse—preferably.

XIV. When the Young Women are fit for Marriage, they wear something upon their Heads for an Advertisement, but so as their Faces are hardly to be seen, but when they please: The Age they Marry at, if Women, is about thirteen and Fourteen; if Men, seventeen and eighteen; they are rarely elder.

XV. Their Houses are Mats, or Barks of Trees set on Poles, in the fashion of an English Barn, but out of the power of the Winds, for they are hardly higher than a Man; they lie on Reeds or Grass. In Travel they lodge in the Woods about a great Fire, with the Mantle of Duffills[8] they wear by day, wrapt about them, and a few Boughs stuck round them.

XVI. Their Diet is Maze, or Indian Corn, divers ways prepared: sometimes Roasted in the Ashes, sometimes beaten and Boyled with Water, which they call *Homine*; they also make Cakes, not unpleasant to eat: They have likewise several sorts of Beans and Pease that are good Nourishment; and the Woods and Rivers are their Larder.

XVII. If an European comes to see them, or calls for Lodging at their House or *Wigwam* they give him the best place and first cut. If they come to visit us, they salute us with an *Itah* which is as much as to say, Good be to you, and set them down, which is mostly on the Ground close to their Heels, their Legs upright; may be they speak not a word more, but observe all Passages:[9] If you give them anything to eat or drink, well, for they will not ask; and be it little or much, if it be with Kindness, they are well pleased, else they go away sullen, but say nothing.

XVIII. They are great Concealers of their own Resentments, brought to it, I believe, by the Revenge that hath been practised among them; in either of these, they are not exceeded by the Italians. A Tragical Instance fell out since I came into the Country; a King's Daughter thinking her self slighted by her Husband, in suffering another Woman to lie down between them, rose up, went out, pluck't a Root out of the Ground, and ate it, upon which she immediately dyed; and for which, last Week he made an Offering to her Kindred for Attonement and liberty of Marriage; as two others did to the Kindred of their Wives, that dyed a natural Death: For till Widdowers have done so, they must not marry again. Some of the young Women are said to take undue liberty before Marriage for a Portion; but when marryed, chaste; when with Child, they know their Husbands no more, till delivered; and during their Moneth, they touch no Meat, they eat, but with a Stick, least they should defile it; nor do their Husbands frequent them, till that time be expired.

XIX. But in Liberality they excell, nothing is too good for their friend; give them a fine Gun, Coat, or other thing, it may pass twenty hands, before it sticks; light of Heart, strong Affections, but soon spent; the most merry Creatures that live, Feast and Dance perpetually; they never have much, nor want much:

---

8. Duffils—coarse woolen cloths.
9. observe all Passages—respect all customs.

Wealth circulateth like the Blood, all parts partake; and though none shall want what another hath, yet exact Observers of Property. Some Kings have sold, others presented me with several parcels of Land; the Pay or Presents I made them, were not hoarded by the particular Owners, but the neighbouring Kings and their Clans being present when the Goods were brought out, the Parties chiefly concerned consulted, what and to whom they should give them? To every King then, by the hands of a Person for that work appointed, is a proportion sent, so sorted and folded, and with that Gravity, that is admirable. Then that King subdivideth it in like manner among his Dependents, they hardly leaving themselves an Equal share with one of their Subjects: and be it on such occasions, at Festivals, or at their common Meals, the Kings distribute, and to themselves last. They care for little, because they want but little; and the Reason is, a little contents them: In this they are sufficiently revenged on us; if they are ignorant of our Pleasures, they are also free from our Pains. . . . We sweat and toil to live; their pleasure feeds them, I mean, their Hunting, Fishing and Fowling, and this Table is spread every where; they eat twice a day, Morning and Evening; their Seats and Table are the Ground. Since the European came into these parts, they are grown great lovers of strong Liquors, Rum especially, and for it exchange the richest of their Skins and Furs: If they are heated with Liquors, they are restless till they have enough to sleep; that is their cry, Some more, and I will go to sleep; but when Drunk, one of the most wretchedst Spectacles in the world.

XX. In sickness impatient to be cured, and for it give any thing, especially for their Children, to whom they are extremly natural; they drink at those times a *Teran* or Decoction[10] of some Roots in spring Water; and if they eat any flesh, it must be of the Female of any Creature; if they dye, they bury them with their Apparel, be they Men or Women, and the nearest of Kin fling in something precious with them, as a token of their Love: Their Mourning is blacking of their faces, which they continue for a year; They are choice[11] of the Graves of their Dead; for least they should be lost by time, and fall to common use, they pick off the Grass that grows upon them, and heap up the fallen Earth with great care and exactness.

XXI. These poor People are under a dark Night in things relating to Religion, to be sure, the Tradition of it; yet they believe a God and Immortality, without the help of Metaphysicks;[12] for they say, There is a great King that made them, who dwells in a glorious Country to the Southward of them, and that the Souls of the good shall go thither, where they shall live again. Their Worship consists of two parts, Sacrifice and *Cantico*. Their Sacrifice is their first Fruits; the first and fattest Buck they kill, goeth to the fire, where he is all burnt with a Mournful Ditty of

---

10. Decoction—broth.

11. choice—careful, concerned with.

12. Metaphysicks—the branch of philosophy which deals with that reality beyond the physical or experiential; here, the over-subtle abstract reasoning of orthodox theologians.

him that performeth the Ceremony, but with such marvellous Fervency and Labour of Body, that he will even sweat to a foam. The other part is their *Cantico*, performed by round-Dances, sometimes Words, sometimes Songs, then Shouts, two being in the middle that begin, and by Singing and Drumming on a Board direct the Chorus: Their Postures in the Dance are very Antick and differing, but all keep measure. This is done with equal Earnestness and Labour, but great appearance of Joy. In the Fall, when the Corn cometh in, they begin to feast one another; there have been two great Festivals already, to which all come that will: I was at one my self; their Entertainment was a green Seat by a Spring, under some shady Trees, and twenty Bucks, with hot Cakes of new Corn, both Wheat and Beans, which they make up in a square form, in the leaves of the Stem, and bake them in the Ashes: And after that they fell to Dance, But they that go, must carry a small Present in their Money, it may be six Pence, which is made of the Bone of a fish; the black is with them as Gold, the white, Silver; they call it all *Wampum*.

XXII. Their Government is by Kings, which they call *Sachema*, and those by Succession, but always of the Mothers side; for Instance, the Children of him that is now King, will not succeed, but his Brother by the Mother, or the Children of his Sister, whose Sons (and after them the Children of her Daughters) will reign; for no Woman inherits; the Reason they render for this way of Descent, is, that their Issue may not be spurious.

XXIII. Every King hath his Council, and that consists of all the Old and Wise men of his Nation, which perhaps is two hundred People: nothing of Moment is undertaken, be it War, Peace, Selling of Land or Traffick, without advising with them; and which is more, with the Young Men too. 'Tis admirable to consider, how Powerful the Kings are, and yet how they move by the Breath of their People. I have had occasion to be in Council with them upon Treaties for Land, and to adjust the terms of Trade; their Order is thus: The King sits in the middle of an half Moon, and hath his Council, the Old and Wise on each hand; behind them, or at a little distance, sit the younger Fry, in the same figure. . . . When the Purchase was agreed, great Promises past between us of Kindness and good Neighbourhood, and that the Indians and English must live in Love, as long as the Sun gave light. Which done, another made a Speech to the Indians, in the Name of all the *Sachamakers* or Kings, first to tell them what was done; next, to charge and command them, To Love the Christians, and particularly live in Peace with me, and the People under my Government: That many Governours had been in the River, but that no Governour had come himself to live and stay here before; and having now such a one that had treated them well, they should never do him or his any wrong. At every sentence of which they shouted, and said, Amen in their way.

XXIV. The Justice they have is Pecuniary: In case of any Wrong or evil Fact, be it Murther it self, they Attone by Feasts and Presents of their *Wampon*, which is proportioned to the quality of the Offence or Person injured, or of the Sex they are of: for in case they kill a Woman, they pay double, and the Reason they render, is, That she breedeth Children, which Men cannot do. 'Tis rare that they fall out, if Sober; and if Drunk, they forgive it, saying, It was the Drink, and not the Man, that abused them.

XXV. We have agreed, that in all Differences between us, Six of each side shall end the matter: Don't abuse them, but let them have Justice, and you win them: The worst is, that they are the worse for the Christians, who have propagated their Vices, and yielded them Tradition for ill, and not for good things. . . .

XXVI. For their Original, I am ready to believe them of the Jewish Race, I mean, of the stock of the Ten Tribes, and that for the following Reasons; first, They were to go to a Land not planted or known, which to be sure Asia and Africa were, if not Europe; and he that intended that extraordinary Judgment upon them, might make the Passage not uneasie to them, as it is not impossible in it self, from the Easter-most parts of Asia, to the Wester-most of America. In the next place, I find them of like Countenance and their Children of so lively Resemblance, that a man would think himself in Dukes-place or Berry-street[13] in London, when he seeth them. But this is not all, they agree in Rites, they reckon by Moons: they offer their first Fruits, they have a kind of Feast of Tabernacles; they are said to lay their Alter upon twelve Stones; their Mourning a year, Customs of Women, with many things that do not now occur. So much for the Natives, next the Old Planters will be considered in this Relation, before I come to our Colony, and the Concerns of it.

XXVII. The first Planters in these parts were the Dutch, and soon after them the Sweeds and Finns. The Dutch applied themselves to Traffick,[14] the Sweeds and Finns to Husbandry. . . .

XXVIII. The Dutch inhabit mostly those parts of the Province, that lie upon or near to the Bay, and the Sweeds the Freshes of the River Delaware. There is no need of giving any Description of them, who are better known there then here; but they are a plain, strong, industrious People, yet have made no great progress in Culture or propagation of fruit-Trees, as if they desired rather to have enough, than Plenty or Traffick. But I presume, the Indians made them the more careless, by furnishing them with the means of Profit, to wit, Skins and Furs, for Rum, and such strong Liquors. They kindly received me, as well as the English, who were few, before the People concerned with me came among them; I must needs commend their Respect to Authority, and kind Behaviour to the English; they do not degenerate from the Old friendship between both Kingdoms. As they are People proper and strong of Body, so they have fine Children, and almost every house full; rare to find one of them without three or four Boys, and as many Girls; some six, seven and eight Sons: And I must do them that right, I see few Young men more sober and laborious.

---

13. Dukes-place or Berry-street—addresses in the Jewish quarter of London.
14. Traffick—trade.

XXIX. The Dutch have a Meeting-place for Religious Worship at New Castle, and the Sweedes three, one at Christina, one at Tenecum, and one at Wicoco, within half a Mile of this Town.

XXX. There rests, that I speak of the Condition we are in, and what Settlement we have made, in which I will be as short as I can; for I fear, and not without reason, that I have tryed your Patience with this long Story. The Country lieth bounded on the East, by the River and Bay of Delaware, and Eastern Sea; it hath the Advantage of many Creeks or Rivers rather, that run into the main River or Bay; some Navigable for great Ships, some for small Craft: Those of most Eminency are Christina, Brandywine, Skilpot, and Skulkill; any one of which have room to lay up the Royal Navy of England, there being from four to eight Fathom Water.

XXXI. The lesser Creeks or Rivers, yet convenient for Sloops and Ketches of good Burthen, are Lewis, Mespilion, Cedar, Dover, Cranbrook, Feversham, and Georges, below, and Chichester, Chester, Toacawny, Pemmapecka, Portquessin, Neshimenck and Pennberry in the Freshes; many lesser that admit Boats and Shallops. Our people are mostly settled upon the upper Rivers, which are pleasant and sweet, and generally bounded with good Land. The Planted part of the Province and Territories is cast into six Counties, Philadelphia, Buckingham, Chester, New Castle, Kent and Sussex, containing about Four Thousand Souls. Two General assemblies have been held, and with such Concord and Dispatch, that they sate but three Weeks, and at least seventy Laws were past without one Dissent in any material thing. . . . And for the well Government of the said Counties, Courts of Justice are establisht in every County, with proper Officers, as Justices, Sheriffs, Clarks, Constables, etc., which Courts are held every two Moneths: But to prevent Law-Suits, there are three Peace-makers chosen by every County-Court, in the nature of common Arbitrators, to hear and end Differences betwixt man and man; and Spring and Fall there is an Orphan's Court in each County, to inspect, and regulate the Affairs of Orphans and Widdows.

XXXII. Philadelphia, the Expectation of those that are concern'd in this Province, is at last laid out to the great Content of those here, that are any wayes Interested therein; The Scituation is a Neck of Land, and lieth between two Navigable Rivers, Delaware and Skulkill, whereby it hath two Fronts upon the Water, each a Mile, and two from River to River. Delaware is a glorious River, but the Skulkill being an hundred Miles Boatable above the Falls, and its Course North-East toward the Fountain of Susquahannah (that tends to the Heart of the Province, and both sides our own) it is like to be a great part of the Settlement of this Age. I say little of the Town it self, because a *Plat-form*[15] will be shewn you by my Agent, in which those who are Purchasers of me, will find their Names and Interests: But this I will say for the good Providence of God, that of all the many Places I have seen in the World, I remember not one better seated; so that it seems

---

15. Plat-form—a plat or plan.

to me to have been appointed for a Town, whether we regard the Rivers, or the conveniency of the Coves, Docks, Springs, the loftiness and soundness of the Land and the Air, held by the People of these parts to be very good. It is advanced within less than a Year to about four Score Houses and Cottages, such as they are, where Merchants and Handicrafts, are following their Vocations as fast as they can, while the Country men are close at their Farms; Some of them got a little Winter-Corn in the Ground last Season, and the generality have had a handsom Summer-Crop, and are preparing for their Winter-Corn. . . .

XXXIII. For your particular Concern, I might entirely refer you to the Letters of the President of the Society; but this I will venture to say, Your Provincial Settlements both within and without the Town, for Scituation and Soil, are without Exception; Your City-Lot is an whole Street, and one side of a Street, from River to River, containing near one hundred Acers, not easily valued, which is besides your four hundred Acers in the City Liberties,[16] part of your twenty thousand Acers in the Countery. Your Tannery hath such plenty of Bark, the Saw-Mill for Timber, the place of the Glass-house so conveniently posted for Water-carriage, the City-Lot for a Dock, and the Whalery for a sound and fruitful Bank, and the Town Lewis[17] by it to help your People, that by Gods blessing the Affairs of the Society will naturally grow in their Reputation and Profit. I am sure I have not turned my back upon any Offer that tended to its Prosperity; and though I am ill at Projects, I have sometimes put in for a Share with her Officers, to countenance and advance her Interest. You are already informed what is fit for you further to do, whatsoever tends to the Promotion of Wine, and to the Manufacture of Linnen in these parts, I cannot but wish you to promote it; and the French People are most likely in both respects to answer that design: To that end, I would advise you to send for some Thousands of Plants out of France, with some able Vinerons, and People of the other Vocation: But because I believe you have been entertained with this and some other profitable Subjects by your President, I shall add no more, but to assure you, that I am heartily inclined to advance your just Interest, and that you will always find me

Your Kind Cordial Friend,
WILLIAM PENN
Philadelphia, the 16th of the
6th Moneth, call'd August,
1683.

---

16. City Liberties—district outside the bounds of the city subject to municipal authority.
17. Town Lewis—the town of Lewes (now in Delaware).

# INTRODUCTION & QUESTIONS

## PENN'S PLAN AND ITS REALIZATION

In his letter to the Free Society, William Penn makes mention of a "plat-form" for the city of Philadelphia. This planned "great town" was part of the Proprietor's larger, comprehensive scheme to assure his own and his religion's success in this colonial venture.

Designed to be the uncontested center of the "holy experiment," Philadelphia's plan was largely the work of Thomas Holme (1624–1695), an Irish Quaker, First Purchaser of Pennsylvania, member of the colonial assembly and council and after 1682, Penn's surveyor-general. Armed with some general instructions from the Proprietor and a list of First Purchasers, Holme headed a commission which in the summer of 1682 designed and surveyed the city depicted in this "Portraiture of the City of Philadelphia" and the accompanying description.

Portrayed here is the commercial heart of an urban complex of over 10,000 acres, for the city proper was bounded on north and west by the "Liberties" Penn mentions in his letter. On these tracks of rural greenery surrounding the trading center of Philadelphia, First Purchasers could develop speculative suburbs or indulge any inclinations to live the lives of country gentlemen (at least on weekends) and still remain near their mercantile activities.

1. The city's central portion, however, received Holme's most concentrated attention. As you study it and the attendant "advertisement," ask yourself:

2. What does the city's projected size, especially in relation to the lots actually sold, indicate as to Penn's expectation for future development? Could the massing of First Purchasers' lots used here be economically beneficial to him as a urban realtor?

3. What were the critical determinants of the city's site? What then is considered the city's primary function? What principal qualities was it designed to possess?

4. What determined the specific location of a purchaser's urban real estate? What ratio was employed here? What special considerations were given to small purchasers?

5. Note the variation in street widths. What concerns might have been important in accounting for these considered discriminations?

6. What uses were envisioned for center square? For the four subsidiary squares? To what cultural priorities do these testify?

7. What distinguishing characteristics mark the land allocation scheme produced by the general street layout? What major cultural traits and social interests may be expressed in such a land distribution scheme and street plan?

8. To clarify these and other elements of "Penn's Plan and It's Realization" one should consider the audio-visual program by that name. As you do, try to determine:

9. Exactly what was, for Penn, a major problem arising from attempting to establish a colony which was both Quaker and English? How did the conditions of his grant from Charles II provide him with a tool for solving his quandary?

10. What were the major objectives of his planning? Are there any obvious contradictions among them?

11. Under what specific terms did the "first purchasers" of Pennsylvania receive their lands? What were the consequences of each of these conditions? How do such arrangements advance the three major aims of Penn's plan?

12. What, in particular, are the consequences of Penn's method of opening up new land for European purchase and settlement?

13. What characterized Penn's rural land offerings? What was promoted by such features?

14. What specialized ends did Penn's sale of "manors" in Pennsylvania serve?

15. What special opportunities and conditions were extended to communal or corporate groups who might be prospective buyers? Of what consequence were these arrangements?

16. What objectives were served by Penn's assurance that the planned city of Philadelphia would be of central concern to all of his settlers? What were his priorities in locating the site of his prospective city?

17. What functions were to be served by the "liberties" of Philadelphia? To what class of purchaser were they expected to appeal?

18. In Holmes' scheme for the city, of what consequence is the street plan? The grid plan? The variation in street widths? The concentration of wealthy Quaker merchants along the river fronts?

19. What are the central features of the house lots of Philadelphia? Do you see any relation here to Penn's Quakerism?

20. What roles were the squares of Philadelphia designed to play?

21. What conditions and urban priorities are evident in the Peter Cooper view of the city? What evidence does it provide regarding the relative success of Penn's planning?

22. What considerations and preferences are apparent in Penn's endorsement of a structure like the Letitia Street house and its placement on its house lot as his model for urban building? What significant changes in this ideal were made by Philadelphia's settlers?

23. Of what consequence to the urban architecture of Philadelphia was Penn's house lot scheme? What do the examples of rural building in the area surrounding the city suggest about Philadelphia's role in the colony?

24. What are the principal features of the Quaker meeting house? What ideals and values are implied in them?

25. What particular priorities and developments in social planning are suggested by the Greater Meeting House and Philadelphia's Town House? How are such features confirmed in the Second Street market sheds?

26. In what form did the Quaker represent his physical appearance? Commemorate his death? How do such art forms differ from previous American colonial examples you have seen?

27. What special circumstances arose in the mid-eighteenth century to seriously challenge the outlines of Penn's plan? How was this problem resolved? To what end?

# A SHORT ADVERTISEMENT
# UPON THE SCITUATION AND EXTENT
# OF THE CITY OF PHILADELPHIA
# AND THE ENSUING PLAT-FORM THEREOF,
# BY THE SURVEYOR GENERAL

*William Penn*

The City of Philadelphia, now extends in Length, from River to River, two Miles, and in Breadth near a Mile; and the Governour, as a further manifestation of his Kindness to the Purchasers, hath freely given them their respective Lots in the City, without defalcation[1] of any their Quantities of purchased Lands; and as its now placed and modelled between two Navigable Rivers upon a Neck of Land, and that Ships may ride in good Anchorage, in six or eight Fathom Water in both Rivers, close to the City, and the Land of the City level, dry and wholsom: such a Scituation is scarce to be paralle'd.

The Model of the City appears by a small Draught now made, and may hereafter, when time permits, be augmented; and because there is not room to express the Purchasers Names in the Draught, I have therefore drawn Directions of Reference, by ways of Number, whereby may be known each mans Lot and Place in the City.

The City is so ordered now, by the Governour's Care and Prudence, that it hath a Front to each River, one half at Delaware, the other at Skulkill; and though all this cannot make way for small Purchasers to be in the Fronts, yet they are placed in the next Streets, contiguous to each Front, *viz.* all Purchasers of One Thousand Acres, and upwards, have the Fronts, (and the High-street) and to every five Thousand Acres Purchase, in the Front about an Acre, and the smaller Purchasers about half an Acre in the backward Streets; by which means the least hath room enough for House, Garden and small Orchard, to the great Content and Satisfaction of all here concerned.

The City, (as the Model shews) consists of a large Front-street to each River, and a High-street (near the middle) from Front (or River) to Front, of

---

1. defalcation—deduction.

Penn's Plan 1682

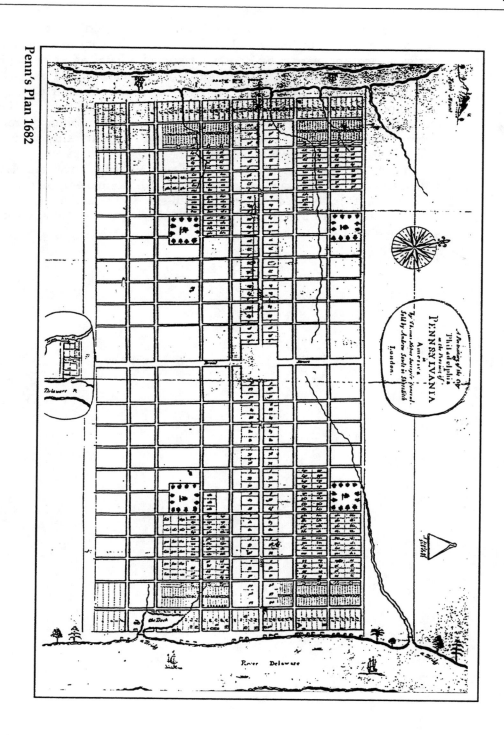

one hundred Foot broad, and a Broad-street in the middle of the City, from side to side, of the like breadth. In the Center of the City is a Square of ten Acres; at each Angle are to be Houses for publick Affairs, as a Meeting-House, Assembly or State-House, Market-House, School-House, and several other Buildings for Public Concerns. There are also in each Quarter of the City a Square of eight Acres, to be for the like Uses, as the Moore-fields[2] in London; and eight Streets, (besides the High-street, that run from Front to Front, and twenty Streets, (besides the Broad-street) that run cross the City, from side to side; all these Streets are of fifty Foot breadth.

In each Number in the Draught, in the Fronts and High-street, are placed the Purchasers of One Thousand Acres, and upwards, to make up five Thousand Acres Lot, both in the said Fronts and High-street, and the Numbers direct to each Lot, and where in the City; so that thereby they may know where their Concerns are therein. . . .

---

2. Moore-fields—a municipal green in London.

# INTRODUCTION & QUESTIONS

## THE PROBLEMS OF COMPARISON AND CHANGE

At this point, we have surveyed the culture of three distinct societies, generally contemporaneous with one another but located within differing geographical areas in colonial North America.

With each of these examples we have observed representative data illustrating each society's behavior patterns. For each of these cases, we might, as we did with the Puritan example, have catagorized this behavior in terms of:

1. Politics

2. Religion

3. Sociology

4. Economics

5. The Family and Education

6. Science Artifacts

We could also observe and describe, as with the Puritan illustration, the complex of ideas by which each society "explains" or justifies its actions and products in each of these areas of behavioral expression.

The totality of these explanations of "reality" constitutes the cultural system for each society, yet, as was initially indicated, to simply "list" the cultural definitions prevailing in a society is not to describe the systematic character of a cultural system. We must still indicate the relationships that existed among these definitions.

Before class, see if you can begin this process of determining some of the relationships that prevail in the cultural example you know most thoroughly. Using the Puritan example, see if you can locate and isolate any definitions, assumptions, premises or values which are *basic* to that system. That is, are there not certain concepts which are apparent in all the areas of thought and action outlined above? In short, are there not certain *fundamental* propositions which are present in each of the specialized contexts listed above? Try then to develop a list of such concepts, ideas which you see as fundamental to the Puritan cultural system. Using the results of your analysis, we can then proceed to investigate the problems of cultural comparison and change.

# INTRODUCTION & QUESTIONS

## THE GREAT AWAKENING AND ITS GENERATION

Included in the *Spiritual Travels* of one Nathan Cole is this description of the arrival of the Reverend George Whitefield in 1740. Cole was an average Connecticut farmer and carpenter who, with his personal journal, presents yet another example of Puritan introspection. In this work he noted that until the age of 29, prior to Whitefield's arrival, he had erroneously "intended to be saved by my own works such as prayers and good deeds."

George Whitefield was, while an Anglican minister, a dissenter within the Church of England and a sharp critic of its rationalistic ministry. His own theological position was squarely on the side of strict Calvinism and totally acceptable by Massachusetts' standards. Yet in his wake through New England, he left no orthodox reactions. Cole, for one, testified to his effect by beginning his *Spiritual Travels* with the line, "I was born Feb 15th 1711 and born again Oct. 1741." Part of the meaning of this reference, both for Cole and for his cultural system, lies in the first selection which follows.

Yet Whitefield was not the only minister in New England who left such an imprint. Chief among his native American sympathizers was Jonathan Edwards (1703–58), of Northampton, Connecticut. Included in this assignment is Edward's most famous sermon, *Sinners in the Hands of an Angry God* delivered first to a frenzied reception in 1741. In it one sees some of the central themes that characterize the phenomenon known as the Great Awakening. Consider:

1. In Edwards description, what are the primary attributes of God? Of man?

2. What means does he use to convey his message here? What specific analogies does he employ?

3. What fate does Edwards forecast for natural man? What possibilities exist for escaping this outcome? How do these prerequisites for attaining salvation differ from the conditions of those who have deluded themselves into believing they are of the elect?

4. What similarities and differences do you see between this position and presentation, and previous Puritan examples? What implications might this have for the cultural system?

5. How significant does Cole consider Whitefield's arrival? What is his response? Does this evaluation appear to be his alone?

6. What does he note about Whitefield's appearance? His effect? How does Cole account for his personal reaction to Whitefield's message?

7. Are there elements in this event that make it unique to the Puritan cultural system? By its nature, would it have any effects on that system? What might they be?

# SPIRITUAL TRAVELS

*Nathan Cole*

## ENTRY OF OCTOBER 23, 1740

Now it pleased God to send Mr. Whitefield into this land; and my hearing of his preaching at Philadelphia, like one of the old apostles, and many thousands flocking to hear him preach the Gospel, and great numbers were converted to Christ, I felt the Spirit of God drawing me by conviction; I longed to see and hear him and wished he would come this way. I heard he was come to New York and the Jerseys and great multitudes flocking after him under great concern for their souls which brought on my concern more and more, hoping soon to see him; but next I heard he was at Long Island, then at Boston, and next at Northampton. Then on a sudden, in the morning about 8 or 9 of the clock there came a messenger and said Mr. Whitefield preached at Hartford and Wethersfield yesterday and is to preach at Middletown this morning at ten of the clock. I was in my field at work. I dropped my tool that I had in my hand and ran home to my wife, telling her to make ready quickly to go and hear Mr. Whitefield preach at Middletown, then ran to my pasture for my horse with all my might, fearing that I should be too late. Having my horse, I with my wife soon mounted the horse and went forward as fast as I thought the horse could bear; and when my horse got much out of breath, I would get down and put my wife on the saddle and bid her ride as fast as she could and not to stop or slack for me except I bade her, and so I would run until I was much out of breath and then mount my horse again, and so I did several times to favour my horse. We improved every moment to get along as if we were fleeing for our lives, all the while fearing we should be too late to hear the sermon, for we had twelve miles to ride double in little more than an hour and we went round by the upper housen parish. And when we came within about half a mile or a mile of the road that comes down from Hartford, Wethersfield, and Stepney to Middletown, on high land I saw before me a cloud of fog arising. I first thought it came from the great river, but as I came nearer the road I heard a noise of horses' feet coming down the road, and this cloud was a cloud of dust made by the horses' feet. It arose some rods into the air over the tops of hills and trees; and when I came within about 20 rods of the road, I could see men and horses slipping along in the cloud like shadows, and as I drew nearer it seemed like a steady stream of horses and their riders, scarcely a horse more than his length behind another, all of a lather and foam with sweat, their breath rolling out of their nostrils every jump. Every horse seemed to go with all his might to carry his rider to hear news from heaven for the saving of souls. It made me tremble to see the sight, how the world was in a struggle. I found a vacancy between two horses to slip in mine and my wife said "Law, our clothes will be all spoiled, see how they look," for they were so covered with dust that they looked almost all of a colour, coats, hats, shirts, and horse. We went down in the stream but heard no man speak a word all the way for 3 miles but every one pressing forward in great haste; and when we got to Middletown old meeting house, there was a great multitude, it was said to be 3 or 4,000 of people, assembled together. We dismounted and shook off our dust, and the ministers were then coming to the meeting house. I turned and looked towards the Great River and saw the ferry boats running swift backward and forward bringing over loads of people, and the oars rowed nimble and quick. Everything, men, horses, and boats seemed to be struggling for life. The land and banks over the river looked black with people and horses; all along the 12 miles I saw no man at work in his field, but all seemed to be gone. When I saw Mr. Whitefield come upon the scaffold, he looked almost angelical; a young, slim, slender youth, before some thousands of people with a bold undaunted countenance. And my hearing how God was with him everywhere as he came along, it solemnized my mind and put me into a trembling fear before he began to preach; for he looked as if he was clothed with authority from the Great God, and a sweet solemn solemnity sat upon his brow, and my hearing him preach gave me a heart wound. By God's blessing, my old foundation was broken up, and I saw that my righteousness would not save me.

# SINNERS IN THE HANDS
# OF AN ANGRY GOD

*Jonathan Edwards*

> *Their foot shall slide in due time.*
> —Deuteronomy 32:35

In this verse is threatened the vengeance of God on the wicked, unbelieving Israelites, that were God's visible people, and lived under means of grace; and that notwithstanding all God's wonderful works that He had wrought towards that people, yet remained, as is expressed in verse 28, void of counsel, having no understanding in them. . . .

The observation from the words that I would now insist upon is this: There is nothing that keeps wicked men at any one moment out of hell but the mere pleasure of God.

By the mere pleasure of God, I mean His sovereign pleasure, His arbitrary will, restrained by no obligation, hindered by no manner of difficulty, anymore than if nothing else but God's mere will had in the least degree or in any respect whatsoever, any hand in the preservation of wicked men one moment.

The truth of this observation may appear by the following considerations.

There is no want of power in God to cast wicked men into hell at any moment. Men's hands cannot be strong when God rises up: the strongest have no power to resist Him, nor can any deliver out of His hands. He is not only able to cast wicked men into hell, but He can most easily do it.

Sometimes an earthly prince meets with a great deal of difficulty to subdue a rebel, that has found means to fortify himself, and has made himself strong by the number of his followers. But it is not so with God. There is no fortress that is any defence against the power of God. Though hand join in hand, and vast multitudes of God's enemies combine and associate themselves, they are easily broken in pieces; they are as great heaps of light chaff before the whirlwind, or large quantities of dry stubble before devouring flames. We find it easy to tread on and crush a worm that we see crawling on the earth; so it is easy for us to cut or singe a slender thread that anything hangs by; thus easy is it for God, when He pleases, to cast His enemies down to hell. What are we, that we should think to stand before Him, at whose rebuke the earth trembles, and before whom the rocks are thrown down! . . . .

It is no security to wicked men, for one moment, that there are no visible means of death at hand. It is no security to a natural man that he is now in health, and that he does not see which way he should now immediately go out of the world by any accident, and that there is no visible danger in any respect in his circumstances. The manifold and continual experience of the world in all ages shows that this is no evidence that a man is not on the very brink of eternity, and that the next step will not be into another world. The unseen, unthought of ways and means of persons going suddenly out of the world are innumerable and inconceivable. Unconverted men walk over the pit of hell on a rotten covering, and there are innumerable places in this covering so weak that they will not bear their weight, and these places are not seen. The arrows of death fly unseen at noonday; the sharpest sight cannot discern them. God has so many different, unsearchable ways of taking wicked men out of the world and sending them to hell that there is nothing to make it appear that God had need to be at the expense of a miracle, or go out of the ordinary course of His providence to destroy any wicked man, at any moment. All the means that there are of sinners going out of the world are so in God's hands, and so absolutely subject to His power and determination, that it does not depend at all less on the mere will of God, whether sinners shall at any moment go to hell, than if means were never made use of, or at all concerned in the case. . . .

God has laid Himself under no obligation, by any promise, to keep any natural man out of hell one moment. God certainly has made no promises either of eternal life or of any deliverance or preservation from eternal death, but what are contained in the Covenant of Grace, the promises that are given in Christ, in whom all the promises are yea and amen. . . .

So that thus it is that natural men are held in the hand of God over the pit of hell; they have deserved the fiery pit and are already sentenced to it; and God is dreadfully provoked—His anger is as great toward them as to those that are actually suffering the executions of the fierceness of His wrath in hell, and they have done nothing in the least to appease or abate that anger; neither is God in the least bound by any promise to hold them up one moment. The devil is waiting for them; hell is gaping for them; the flames gather and flash about them, and would fain lay hold on them and swallow them up; the fire pent up in their own hearts is struggling to break out; and they have no interest in any Mediator—there are no means within reach that can be any security to them. In short, they have no refuge, nothing to take hold of; all that preserves them every moment is the mere arbitrary will and uncovenanted, unobliged forbearance of an incensed God.

## APPLICATION

The use may be of awakening to unconverted persons in this congregation. This that you have heard is the case of every one of you that are out of Christ.

That world of misery, that lake of burning brimstone, is extended abroad under you. There is the dreadful pit of the glowing flames of the wrath of God; there is hell's wide gaping mouth open; and you have nothing to stand upon, nor anything to take hold of. There is nothing between you and hell but the air; it is only the power and mere pleasure of God that holds you up. . . .

The bow of God's wrath is bent, and the arrow made ready on the string, and justice bends the arrow at your heart, and strains the bow, and it is nothing but the mere pleasure of God, and that of an angry God, without any promise or obligation at all, that keeps the arrow one moment from being made drunk with your blood.

Thus are all you that never passed under a great change of heart, by the mighty power of the Spirit of God upon your souls; all that were never born again, and made new creatures, and raised from being dead in sin to a state of new, and before altogether unexperienced, light and life (however you may have reformed your life in many things, and may have had religious affections, and may keep up a form of religion in your families and closets[1] and in the houses of God, and may be strict in it), you are thus in the hands of an angry God; it is nothing but His mere pleasure that keeps you from being this moment swallowed up in everlasting destruction. . . .

The God that holds you over the pit of hell, much as one holds a spider, or some loathsome insect over the fire, abhors you, and is dreadfully provoked. His wrath toward you burns like fire; He looks upon you as worthy of nothing else, but to be cast into the fire; He is of purer eyes than to bear to have you in His sight; you are ten thousand times so abominable in His eyes, as the most hateful and venomous serpent is in ours. You have offended Him infinitely more than ever a stubborn rebel did his prince; and yet it is nothing but His hand that holds you from falling into the fire every moment. It is ascribed to nothing else that you did not go to hell the last night; that you was suffered to awake again in this world after you closed your eyes to sleep; and there is no other reason to be given why you have not dropped into hell since you arose in the morning, but that God's hand has held you up. There is no other reason to be given why you have not gone to hell, since you have sat here in the house of God, provoking His pure eyes by your sinful, wicked manner of attending His solemn worship; yea, there is nothing else that is to be given as a reason why you do not this very moment drop down into hell.

O sinner! consider the fearful danger you are in: it is a great furnace of wrath, a wide and bottomless pit, full of the fire of wrath, that you are held over in the hand of that God, whose wrath is provoked and incensed as much against you as many of the damned in hell. You hang by a slender thread, with the flames of divine wrath flashing about it, and ready every moment to singe it and burn it asunder; and you have no interest in any Mediator, and nothing to lay hold of to

---

1. closets—studies

save yourself, nothing to keep off the flames of wrath, nothing of your own, nothing that you ever have done, nothing that you can do to induce God to spare you one moment. . . .

How dreadful is the state of those that are daily and hourly in danger of this great wrath and infinite misery! But this is the dismal case of every soul in this congregation that has not been born again, however moral and strict, sober and religious they may otherwise be. Oh, that you would consider it, whether you be young or old! There is reason to think that there are many in this congregation now hearing this discourse that will actually be the subjects of this very misery to all eternity. We know not who they are, or in what seats they sit, or what thoughts they now have. It may be they are now at ease, and hear all these things without much disturbance, and are now flattering themselves that they are not the persons—promising themselves that they shall escape. If we knew that there was one person, and but one, in the whole congregation, that was to be the subject of this misery, what an awful thing it would be to think of! If we knew who it was, what an awful sight would it be to see such a person! How might all the rest of the congregation lift up a lamentable and bitter cry over him! But alas! Instead of one, how many is it likely will remember this discourse in hell! And it would be a wonder if some that are now present should not be in hell in a very short time, before this year is out. And it would be no wonder if some person sthat now sit here in some seats of this meetinghouse in health, and quiet and secure, should be there before tomorrow morning.

# INTRODUCTION & QUESTIONS

## THE ICONOGRAPHY OF CHANGE

"The Iconography of Change" reveals some of the visual record of the Great Awakening on American culture. Ask yourself:

1. How can you explain the failure of the artists of the day to capture the revolutionary nature of Jonathan Edwards or George Whitefield? What do they reveal about the latter?

2. What are the primary features of American portraiture evident in John Smibert's *George Berkeley and His Entourage*? Which of these reappear in his portraits of Nathaniel Byfield and the Oliver boys?

3. What points of resemblance do you see between Smibert's *George Berkeley and His Entourage* and Robert Feke's *Isaac Royall and Family*? What do such similarities indicate about the nature of colonial portraiture?

4. What personal artistic characteristics of Feke are illustrated in his studies of Isaac Winslow and the unknown woman? Could the acceptance of these individual traits also suggest certain cultural priorities in American portraiture?

5. What standard artistic conventions are shared by Peter Pelham and John Singleton Copley in their portraits of Puritan ministers?

6. In what precise ways does Copley in his early works echo or augment the conventions of American colonial portraiture?

7. What revolutionary changes do you see appearing in Copley's work beginning with his *Boy with a Squirrel*? What new priorities are suggested here?

8. Both Joseph Barrell and Epes Sargent were businessmen painted by Copley. What relative importance does the painter assign to their social role in his portraits of them? Is the same decision evident in Copley's study of Mrs. Nathaniel Appleton?

9. What new elements of portrait presentation does Copley introduce in his portrayal of Nathaniel Hurd? How are these elaborated on in his portrait of Paul Revere?

10. What distinguishing traits mark Copley's studies of married couples like the Winslows and the Mifflens?

11. What specific circumstances caused Copley's emigration from America? What American cultural values are suggested in his painting marking his reunion with his family in England?

12. Which of Copley's characteristics are continued in Ralph Earle's studies of the elite of New Milford, Connecticut? Are there any resemblances between Earle's *Chief Justice and Mrs. Oliver Ellsworth* and Copley's presentations of couples and families?

13. Make a detailed study of the similarities between Earle's *Mrs. William Moseley and Her Son* and Copley's *Boy with a Squirrel*. What similarities do you see and what new cultural values could be illustrated by such features?

# INTRODUCTION & QUESTIONS

## THE AMERICAN—
## BENJAMIN FRANKLIN

Benjamin Franklin was, during his own lifetime, the most famous and rewarded American of his day. Both in his own country and in the world abroad, he represented *the* American, all the virtues and attributes of the new man of the United States. Named "the father of his country" before Washington received the title, he served America as a kind of eighteenth-century Uncle Sam.

This assessment of Franklin as the symbol of the new nation was virtually universal, both during his lifespan and throughout the nineteenth century. Thus, Thomas Jefferson, immediately upon Franklin's death, referred to him as "the greatest man and ornament of the age and country in which he lived." This same appraisal was still to be heard just before the Civil War. Then the religious spokesman Theodore Parker called him "the most popular man in America . . . No man now has so strong a hold on the habits and manners of the people." A few years later in 1862, another national spokesman, Horace Greeley, dubbed him "the consummate type and flowering of human nature under the skies of colonial America."

In reviewing Franklin's *Autobiography* then, keep in mind that you are reading more than the personal narrative of one man's life but, by the Americans' own evaluation, a personification of the national character. Try, then, to determine the qualities exemplified by Franklin with which so many Americans over so many years chose to be identified. Attempt, too, to determine the factors that influenced Franklin's own development out of a background in Puritan culture.

### PART ONE

If you are using the New American Library (Signet) edition of *The Autobiography and Other Writings*, read the introduction and the first part of the autobiography. (This ends on page 55) The questions that follow should be useful in studying this assignment.

1. What reasons does Franklin present for writing his autobiography? What effect could these motives have on the final product?

2. What were, in Franklin's estimation, the most significant facets of his ancestry? With which of his forefathers and relatives was he most sympathetic?

3. What were Franklin's earliest memories of his father? What, by his accounting, were the major influences his father had upon his development?

4. How significant does he regard his early reading? What were the sources for his books? What readings does he consider most valuable and why? Carefully note both the types of literature referred to as well as representative titles.

5. The *Spectator* refers to a daily paper published in London during 1711 and 1712 by Joseph Addison and Richard Steele. It contained essays on literature and aesthetics as well as satires of society and manners. What use does Franklin make of this work?

6. What was his experience with the ideas and methods of Socrates? What does this suggest about his character?

7. What, according to Franklin, was the basis for the estrangement between himself and his brother? Do his subsequent actions regarding his brother appear justified by his reasoning? What were the specific circumstances surrounding their final break?

8. Under what conditions did he leave Boston? What, in particular, was his father's response to his actions?

9. What events befall him on his journey to and entry into Philadelphia? What do these incidents add to the autobiography and to Franklin's presentation of himself?

10. For what reasons does Franklin return to Boston? How does he behave toward his family? What is their response to him?

## PART TWO

Read the second part of the *Autobiography,* then edited pages 69–82 which follow the "Proposal" below, then pages 89–135 (in the NAL edition) Also those sections concerning George Whitefield and Franklin's social projects. (The page numbers of these sections in the NAL edition are indicated below)

1. What were the stages in the evolution of Franklin's religious position? What does he finally conclude are valid religious principles? How specific are they?

2. What was his attitude toward religious organizations? How was this demonstrated? What criteria does he use to judge a religious body's worth?

3. What does he substitute for religious observance? What is the source of this plan and its ideals? What are the means he uses to accomplish it? What is its announced goal?

4. Franklin was on hand to witness the arrival and activities of George White-field in Philadelphia (pp. 116–120). What aspects of Whitefield's campaign did he participate in? What specific features of the evangelist merit his closest attention?

5. Review Franklin's descriptions of his famous social projects listed below. Are there any characteristics shared by all of these activities? Are they in any way similar in goals and the methods used to achieve their ends?

6. The Junto (pp. 72–73). What was to be the chief purpose of the Junto? What kinds of individuals were members? What were the advantages and consequences of membership?

7. The library (pp. 82; 90–91). What were the most conspicuous effects the library had upon the community? What special lesson did Franklin learn in establishing the library?

8. The fire company (pp. 115–116). What were the obligations of those who received the services of the company? How were major pieces of fire-fighting apparatus obtained?

9. The militia (pp. 101–107). What were the circumstances that called forth this project? How were its officers selected? What were the means used to supply fortifications? How did the church assist Franklin here? How did Franklin deal with Quaker opposition?

10. The Academy; later, the University of Pennsylvania (pp. 108–111). What special arrangements were made for housing the new school? What credit did Franklin take in initiating the project?

11. The Pennsylvania Hospital (pp. 113–114). What special assistance did Franklin give to Dr. Thomas Bond in establishing the hospital? What role did the state play in this endeavor?

12. The American Philosophical Society (p. 101), Franklin's "Proposal" is reproduced below. What was the function of the society? What kinds of people were members? How did it operate?

# A PROPOSAL FOR PROMOTING USEFUL KNOWLEDGE AMONG THE BRITISH PLANTATIONS IN AMERICA

*Benjamin Franklin*

**Philadelphia, May 14, 1743**

The English are possessed of a long tract of continent, from Nova Scotia to Georgia, extending north and south through different climates, having different soils, producing different plants, mines, and minerals, and capable of different improvements, manufacturers, &c.

The first drudgery of settling new colonies, which confines the attention of people to mere necessaries, is now pretty well over; and there are many in every province in circumstances that set them at ease, and afford leisure to cultivate the finer arts and improve the common stock of knowledge. To such of these who are men of speculation, many hints must from time to time arise, many observations occur, which if well examined, pursued, and improved, might produce discoveries to the advantage of some or all of the British plantations, or to the benefit of mankind in general.

But as from the extent of the country such persons are widely separated, and seldom can see and converse or be acquainted with each other, so that many useful particulars remain uncommunicated, die with the discoverers, and are lost to mankind; it is, to remedy this inconvenience for the future, proposed,

That one society be formed of *virtuosi* or ingenious men, residing in the several colonies, to be called *The American Philosophical Society*, who are to maintain a constant correspondence.

That Philadelphia, being the city nearest the centre of the continent colonies, communicating with all of them northward and southward by post, and with all the islands by sea, and having the advantage of a good growing library, be the centre of the Society.

That at Philadelphia there be always at least seven members, viz. a physician, a botanist, a mathematician, a chemist, a mechanician, a geographer, and a general natural philosopher, besides a president, treasurer, and secretary.

That these members meet once a month, or oftener, at their own expense, to communicate to each other their observations and experiments, to receive, read, and consider such letters, communications, or queries as shall be sent from distant members; to direct the dispersing of copies of such communications as are valuable, to other distant members, in order to procure their sentiments thereupon.

That the subjects of the correspondence be: all new-discovered plants, herbs, trees, roots, their virtues, uses, &c.; methods of propagating them, and making such as are useful, but particular to some plantations, more general; improvements of vegetable juices, as ciders, wines, &c.; new methods of curing or preventing diseases; all new-discovered fossils in different countries, as mines, minerals, and quarries; new and useful improvements in any branch of mathematics; new discoveries in chemistry, such as improvements in distillation, brewing, and assaying of ores; new mechanical inventions for saving labour, as mills and carriages, and for raising and conveying of water, draining of meadows, &c., all new arts, trades, and manufactures, that may be proposed or thought of; surveys, maps, and charts of particular parts of the seacoasts or inland countries; course and junction of rivers and great roads, situation of lakes and mountains, nature of the soil and productions; new methods of improving the breed of useful animals; introducing other sorts from foreign countries; new improvements in planting, gardening, and clearing land; and all philosophical experiments that let light into the nature of things, tend to increase the power of man over matter, and multiply the conveniences or pleasures of life.

That a correspondence, already begun by some intended members, shall be kept up by this Society with the *Royal Society* of London, and with the *Dublin Society*.

That every member shall have abstracts sent him quarterly, of every thing valuable communicated to the Society's Secretary at Philadelphia; free of all charge except the yearly payment hereafter mentioned.

That, by permission of the postmaster-general, such communications pass between the Secretary of the Society and the members, postage-free.

That, for defraying the expense of such experiments as the Society shall judge proper to cause to be made, and other contingent charges for the common good, every member send a piece of eight per annum to the treasurer, at Philadelphia, to form a common stock, to be disbursed by order of the President with the consent of the majority of the members that can conveniently be consulted thereupon, to such persons and places where and by whom the experiments are to be made, and otherwise as there shall be occasion; of which disbursements an exact account shall be kept, and communicated yearly to every member.

That, at the first meetings of the members at Philadelphia, such rules be formed for regulating their meetings and transactions for the general benefit, as shall be convenient and necessary; to be afterwards changed and improved as there shall be occasion, wherein due regard is to be had to the advice of distant members.

That, at the end of every year, collections be made and printed, of such experiments, discoveries, and improvements, as may be thought of public advantage; and that every member have a copy sent him.

That the business and duty of the Secretary be to receive all letters intended for the Society, and lay them before the President and members at their meetings; to abstract, correct, and methodize such papers as require it, and as he shall be directed to do by the President, after they have been considered, debated, and digested in the Society; to enter copies thereof in the Society's books, and make out copies for distant members; to answer their letters by direction of the President, and keep records of all material transactions of the Society.

Benjamin Franklin, the writer of this Proposal, offers himself to serve the Society as their secretary, till they shall be provided with one more capable.

# THE AUTOBIOGRAPHY
# OF BENJAMIN FRANKLIN

*At this point in the* Autobiography, *Franklin recalls his eighteen month stay in England. On his return to Philadelphia, he becomes established in the printing trade.*

Before I enter upon my public appearance in business, it may be well to let you know the then state of my mind with regard to my principles and morals, that you may see how far those influenced the future events of my life. My parents had early given me religious impressions, and brought me through my childhood piously in the dissenting way. But I was scarce fifteen when, after doubting by turns of several points, as I found them disputed in the different books I read, I began to doubt of revelation itself. Some books against deism fell into my hands; they were said to be the substance of the sermons which had been preached at Boyle's lectures. It happened that they wrought an effect on me quite contrary to what was intended by them, for the arguments of the deists which were quoted to be refuted appeared to me much stronger than the refutations. In short, I soon became a thorough deist. My arguments perverted some others, particularly Collins and Ralph; but each of them having afterwards wronged me greatly without the least compunction, and recollecting Keith's conduct towards me (who was another freethinker) and my own towards Vernon and Miss Read (which at times gave me great trouble), I began to suspect that this doctrine, tho' it might be true, was not very useful. My London pamphlet which had for its motto these lines of Dryden

> *Whatever is, is right*
> *Tho' purblind man*
> *Sees but a part of the chain, the nearest link,*
> *His eyes not carrying to the equal beam,*
> *That poizes all above.*

And which from the attributes of God, his infinite wisdom, goodness, and power, concludes that nothing could possibly be wrong in the world and that vice and virtue were empty distinctions, no such things existing, appeared now not so clever a performance as I once thought it; and I doubted whether some error had not insinuated itself unperceived into my argument so as to infect all that followed, as is common in metaphysical reasonings. I grew convinced that *truth*, *sincerity* and *integrity* in dealings between man and man were of the utmost importance to the felicity of life, and I formed written resolutions (which still remain in my Journal book) to practise them ever while I lived. Revelation had indeed no weight with me as such; but I entertained an opinion that tho' certain actions might not be bad *because* they were forbidden by it, or good *because* it commanded them, yet probably those actions might be forbidden *because* they were bad for us or commanded *because* they were beneficial to us, in their own natures, all the circumstances of things considered. And this persuasion, with the kind hand of Providence, or some guardian angel, or accidental favourable circumstances and situations, or all together, preserved me (thro' this dangerous time of youth and the hazardous situations I was sometimes in among strangers, remote from the eye and advice of my father) without any *wilful*, gross immorality or injustice that might have been expected from my want of religion. I say *wilful* because the instances I have mentioned had some thing of necessity in them, from my youth, inexperience, and the knavery of others. I had, therefore, a tolerable character to begin the world with; I valued it properly and determined to preserve it.

We had not been long returned to Philadelphia, before the new types arrived from London. We settled with Keimer and left him by his consent before he heard of it. We found a house to hire near the market and took it. To lessen the rent (which was then but £24 a year tho' I have since known it let for seventy) we took in. Thomas Godfrey, a glazier, and his family, who were to pay a considerable part of it to us, and we to board with them. We had scarce opened our letters and put our press in order before George House, an acquaintance of mine, brought a country man to us whom he had met in the street enquiring for a printer. All our cash was expended in the variety of particulars we had been obliged to procure, and this country man's five shillings being our first fruits and coming so seasonably, gave me more pleasure than any crown I have since earned, and from the gratitude I felt towards House, has made me often more ready than perhaps I should otherwise have been to assist young beginners.

There are croakers in every country always boding it ruin. Such a one then lived in Philadelphia, a person of note, an elderly man with a wise look and very grave manner of speaking. His name was Samuel Mickle. This gentleman, a stranger to me, stopped one day at my door and asked me if I was the young man who had lately opened a new printing house. Being answered in the affirmative, he said he was sorry for me because it was an expensive undertaking and the expence would be lost, for Philadelphia was a sinking place, the people already half bankrupts or near being so—all appearances of the contrary, such as new buildings and the rise of rents, being to his certain knowledge fallacious, for they were in fact among the things that would soon ruin us. And he gave me such a detail of misfortunes now existing, or that were soon to exist, that he left me half-melancholy. Had I known him before I engaged in this business, probably I never should have done it. This man continued to live in this decaying place and to declaim in the same strain, refusing for many years to buy a house there because all was going to destruction, and at last I had the pleasure of seeing him give five times as much for one as he might have bought it for when he first began his croaking.

I should have mentioned before that in the autumn of the preceding year I had formed most of my ingenious acquaintance into a club for mutual improvement which we called the Junto. We met on Friday evenings. The rules I drew up required that every member in his turn should produce one or more queries on any point of morals, politics, or natural philosophy, to be discussed by the company, and once in three months produce and read an essay of his own writing on any subject he pleased. Our debates were to be under the direction of a president, and to be conducted in the sincere spirit of enquiry after truth, without fondness for dispute or desire of victory; and to prevent warmth, all expressions of positiveness in opinion or of direct contradiction were after some time made contraband and prohibited under small pecuniary penalties.

The first members were, Joseph Breintnal, a copier of deeds for the scriveners, a good-natured, friendly, middle-aged man, a great lover of poetry—reading all he could meet with and writing some that was tolerable—very ingenious in many little nicknackeries, and of sensible conversation.

Thomas Godfrey, a self-taught mathematician, great in his way, and afterwards inventor of what is now called Hadley's Quadrant. But he knew little out of his way and was not a pleasing companion, as like most great mathematicians I have met with, he expected unusual precision in everything said, or was forever denying or distinguishing upon trifles to the disturbance of all conversation. He soon left us.

Nicholas Scull, a surveyor, afterwards Surveyor-General, who loved books, and sometimes made a few verses.

William Parsons, bred a shoemaker, but loving reading, had acquired a considerable share of mathematics, which he first studied with a view to astrology that he afterwards laughed at. He also became Surveyor-General.

William Maugridge, a joiner, but a most exquisite mechanic, and a solid, sensible man.

Hugh Meredith, Stephen Potts, and George Webb I have characterised before.

Robert Grace, a young gentleman of some fortune, generous, lively, and witty, a lover of punning and of his friends.

Lastly, William Coleman, then a merchant's clerk, about my age, who had the coolest, clearest head, the best heart, and the exactest morals of almost any man I ever met with. He became afterwards a merchant of great note, and one of our provincial judges. Our friendship continued without interruption to his death, upwards of forty years. And the club continued almost as long and was the best school of philosophy, and politics that then existed in the province; for our queries which were read the week preceding their discussion, put us on reading with attention upon the several subjects that we might speak more to the purpose; and here, too, we acquired better habits of conversation, everything being studied in our rules which might prevent our disgusting each other—from hence the long continuance of the club, which I shall have frequent occasion to speak further of hereafter. But my giving this account of it here is to show something of the interest I had, every one of these exerting themselves in recommending business to us. Breintnal particularly procured us from the Quakers the printing forty sheets of their history, the rest being to be done by Keimer; and upon this we worked exceeding hard, for the price was low. It was a folio, *pro patria* size, in pica with long primer notes. I composed of it a sheet a day, and Meredith worked it off at press. It was often eleven at night, and sometimes later, before I had finished my distribution for the next day's work. For the little jobs sent in by our other friends now and then put us back. But so determined I was to continue doing a sheet a day of the folio, that one night when having imposed my forms I thought my day's work over, one of them by accident was broken and two pages reduced to pie, I immediately distributed and composed it over again before I went to bed. And this industry visible to our neighbours began to give us character and credit—particularly, I was told, that mention being made of the new printing office at the merchants' Every-night Club, the general opinion was that it must fail, there being already two printers in the place, Keimer and Bradford; but Doctor Baird (whom you and I saw many years after at his native place, St. Andrew's in Scotland) gave a contrary opinion: "For the industry of that Franklin," says he, "is superior to anything I ever saw of the kind; I see him still at work when I go home from club, and he is at work again before his neighbours are out of bed." This struck the rest, and we soon after had offers from one of them to supply us with stationery; but as yet we did not choose to engage in shop business.

I mention this industry the more particularly and the more freely, tho' it seems to be talking in my own praise, that those of my posterity who shall read it may know the use of that virtue, when they see its effects in my favour throughout this relation. . . .

*Here Franklin discusses at length his career as a printer, including his relations with his employees and his contracts with the legislature to print the paper currency of Pennsylvania.*

I began now gradually to pay off the debt I was under for the printing house. In order to secure my credit and character as a tradesman, I took care not only to be in *reality* industrious and frugal, but to avoid all *appearances* of the contrary. I dressed plain and was seen at no places of idle diversion. I never went out a fishing or shooting; a book, indeed, sometimes debauched me from my work, but that was seldom, snug, and gave no scandal; and to show that I was not above my business, I sometimes brought home the paper I purchased at the stores, thro' the streets on a wheelbarrow. Thus being esteemed an industrious, thriving, young man, and paying duly for what I bought, the merchants who imported stationery solicited my custom; others proposed supplying me with books, and I went on swimmingly. In the meantime Keimer's credit and business declining daily, he was at last forced to sell his printing house to satisfy his creditors. He went to Barbadoes and there lived some years in very poor circumstances. . . .

A friendly correspondence as neighbours and old acquaintances had continued between me and Miss Read's family, who all had a regard for me from the time of my first lodging in their house. I was often invited there and consulted in their affairs, wherein I sometimes was of service. I pitied poor Miss Read's unfortunate situation, who was generally dejected, seldom cheerful, and avoided company. I considered my giddiness and inconstancy when in London as in a great degree the cause of her unhappiness, tho' the mother was good enough to think the fault more her own than mine, as she had prevented our marrying before I went thither and persuaded the match in my absence. Our mutual affection was revived, but there were now great objections to our union. That match was indeed looked upon as invalid, a preceding wife being said to be living in England; but this could not easily be proved because of the distance. And tho' there was a report of his death, it was not certain. Then, tho' it should be true, he had left many debts which his successor might be called upon to pay. We ventured, however, over all these difficulties, and I took her to wife, Sept. 1, 1730. None of the inconveniencies happened that we had apprehended; she proved a good and faithful helpmate, assisted me much by attending the shop; we throve together and ever mutually endeavoured to make each other happy. Thus I corrected that great erratum as well as I could.

About this time our club meeting, not at a tavern, but in a little room of Mr. Grace's set apart for that purpose, a proposition was made by me that since our books were often referred to in our disquisitions upon the queries, it might be convenient to us to have them all together where we met, that upon occasion they might be consulted; and by thus clubbing our books to a common library, we should, while we liked to keep them together, have each of us the advantage of using the books of all the other members, which would be nearly as beneficial as if each owned the whole. It was liked and agreed to, and we filled one end of the room with such books as we could best spare. The number was not so great as we expected; and tho' they had been of great use, yet some inconveniencies occurring for want of due care of them, the collection after about a year was separated, and each took his books home again.

And now I set on foot my first project of a public nature, that for a subscription library. I drew up the proposals, got them put into form by our great scrivener, Brockden, and by the help of my friends in the Junto, procured fifty subscribers of forty shillings each to begin with, and ten shillings a year for fifty years—the term our company was to continue. We afterwards obtained a charter, the company being increased to one hundred. This was the mother of all the North American subscription libraries, now so numerous. It is become a great thing itself and continually increasing. These libraries have improved the general conversation of the Americans, made the common tradesmen and farmers as intelligent as most gentlemen from other countries, and perhaps have contributed in some degree to the stand so generally made throughout the Colonies in defence of their privileges.

*Memo*: Thus far was written with the intention expressed in the beginning and therefore contains several little family anecdotes of no importance to others. What follows was written many years after, in compliance with the advice contained in these letters, and accordingly intended for the public. The affairs of the Revolution occasioned the interruption.

# INTRODUCTION & QUESTIONS

## THE FACES OF FRANKLIN

For this audio-visual program, consider the following questions:

1. What connection do you see between the amazing versatility of Benjamin Franklin and his demonstrated abilities at role playing?

2. In the many artistic portrayals of Franklin in ceramics, portraiture, engravings and the like, he appears subtly different in each visual presentation. Excluding physical naturalism, what could explain this?

3. Why would Franklin, at the beginning of his career in Philadelphia, prefer a portrait like the one of 1746 by Robert Feke, which portrays him in Quaker garb and a simple brown wig?

4. How can one explain the absence of the brown wig and Quaker costume in Charles Willson Peale's 1785 painting of Franklin? What aspects of the individual are stressed in this representation? What does this portrayal suggest about Franklin's public reputation by 1785?

5. Why would Franklin, given the special opportunities for architectural innovation available on his Philadelphia building site, elect to construct a dwelling very similar in design to those of his Philadelphia neighbors?

6. What social ideals are expressed by Franklin's choosing to rent the street front dependencies that flanked his entrance gate?

7. How similar in character to the exterior of the structure were the interiors of Franklin's home? What could explain this?

8. What personal and social attributes are stressed in the David Martin portrait of Franklin? How would such a public presentation be appropriate at this stage of his career?

9. Sir Isaac Newton was the leading intellectual figure of his time, the human symbol and representative of rationality during the European Enlightenment. Given this, what significance is there in the inclusion of Newton's bust in Franklin's English portrait?

10. In the painting by Benjamin West, Franklin is presented as a Greek or Roman god, surrounded by cherubs, figures frequently seen in the art of the Italian

Renaissance. What kind of audience would have appreciated and sympathized with this presentation?

11. How has the portrayal of Franklin the scientist changed in the 1787 Peale portrait? To what could this be attributed?

12. Contemporary Europeans expressed great admiration for the presumed order and rationality of classical Greek and Roman culture. How are such attributes introduced into the Wedgewood medallion portraits of Franklin?

13. Again, in the Wedgewood medallions we find Franklin associated with Sir Isaac Newton, but here the American is equated to this embodiment of the European Enlightenment by an English pottery merchant. What measure of Franklin's reputation is available in this?

14. What were Franklin's major objectives as the American Ambassador in France? What expectations about America on the part of some Frenchmen did he make use of to achieve these? How do his French portraits reveal this tactic?

15. What measure of Franklin's success in France is evident in his being chosen as a subject by the French painter, Joseph Duplessis?

16. What aspects of Franklin's character are revealed in his note to an English friend about his appearance?

17. In the unfinished work by Benjamin West of the negotiators of the Treaty of Paris, how significant is Franklin's costume?

18. In what symbolic guises is Franklin portrayed in the series of French cartoons and engravings shown? With what values was he and his country then identified?

19. What aspects of Franklin's European reputation are stressed in John Adam's assessment of it?

20. What special elements in Franklin's career and reputation are associated in the engraving, "the apotheosis of Franklin?" What underlying similarity was presumed to unite these elements?

21. How can Franklin's success in the game of sophisticated literary seduction be explained, given the character of his American background? How could he have learned the principles of this exercise?

22. What special features of his American upbringing are particularly stressed in his appeal to his French "confessor?" Which of these is used for comic purposes by Franklin?

23. What comment is made about Franklin in the special chamber pot or portable toilet ordered by Louis XVI for one of his mistresses?

24. What elements and characteristics of his career are apparent in Franklin's description of himself in his will? In his epitaph?

25. What significance has the central metaphor used by Franklin in this epitaph?

# INTRODUCTION & QUESTIONS

## THE MAN OF NATURAL SCIENCE

Benjamin Franklin was not the only American in this period to receive universal recognition for his scientific accomplishments. Hardly less renowned was his friend and fellow Philadelphian, William Bartram. His life and work display a number of the representative features of the science of this new American cultural system.

William Bartram's scientific achievements and reputation were inextricably linked to the accomplishments of his father John Bartram (1699–1777). The elder Bartram, born on a Quaker farm near Philadelphia and self educated in botany, was the founder, in 1728, of the first botanical garden in America. From this world-famous nursery, on the west bank of the Schuylkill, he supplied American specimen plants to his patrons, aristocratic English amateur scientists and gardeners. Recipient of Benjamin Franklin's friendship and assistance, John Bartram shared Franklin's deistic rationalism and was on this basis disowned by the Quaker meeting in 1757.

His second son William was born in 1739 and early taken on botanical expeditions with his famous father. At eighteen, he was placed with a Philadelphia merchant to learn the essentials of commerce. His leisure time was spent in the study of natural history and drawing illustrations of plants and animals which captured the attention of some of his father's English patrons.

He continued these activities after becoming a trader in North Carolina, much to the detriment of his business. This mercantile career ended in 1765 when he left North Carolina to accompany his father on a botanical exploration of Florida. The next year found him, still in Florida, as an indigo planter. The pursuit ended soon after in the most disastrous failure of his business ventures. Abandoning his plantation, he returned to Philadelphia to eke out a living on a small farm near his father's.

After still more financial reverses, he obtained the sponsorship of one of his father's English patrons to undertake a four year expedition through the American Southeast. The record of this experience of 1773–1777, published in English, Dutch, German and French as the *Travels Through North and South Carolina, Georgia, East and West Florida*, gained him universal fame.

The latter part of his life was spent in a simple, quiet, single existence combining scientific investigation and the management of the botanical gardens. Visited and honored by the most prestigious, scientific and social personalities of the day, Bartram was offered distinguished teaching positions and a place with the Lewis and Clark expedition, all of which he refused. He died, while surveying his beloved garden, in 1823.

1. What features of the landscape attract his attention? What are, for him, the most notable characteristics of the natural world? What facets of the natural environment are not discussed by him?

2. What kinds of data are important for Bartram in his description of the Rhododendron? What areas and characteristics of the subject does he consider? What facilities does he employ to investigate such data?

3. What is his mode of travel? Who is with him at this point? How planned and directed is his itinerary?

4. Do the waters of the brook, Falling Creek and the "mountain vegetable beauties" possess any features in common? Are such attributes attached to other parts of nature as well?

5. What scientific knowledge could be gained from his analysis of the storm? What role does it play in his presentation?

6. How much concern does he show for his daily routine? What attention has been given to supplying the expedition?

7. What references are made to Indian artifacts? How precise is his archaeological description?

8. What features of the Indian settlement are noted? What elements of the Indians' social system are revealed in this description?

9. To what does he attribute the agricultural success of the Indians? Are institutional or ecological features considered important here?

10. What physical features and character traits of the Indians does he notice? What accounts for such traits? What is implied in such an hypothesis?

11. How precise are the directional notations of his travels? Would this be of consequence for ecological studies of plant distribution, for instance?

12. To what does he allude to give his readers standards for comparing the landscape? To describe the Indian maidens?

13. What characteristics do the trader's horses display? Is this the only occasion when Bartram has described animals in such terms?

14. What, according to Bartram, were his and the trader's intentions on seeing the strawberry pickers? What prevented them from carrying through with their plans?

# TRAVELS THROUGH NORTH AND SOUTH CAROLINA, GEORGIA, EAST AND WEST FLORIDA

*William Bartram*

## CHAPTER THREE

### PART THREE

. . . . My next flight was up a very high peak, to the top of the Occonne mountain, where I rested; and turning about, found that I was now in a very elevated situation, from whence I enjoyed a view inexpressibly magnificent and comprehensive. The mountainous wilderness through which I had lately traversed, down to the region of Augusta, appearing regularly undulated as the great ocean after a tempest; the undulations gradually depressing, yet perfectly regular, as the squama of fish or imbrications of tile on a roof: the nearest ground to me of a perfect full green; next more glaucous; and lastly almost blue as the ether with which the most distant curve of the horizon seemed to be blended.

My imagination thus wholly engaged in the contemplation of this magnificent landscape, infinitely varied, and without bound, I was almost insensible or regardless of the charming objects more within my reach: a new species of Rhododendron foremost in the assembly of mountain beauties; next the flaming Azalea, Kalmia latifolia, incarnate Robinia, snowy mantled Philadelphus inodorus, perfumed Calycanthus, etc.

This species of Rhododendron grows six or seven feet high, many nearly erect stems arise together from the root, forming a group or coppice. The leaves are three or four inches in length, of an oblong figure, broadest toward the extremity, and terminating with an obtuse point; their upper surface of a deep green and polished; but the nether surface of a rusty iron colour, which seems to be effected by innumerable minute reddish vesicles, beneath a fine short downy pubescence; the numerous flexile branches terminate with a loose spiked raceme, or cluster of large deep rose coloured flowers, each flower being affixed in the diffused cluster of a long peduncle, which, with the whole plant possesses an agreeable perfume. . . .

Now I enter a charming narrow vale, through which flows a rapid large creek, on whose banks are happily associated the shrubs already recited, together with the following; Staphylaea, Euonismus Americana, Hamamelis, Azalea, various species, Aristolochia frutescens, s. odoratissima, which rambles over the trees and shrubs on the prolific banks of these mountain brooks. Passed through magnificent high forests, and then came upon the borders of an ample meadow on the left, embroidered by the shade of a high circular amphitheatre of hills, the circular ridges rising magnificently one over the other. On the green turfy bases of these ascents appear the ruins of a town of the ancients.[1] The upper end of this spacious green plain is divided by a promontory or spur of the ridges before me, which projects into it; my road led me up into an opening of the ascents through which the glittering brook which watered the meadows ran rapidly down, dashing and roaring over high rocky steps. Continued yet ascending until I gained the top of an elevated rocky ridge, when appeared before me a gap or opening between other yet more lofty ascents, through which continued as the rough rocky road led me, close by the winding banks of a large rapid brook, which at length turning to the left, pouring down rocky precipices, glided off through dark groves and high forests, conveying streams of fertility and pleasure to the fields below. . . .

The day being remarkably warm and sultry, together with the labour and fatigue of ascending the mountains, made me very thirsty and in some degree sunk my spirits. Now past mid-day, I sought a cool shaded retreat, where was water for refreshment and grazing for my horse, my faithful slave and only companion. After proceeding a little farther, descending the other side of the mountain, I perceived at some distance before me, on my right hand, a level plain supporting a grand high forest and groves: the nearer I approached, my steps were the more accelerated from the flattering prospect opening to view. I now entered upon the verge of the dark forest, charming solitude! as I advanced through the animating shades, observed on the farther grassy verge a shady grove; thither I directed my steps. On approaching these shades, between the stately columns of the superb forest trees, presented to view, rushing from rocky precipices under the shade of the pensile hills, the unparalleled cascade of Falling Creek, rolling and leaping off the rocks: the waters uniting below, spread a broad glittering sheet, over a vast convex elevation of plain smooth rocks, and are immediately received by a spacious bason, where trembling in the centre through hurry and agitation, they gently subside, encircling the painted still verge; from whence gliding swiftly, they soon form a delightful little river, which continuing to flow more moderately, is restrained for a moment, gently undulating in a little lake: then they pass on rapidly to a high perpendicular steep of rocks, from whence these delightful waters are hurried down with irrestible rapidity. I here seated myself on the

---

1. town of the ancients—Bartram here, as elsewhere, is referring to the American Indians.

moss-clad rocks, under the shade of spreading trees and floriferous fragrant shrubs, in full view of the cascades.

At this rural retirement were assembled a charming circle of mountain vegetable beauties; Magnolia auriculata, Rhododendron ferrigineum, Kalmia latifolia, Robinia montana, Azalea flammula, Rosa paniculata, Calycanthus Floridus, Philadelphus inodorus, perfumed Convalaria majalis, Anemone thalictroides, Anemone hepatica, Erythronium maculatum, Leontice thalictroides, Trillium sessile, Trillium cesnum, Cypripedium, Arethusa, Ophrys, Sanguinaria, Viola uvalaria, Epigea, Mitchella repens, Stewartia, Halesia, Styrax, Lonicera, & c. Some of these roving beauties stroll over the mossy, shelving, humid rocks, or from off the expansive wavy boughs of trees, bending over the floods, salute their delusive shades, playing on the surface; some plunge their perfumed heads and bathe their flexile limbs in the silver stream; whilst others by the mountain breezes are tossed about, their blooming tufts bespangled with pearly and chrystaline dew-drops collected from the falling mists, glistening in the rainbow arch. Having collected some valuable specimens at this friendly retreat, I continued my lonesome pilgrimage. My road for a considerable time led me winding and turning about the steep rocky hills; the descent of some of which were very rough and troublesome, by means of fragments of rocks, slippery clay and talc: but after this I entered a spacious forest, the land having gradually acquired a more level surface: a pretty grassy vale appears on my right, through which my wandering path led me, close by the banks of a delightful creek, which sometimes falling over steps of rocks glides gently with serpentine meanders through the meadows.

After crossing this delightful brook and mead, the land rises again with sublime magnificence, and I am led over hills and vales, groves and high forests, vocal with the melody of the feathered songsters; the snow-white cascades glittering on the sides of the distant hills.

It was now afternoon; I approached a charming vale, amidst sublimely high forests, awful shades! Darkness gathers around; far distant thunder rolls over the trembling hills; the black clouds with august majesty and power, move slowly forwards, shading regions of towering hills, and threatening all the destruction of a thunder storm: all around is now still as death; not a whisper is heard, but a total inactivity and silence seem to pervade the earth; the birds afraid to utter a chirrup, in low tremulous voices take leave of each other, seeking covert and safety: every insect is silenced, and nothing heard but the roaring of the approaching hurricane. The mighty cloud now expands its sable wings, extending from North to South, and is driven irresistibly on by the tumultuous winds, spreading its livid wings around the gloomy concave, armed with terrors of thunder and fiery shafts of lightning. Now the lofty forests bend low beneath its fury; their limbs and wavy boughs are tossed about and catch hold of each other; the mountains tremble and seem to reel about, and the ancient hills to be shaken to their foundations: the furious storm sweeps along, smoaking through the vale and over the resounding hills: the face of the earth is obscured by the deluge descending from the firmament, and I am deafened by the din of the thunder. The tempestous scene damps my spirits, and my horse sinks under me at the tremendous peals, as I hasten on for the plain.

The storm abating, I saw an Indian hunting cabin on the side of a hill, a very agreeable prospect, especially in my present condition; I made up to it and took quiet possession, there being no one to dispute it with me except a few bats and whip-poor-wills, who had repaired thither for shelter from the violence of the hurricane.

Having turned out my horse in the sweet meadows adjoining and found some dry wood under shelter of the old cabin, I struck up a fire, dried my clothes, and comforted myself with a frugal repast of biscuit and dried beef, which was all the food my viaticum[2] afforded me by this time, excepting a small piece of cheese which I had furnished myself with at Charleston, and kept till this time.

The night was clear, calm and cool, and I rested quietly. Next morning at day-break I was awakened and summoned to resume my daily task, by the shrill cries of the social night hawk and active merry mock-bird. By the time the rising sun had gilded the tops of the towering hills, the mountains and vales rang with the harmonious shouts of the pious and cheerful tenants of the groves and meads.

I observed growing in great abundance in these mountain meadows, Sanguisorba Canadensis and Heracleum maximum; the latter exhibiting a fine show, being rendered conspicuous even at a great distance, by its great height and spread, vast pennatifid leaves and expansive umbels of snow-white flowers. The swelling bases of the surrounding hills fronting the meadows presented for my acceptance the fragrant red strawberry, in painted beds of many acres surface, indeed I may safely say, many hundreds.

After passing through this meadow, the road led me over the bases of a ridge of hills, which as a bold promontory dividing the fields I had just passed, form expansive green lawns. On these towering hills appeared the ruins of the ancient famous town of Sticoe. Here was a vast Indian mount or tumulus and great terrace, on which stood the council-house, with banks encompassing their circus; here also were old Peach and Plumb orchards; some of the trees appeared yet thriving and fruitful. Presently after leaving these ruins, the vale and fields are divided by means of a spur of the mountains pushing forward: here likewise the road forked; the lefthand path continued up the mountains to the Overhill towns: I followed the vale to the righthand, and soon began to ascend the hills, riding several miles over very rough, stony land, yielding the like vegetable productions as heretofore; and descending again gradually, by a dubious winding path, leading into a narrow vale and lawn, through which rolled on before me a delightful brook, water of the Tanase. I crossed it and continued a

---

2. viaticum—provisions.

mile or two down the meadows; when the high mountains on each side suddenly receding, discovered the opening of the extensive and fruitful vale of Cowe, through which meanders the head branch of the Tanase, almost from its source, sixty miles, following its course down to Cowe.

I left for a little while, the stream passing swiftly and foaming over its rocky bed, lashing the steep craggy banks, and then suddenly sunk from my sight, murmuring hollow and deep under the rocky surface of the ground. On my right hand the vale expands, receiving a pretty silvery brook of water which came hastily down from the adjacent hills, and entered the river a little distance before me. I now turn from the heights on my left, the road leading into the level lawns, to avoid the hollow rocky grounds, full of holes and cavities, arching over the river through which the waters are seen gliding along: but the river is soon liberated from these solitary and gloomy recesses, and appears waving through the green plain before me. I continued several miles, pursuing my serpentine path, through and over the meadows and green fields, and crossing the river, which is here incredibly increased in size, by the continual accession of brooks flowing in from the hills on each side, dividing their green turfy beds, forming them into parterres, vistas, and verdant swelling knolls, profusely productive of flowers and fragrant strawberries, their rich juice dying my horses feet and ancles. . . .

Next morning, after breakfasting on excellent coffee, relished with bucanned[3] venison, hot corn cakes, excellent butter and cheese, set forwards again for Cowe, which was about fifteen miles distance, keeping the trading path which coursed through the low lands between the hills and the river, now spacious and well beaten by travellers, but somewhat intricate to a stranger, from the frequent collateral roads falling into it from villages and towns over the hills. After riding about four miles mostly through fields and plantations, the soil incredibly fertile, arrived at the town of Echoe, consisting of many good houses, well inhabited. I passed through, and continued three miles farther to Nucasse, and three miles more brought me to Whatoga. Riding through this large town, the road carried me winding about through their little plantations of Corn, Beans, &c. up to the council-house, which was a very large dome or rotunda, situated on the top of an ancient artificial mount, and here my road terminated. All before me and on every side, appeared little plantations of young Corn, Beans, &c. divided from each other by narrow strips or borders of grass, which marked the bounds of each one's property, their habitation standing in the midst. Finding no common high road to lead me through the town, I was now at a stand how to proceed farther; when observing an Indian man at the door of his habitation, three or four hundred yards distance from me, beckoning me to come to him, I ventured to ride through their lots, being careful to do no injury to the young plants, the rising hopes of their labour and industry; crossed a little grassy vale watered by a silver stream, which gently undulated through; then ascended a green hill to the house,

---

3. bucanned—smoked or barbequed.

where I was chearfully welcomed at the door, and led in by the chief, giving the care of my horse to two handsome youths, his sons. During my continuance here, about half an hour, I experienced the most perfect and agreeable hospitality conferred on me by these happy people; I mean happy in their dispositions, in their apprehensions of recititude with regard to our social or moral conduct. O divine simplicity and truth, friendship without fallacy or guile, hospitality disinterested, native, undefiled, unmodifyed by artificial refinements!

My venerable host gracefully and with an air of respect, led me into an airy, cool apartment; where being seated on cabins, his women brought in a refreshing repast, consisting of sodden venison, hot corn cakes, &c. with a pleasant cooling liquor made of hommony well boiled, mixed afterwards with milk; this is served up, either before or after eating, in a large bowl, with a very large spoon or ladle to sup it with.

After partaking of this simple but healthy and liberal collation, and the dishes cleared off, Tobacco and pipes were brought; and the chief filling one of them, whose stem, about four feet long, was sheathed in a beautiful spackled snake skin, and adorned with feathers and strings of wampum, lights it and smoaks a few whiffs, puffing the smoak first towards the sun, then to the four cardinal points, and lastly over my breast, hands it toward me, which I chearfully received from him and smoaked; when we fell into conversation. He first enquired if I came from Charleston? if I knew John Stewart, Esq., how long since I left Charleston? &c. Having satisfied him in my answers in the best manner I could, he was greatly pleased; which I was convinced of by his attention to me, his cheerful manners, and his ordering my horse a plentiful bait of corn, which last instance of respect is conferred on those only to whom they manifest the highest esteem, saying that corn was given by the Great Spirit only for food to man. . . .

Next day after my arrival I crossed the river in a canoe, on a visit to a trader who resided amongst the habitations on the other shore.

After dinner, on his mentioning some curious scenes amongst the hills, some miles distance from the river, we agreed to spend the afternoon in observations on the mountains.

After riding near two miles through Indian plantations of Corn, which was well cultivated, kept clean of weeds, and was well advanced, being near eighteen inches in height, and the Beans planted at the Corn-hills were above ground; we left the fields on our right, turning towards the mountains, and ascending through a delightful green vale or lawn, which conducted us in amongst the pyramidal hills, and crossing a brisk flowing creek, meandering through the meads which continued near two miles, dividing and branching in amongst the hills. We then mounted their steep ascents, rising gradually by ridges or steps one above another, frequently crossing narrow fertile vales as we ascended: the air felt cool and animating, being charged with the fragrant breath of the mountain beauties, the blooming mountain cluster Rose, blushing Rhododendron, and fair

Lily of the valley. Having now attained the summit of this very elevated ridge, we enjoyed a fine prospect indeed; the enchanting Vale of Keowe, perhaps as celebrated for fertility, fruitfulness and beautiful prospects, as the Fields of Pharsalia or the Vale of Tempe;[4] the town, the elevated peaks of the Jore mountains, a very distant prospect of the Jore village in a beautiful lawn, lifted up many thousand feet higher than our present situation, besides a view of many other villages and settlements on the sides of the mountains, at various distances and elevations; the silver rivulets gliding by them, and snow white cataracts glimmering on the sides of the lofty hills; the bold promontories of the Jore mountain stepping into the Tanase river, whilst his foaming waters rushed between them.

After viewing this very entertaining scene, we began to descend the mountain on the other side, which exhibited the same order of gradations of ridges and vales as on our ascent; and at length rested on a very expansive, fertile plain, amidst the towering hills, over which we rode a long time, through magnificent high forests, extensive green fields, meadows and lawns. Here had formerly been a very flourishing settlement; but the Indians deserted it in search of fresh planting land, which they soon found in a rich vale but a few miles distance over a ridge of hills. Soon after entering on these charming, sequestered, prolific fields, we came to a fine little river, which crossing, and riding over fruitful strawberry beds and green lawns, on the sides of a circular ridge of hills in front of us, and going round the bases of this promontory, came to a fine meadow on an arm of the vale, through which meandered a brook, its humid vapours bedewing the fragrant strawberries which hung in heavy red clusters over the grassy verge. We crossed the rivulet; then rising a sloping, green, turfy ascent, alighted on the borders of a grand forest of stately trees, which we penetrated on foot a little distance to a horse-stamp, where was a large squadron of those useful creatures belonging to my friend and companion, the trader, on the sight of whom they assembled together from all quarters; some at a distance saluted him with shrill neighings of gratitude, or came prancing up to lick the salt out of his hand, whilst the younger and more timorous came galloping onward, but coyly wheeled off, and fetching a circuit stood aloof; but as soon as their lord and master strewed the crystaline salty bait on the hard beaten ground, they all, old and young, docile and timorous, soon formed themselves in ranks, and fell to licking up the delicious morsel.

It was a fine sight: more beautiful creatures I never saw; there were of them of all colours, sizes and dispositions. Every year, as they become of age, he sends off a troup of them down to Charleston, where they are sold to the highest bidder.

---

4. the Fields of Pharsalia or the Vale of Tempe—sites in Greece much praised for their beauty by classical writers.

Having paid our attention to this useful part of the creation, who, if they are under our dominion, have consequently a right to our protection and favour, we returned to our trusty servants that were regaling themselves in the exuberant sweet pastures and strawberry fields in sight, and mounted again. Proceeding on our return to town, continued through part of this high forest skirting on the meadows: began to ascend the hills of a ridge which we were under the necessity of crossing; and having gained its summit, enjoyed a most enchanting view; a vast expanse of green meadows and strawberry fields; a meandering river gliding through, saluting in its various turnings the swelling, green, turfy knolls, embellished with parterres of flowers and fruitful strawberry beds; flocks of turkies strolling about them; herds of deer prancing in the meads or bounding over the hills; companies of young, innocent Cherokee virgins, some busy gathering the rich fragrant fruit, others having already filled their baskets, lay reclined under the shade of floriferous and fragrant native bowers of Magnolia, Azalea, Philadelphus, perfumed Calycanthus, sweet Yellow Jessamine and cerulean Glycine frutescens, disclosing their beauties to the fluttering breeze, and bathing their limbs in the cool fleeting streams; whilst other parties, more gay and libertine, were yet collecting strawberries, or wantonly chasing their companions, tantalising them, staining their lips and cheeks with the rich fruit.

This sylvan scene of primitive innocence was enchanting, and perhaps too enticing for hearty young men long to continue idle spectators.

In fine, nature prevailing over reason, we wished at least to have a more active part in their delicious sports. Thus precipitately resolving, we cautiously made our approaches, yet undiscovered, almost to the joyous scene of action. Now, although we meant no other than an innocent frolic with this gay assembly of hamadrayades,[5] we shall leave it to the person of feeling and sensibility to form an idea to what lengths our passions might have hurried us, thus warmed and excited, had it not been for the vigilance and care of some envious matrons who lay in ambush, and espying us, gave the alarm, time enough for the nymphs to rally and assemble together. We however, pursued and gained ground on a group of them, who had incautiously strolled to a greater distance from their guardians, and finding their retreat now like to be cut off, took shelter under cover of a little grove; but on perceiving themselves to be discovered by us, kept their station, peeping through the bushes; when observing our approaches, they confidently discovered themselves, and decently advanced to meet us, half unveiling their blooming faces, incarnated with the modest maiden blush, and with native innocence and cheerfulness, presented their little baskets, merrily telling us their fruit was ripe and sound.

We accepted a basket, sat down and regaled ourselves on the delicious fruit, encircled by the whole assembly of the innocently jocose sylvan nymphs: by this

---

5. hamadrayades—wood nymphs.

time the several parties, under the conduct of the elder matrons, had disposed themselves in companies on the green, turfy banks.

My young companion, the trader, by concessions and suitable apologies for the bold intrusion, having compromised the matter with them, engaged them to bring their collections to his house at a stipulated price: we parted friendly.

And now taking leave of these Elysian fields,[6] we again mounted the hills, which we crossed, and traversing obliquely their flowery beds, arrived in town in the cool of the evening.

---

6. Elysian fields—the Greek or Roman version of paradise.

# INTRODUCTION & QUESTIONS

## THE ARTISTRY OF NATURE

1. The cultural priorities present in the scientific perspective of the new America is revealed further in this audio-visual program. Find answers for these study questions as you view it:

2. What particular features of Franklin, the scientist, are repeated in other contemporary investigators of nature? How are such features present in the case of David Rittenhouse?

3. What was the nature of Rittenhouse's involvement with his surrounding community as a child? As an adult?

4. At what stage of his development were his talents recognized? In this, does he repeat any of Franklin's characteristics?

5. What specific cultural assumptions and assessments are manifested in the orrery? What, in short, does it reveal about its creator's views on the nature of the physical world, man's place in it and the extent of human comprehension of the physical environment?

6. In what precise ways does the career of John Bartram represent a different set of cultural priorities from those apparent in Rittenhouse?

7. What cultural changes are apparent in the contrasts between John Bartram and his son, William? How are such differences suggested in the Peale portrait of the latter?

8. What social values are suggested by the life and work of John Audubon? What assumptions about nature are revealed in his products? What purposes were these products designed to serve? How are these purposes underscored by the *Ornithological Biographies* and the changes made between the original watercolor versions and the final lithographs?

9. What cultural features of the time are present in the early experience of Charles Willson Peale? What contemporary commitments are suggested in his portrait studies?

10. Review the observable features of Peale's *George Washington at Princeton* and determine in what ways these traits reflect the cultural system of America at

this time. How are such values illustrated in his *William Buckland*, another example of the contemporary portrait?

11. Itemize the fields in which Peale was active. What do these suggest about the Americans of his period?

12. In what specific ways are his portraits of women different from those of men? In what ways are such studies similar in character and function?

13. What cultural priorities are represented in a *trompe d'oeil* piece such as Peale's *Staircase Group?* In a work like *The Peale Family?*

14. What particular traits and artistic interests of their father are continued by Peale's sons?

15. Consider "The Exhuming of the First American Mastadon," both as event as well as Peale's portrayal of it. What cultural characteristics are represented by it?

16. What priorities of the American cultural system are revealed in the purpose of Peale's museum? By its site? By the organization of its exhibits? By the uses made of Peale's portrait studies? By the economic nature of the institution?

17. Are other traits of the American culture of the day present in Peale's latter years? What are they?

# INTRODUCTION & QUESTIONS

## THE NATURAL SCIENCE OF MAN, REVOLUTIONS AND REPUBLICS

The political theory of the new American nation is perhaps most concisely and directly expressed in the three American public documents in this assignment. With the addition of the United States Constitution, they can serve as classic embodiments of the major values and interests with which late eighteenth-century Americans approached political questions. By their very nature, all three documents were conscious attempts to articulate those shared assumptions and concerns. Their authors struggled to produce syntheses of what they believed to be universally valid political propositions.

Certainly foremost among their sources for political theory were the writings of John Locke (1632–1704), an English philosopher who published his *Second Treatise on Civil Government* in 1689 contemporaneously with the Glorious Revolution, a bloodless coup executed by William of Orange against the arbitrary rule of James II. His treatise, included in this assignment, was unquestionably one of the references used by Thomas Jefferson as he composed the first of the American documents included here.

Some years after authoring the Declaration of Independence, Jefferson insisted that his goal had been:

> Not to find out new principles, or new arguments, never before thought of, not merely to say things which had never been said before; but to place before mankind the common sense of the subject, in terms so plain and firm as to command their assent, and to justify ourselves in the independent stand we are compelled to take. Neither aiming at originality of principle or sentiment, nor yet copied from any particular and previous writing, it was intended to be an expression of the American mind, and to give to that expression the proper tone and spirit called for by the occasion. All its authority rests then on the harmonizing sentiments of the day, whether expressed in conversation, in letters, printed essays, or in the elementary books of public right.

The edition presented here contains the original version of the Declaration prepared by Jefferson and his drafting assistants, who included Benjamin Franklin and John Adams. This first draft was presented to the Continental Congress on June 28, 1776. The final form of the Declaration approved by Congress on July 4 overlays this original version. In addition to the deletions and revisions noted, those portions in brackets were added by the Congress.

184

The Declaration was the product of the American, who, after Benjamin Franklin, was most frequently cited in this period 1750–1850 as a classic example of American virtue and genius. Thomas Jefferson was born in 1743 in the Piedmont area of western Virginia. As a child of the planting aristocracy, he received a private education culminating at the College of William and Mary. With his election in 1769 to the House of Burgesses, he began what became an extremely stormy and uneven political career. An early revolutionist, he was selected in 1775 as a Virginia delegate to the Continental Congress, where, due to his literary reputation, he was selected to write the colonies' Declaration of Independence. Following this initial triumph, he returned to the Virginia political arena to become governor of the new state in 1779. After two turbulent terms, marked by reforms in land law, church-state relations and education, he abandoned his post with an abrupt and inglorious resignation.

Returned to Congress in 1783, he was appointed in the next year to assist Franklin in France. A distinguished diplomatic career gave him, in 1790, the post of first Secretary of State under Washington. In 1796, although anxious to join the first president in retirement, he was prevailed upon to accept the vice-presidency under Adams. In 1800 he gained the presidency in what he dubbed a "second American revolution." After two terms in office, noted above all for the feat of the Louisiana Purchase, he retired for his remaining seventeen years to his plantation estate of "Monticello." The most distinguished accomplishment of these last years was the design, both philosophically and architecturally, of the University of Virginia. This last success was added to a career noted for the breadth of its achievements, including those of statesman, diplomat, author, architect, political philosopher and scientist. This versatile life ended on the fiftieth anniversary of the Declaration of Independence, only a few hours after the death of Jefferson's friend, sometime political adversary and assistant on the Declaration's drafting committee, John Adams.

The second document in this American trilogy was authored by Jefferson's associate and fellow Virginian, George Mason. Mason's life bore certain similarities to that of "the sage of Monticello." Born in 1725 of an established tidewater family, he was given a private education based on an uncle's law library, married well and fathered nine children. In addition to the financial rewards of his substantial Potomac river plantation of "Gunston Hall," Mason actively speculated in western lands.

A member of the local vestry and a justice of the peace, Mason agreed to serve only one term in the colonial House of Burgesses. This refusal to accept public office was one of the most remarkable features of his public life. Although he reluctantly accepted seats in various revolutionary conventions on both the local and continental level, his most active political work was in authoring statements of colonial grievances and in drafting justifications for revolutionary activities. In addition to these literary activities, Mason was a strong campaigner for religious freedom and a consistant advocate of the abolition of slavery.

Following the adoption of the Federal Constitution, Mason returned to Gunston Hall, which he continued to manage without the aid of a supervisor. True to his solitary nature, at his death in 1792, his will advised his sons to shun public service unless "the necessity of the times" required them "to transmit to their posterity those sacred rights to which [they] were born."

George Mason was one of those members of the Constitutional Convention who refused to sign the original version of the Constitution, protesting that it lacked a specific Bill of Rights. In response to similar objections raised during the ratification process, proposals were introduced in the first Federal Congress, which, when ratified in 1791 by two-thirds of the states became the first ten amendments to the Constitution. This Federal Bill of Rights is the last of this triad of American political statements. In large part, it too was the work of Virginians, among them James Madison, Patrick Henry, and Richard Henry Lee, who shared Jefferson's and Mason's intellectual and social commitments. As you consider these documents, approach them as a unit, noting the shared features of each. Additionally, ask yourself questions such as:

1. What are, for Locke, the principal features of man's condition in the state of Nature? What regulates him in this situation?

2. How does government originate? What is its purpose? What preconditions must exist before it can be established? What rights and responsibilities does an individual enjoy under it?

3. What does Locke consider to be the "supreme power" in a political society? Why? Within what limitations must it operate?

4. Under what conditions may government be dissolved? What is the ultimate standard for judging the validity of such actions? What options now are open to the people?

5. To whom is the Declaration of Independence addressed? According to Jefferson, what need must the document fulfill?

6. What does Jefferson declare to be the most basic "cause" of American independence? Especially as defined in the wording of the original draft, what precise changes in the nation's status have occurred?

7. What is assumed by both Jefferson and Mason to be characteristic of the original condition of man? What "rights" did he possess in this original state? Does Mason's list of such rights differ in any way from that contained in the Declaration of Independence?

8. How did man come to possess these rights? On what occasions may he renounce or surrender them?

9. What are, by Mason's reasoning, the principal functions of government? Does Jefferson define the ends of government in a similar but more restricted manner?

10. Who, for both Jefferson and Mason, holds final authority or ultimate sovereignty in a valid government? How then does the magistrate receive his authority?

11. On what occasions are attempts to reform or abolish government justified? What is the ultimate criteria for declaring governmental action to be unjustifiable and cause for legitimate revolution? In Jefferson's opinion, how frequently do such provocations for revolution occur?

12. Who does Jefferson blame for the current situation? What motives does he attribute to this agent? What has consistently been the colonists' response to these activities?

13. In the listing of the British "injuries and usurpations," what has been the role of Parliament? How significant are economic measures in this list? Does there appear to be any order to the listing? Are any actions considered more heinous than others?

14. What is the most significant deletion made by Congress from the list? For what specific crimes is the tyrant blamed here? Does this section denounce an institution per se, or only specific activities associated with the institution?

15. How is Jefferson's argument affected by the omission of the beginning date for Britain's tyranny? What purpose could be served by deleting the descriptions of the English people's response to colonial protest?

16. What specific features must the good government described in Mason's statement have? What do articles 2 and 4 add to the definition of a magistrate? What requirements do articles 5, 6, and 7 make regarding governmental structure and elections?

Compare articles 8 thru 16 of Mason's Virginia Declaration to the items included in the Federal Bill of Rights. How similar are the two documents? Are any concerns of the Federal Bill of Rights not included in Mason's listing? Could these omissions be a result of Mason's more extensive restrictions on the military contained in article 13?

# SECOND TREATISE ON CIVIL GOVERNMENT

*John Locke*

## OF CIVIL GOVERNMENT

### OF THE STATE OF NATURE

To understand political power right and derive it from its original, we must consider what state all men are naturally in, and that is a state of perfect freedom to order their actions and dispose of their possessions and persons as they think fit, within the bounds of the law of nature, without asking leave or depending upon the will of any other man.

A state also of equality, wherein all the power and jurisdiction is reciprocal,[1] no one having more than another; there being nothing more evident than that creatures of the same species and rank, promiscuously[2] born to all the same advantages of nature and the use of the same faculties, should also be equal one amongst another without subordination or subjection. . . .

But though this be a state of liberty, yet it is not a state of license; though man in that state have an uncontrollable liberty to dispose of his person or possessions, yet he has not liberty to destroy himself, or so much as any creature in his possession, but where some nobler use than its bare preservation calls for it. The state of nature has a law of nature to govern it, which obliges every one; and reason, which is that law, teaches all mankind who will but consult it that, being all equal and independent, no one ought to harm another in his life, health, liberty, or possessions; for men being all the workmanship of one omnipotent and infinitely wise Maker—all the servants of one sovereign master, sent into the world by his order, and about his business—they are his property whose workmanship they are, made to last during his, not one another's, pleasure; and being furnished with like faculties, sharing all in one community of nature, there cannot be supposed any such subordination among us that may authorize us to destroy another, as if we were made for one another's uses as the inferior ranks of

1. reciprocal—mutual.
2. promiscuously—indiscriminately, without plan or order.

creatures are for ours. Every one, as he is bound to preserve himself and not to quit his station wilfully, so by the like reason, when his own preservation comes not in competition, ought he, as much as he can, to preserve the rest of mankind, and may not, unless it be to do justice to an offender, take away or impair the life, or what tends to the preservation of life, the liberty, health, limb, or goods of another.

And that all men may be restrained from invading others' rights and from doing hurt to one another, and the law of nature be observed, which wills the peace and preservation of all mankind, the execution of the law of nature is, in that state, put into every man's hands, whereby every one has a right to punish the transgressors of that law to such a degree as may hinder its violation. . . .

And thus in the state of nature one man comes by a power over another; but yet no absolute or arbitrary power to use a criminal, when he has got him in his hands, according to the passionate heats or boundless extravagance of his own will; but only to retribute to him, so far as calm reason and conscience dictate, what is proportionate to his transgression, which is so much as may serve for reparation and restraint. . . .

## OF PROPERTY

God, who has given the world to men in common, has also given them reason to make use of it to the best advantage of life and convenience. The earth and all that is therein is given to men for the support and comfort of their being. And though all the fruits it naturally produces and beasts it feeds belong to mankind in common, as they are produced by the spontaneous hand of nature; and nobody has originally a private dominion exclusive of the rest of mankind in any of them, as they are thus in their natural state; yet, being given for the use of men, there must of necessity be a means to appropriate them some way or other before they can be of any use or at all beneficial to any particular man. The fruit or venison which nourishes the wild Indian, who knows no enclosure[3] and is still a tenant in common, must be his, and so his, i.e., a part of him, that another can no longer have any right to it before it can do him any good for the support of his life.

Though the earth and all inferior creatures be common to all men, yet every man has a property in his own person; this nobody has any right to but himself. The labor of his body and the work of his hands, we may say, are properly his. Whatsoever then he removes out of the state that nature has provided and left it in, he has mixed his labor with, and joined to it something that is his own, and thereby makes it his property. . . .

God gave the world to men in common; but since he gave it them for their benefit and the greatest conveniences of life they were capable to draw from it, it cannot be supposed he meant it should always remain common and

---

3. enclosure—fenced private property.

uncultivated. He gave it to the use of the industrious and rational—and labor was to be his title to it—not to the fancy or covetousness of the quarrelsome and contentious. He that had as good left for his improvement as was already taken up needed not complain, ought not to meddle with what was already improved by another's labor; if he did, it is plain he desired the benefit of another's pains which he had no right to, and not the ground which God had given him in common with others to labor on, and whereof there was as good left as that already possessed, and more than he knew what to do with, or his industry could reach to. . . .

## OF POLITICAL OR CIVIL SOCIETY

Man, being born, as has been proved, with a title to perfect freedom and an uncontrolled enjoyment of all the rights and privileges of the law of nature equally with any other man or number of men in the world, has by nature a power not only to preserve his property—that is, his life, liberty, and estate—against the injuries and attempts of other men, but to judge of and punish the breaches of that law in others as he is persuaded the offense deserves, even with death itself in crimes where the heinousness of the fact in his opinion requires it. But because no political society can be, nor subsist, without having in itself the power to preserve the property and, in order thereunto, punish the offenses of all those of that society, there and there only is political society where every one of the members has quitted[4] his natural power, resigned it up into the hands of the community in all cases that exclude him not from appealing for protection to the law established by it. And thus all private judgment of every particular member being excluded, the community comes to be umpire by settled standing rules, indifferent and the same to all parties, and by men having authority from the community for the execution of those rules decides all the differences that may happen between any members of that society concerning any matter of right, and punishes those offenses which any member has committed against the society with such penalties as the law has established; whereby it is easy to discern who are, and who are not, in political society together. . . .

And thus the commonwealth[5] comes by a power to set down what punishment shall belong to the several transgressions which they think worthy of it committed amongst the members of that society—which is the power of making laws—as well as it has the power to punish any injury done unto any of its members by any one that is not of it—which is the power of war and peace—and all this for the preservation of the property of all the members of that society as far as is possible. . . .

Whenever, therefore, any number of men are so united into one society as to quit every one his executive power of the law of nature and to resign it to

---

4. quitted—given up.
5. commonwealth—the state or political community.

the public, there and there only is a political or civil society. And this is done wherever any number of men, in the state of nature, enter into society to make one people, one body politic, under one supreme government, or else when any one joins himself to, and incorporates with, any government already made; for hereby he authorizes the society or, which is all one, the legislative thereof to make laws for him as the public good of the society shall require, to the execution whereof his own assistance, as to his own decrees, is due. . . .

## OF THE BEGINNING OF POLITICAL SOCIETIES

Men being, as has been said, by nature all free, equal, and independent, no one can be put out of this estate and subjected to the political power of another without his own consent. The only way whereby any one divests himself of his natural liberty, and puts on the bonds of civil society, is by agreeing with other men to join and unite into a community for their comfortable, safe, and peaceable living one among another, in a secure enjoyment of their properties and a greater security against any that are not of it. This any number of men may do, because it injures not the freedom of the rest; they are left as they were in the liberty of the state of nature. When any number of men have so consented to make one community or government, they are thereby presently incorporated and make one body politic wherein the majority have a right to act and conclude the rest. . . .

For if the consent of the majority shall not in reason be received as the act of the whole and conclude every individual, nothing but the consent of every individual can make anything to be the act of the whole; but such a consent is next to impossible ever to be had if we consider the infirmities of health and avocations of business which in a number, though much less than that of a commonwealth, will necessarily keep many away from the public assembly. . . .

## OF THE ENDS OF POLITICAL SOCIETY AND GOVERNMENT

If man in the state of nature be so free, as has been said, if he be absolute lord of his own person and possessions, equal to the greatest, and subject to nobody, why will he part with his freedom, why will he give up his empire and subject himself to the dominion and control of any other power? To which it is obvious to answer that though in the state of nature he has such a right, yet the enjoyment of it is very uncertain and constantly exposed to the invasion of others; for all being kings as much as he, every man his equal, and the greater part no strict observers of equity and justice, the enjoyment of the property he has in this state is very unsafe, very unsecure. This makes him willing to quit a condition which, however free, is full of fears and continual dangers; and it is not without reason that he seeks out and is willing to join in society with others who are already united, or have a mind to unite, for the mutual preservation of their lives, liberties, and estates, which I call by the general name 'property.'

The great and chief end, therefore, of men's uniting into commonwealths and putting themselves under government, is the preservation of their property. To which in the state of nature there are many things wanting:

First, there wants an established, settled, known law, received and allowed by common consent to be the standard of right and wrong and the common measure to decide all controversies between them; for though the law of nature be plain and intelligible to all rational creatures, yet men, being biased by their interest as well as ignorant for want of studying it, are not apt to allow of it as a law binding to them in the application of it to their particular cases.

Secondly, in the state of nature there wants a known and indifferent[6] judge with authority to determine all differences according to the established law; for every one in that state being both judge and executioner of the law of nature, men being partial to themselves, passion and revenge is very apt to carry them too far and with too much heat in their own cases, as well as negligence and unconcernedness to make them too remiss in other men's.

Thirdly, in the state of nature there often wants power to back and support the sentence when right, and to give it due execution. They who by any injustice offend will seldom fail, where they are able, by force, to make good their injustice; such resistance many times makes the punishment dangerous and frequently destructive to those who attempt it.

Thus mankind, notwithstanding all the privileges of the state of nature, being but in an ill condition while they remain in it, are quickly driven into society. Hence it comes to pass that we seldom find any number of men live any time together in this state. The inconveniences that they are therein exposed to by the irregular and uncertain exercise of the power every man has of punishing the transgressions of others make them take sanctuary under the established laws of government and therein seek the preservation of their property. It is this makes them so willingly give up every one his single power of punishing, to be exercised by such alone as shall be appointed to it among them; and by such rules as the community, or those authorized by them to that purpose, shall agree on. And in this we have the original right of both the legislative and executive power, as well as of the governments and societies themselves.

## OF THE EXTENT OF THE LEGISLATIVE POWER

The great end of men's entering into society being the enjoyment of their properties in peace and safety, and the great instrument and means of that being the laws established in that society, the first and fundamental positive law of all commonwealths is the establishing of the legislative power; as the first and fundamental natural law which is to govern even the legislative itself, is the preservation of the society and, as far as will consist with the public good, of every person in it. This legislative is not only the supreme power of the

6. indifferent—impartial, neutral.

commonwealth, but sacred and unalterable in the hands where the community have once placed it; nor can any edict of anybody else, in what form soever conceived or by what power soever backed, have the force and obligation of a law which has not its sanction from that legislative which the public has chosen and appointed; for without this the law could not have that which is absolutely necessary to its being a law: the consent of the society over whom nobody can have a power to make laws, but by their own consent and by authority received from them. . . .

These are the bounds which the trust that is put in them by the society and the law of God and nature have set to the legislative power of every commonwealth, in all forms of government:

First, they are to govern by promulgated established laws, not to be varied in particular cases, but to have one rule for rich and poor, for the favorite at court and the countryman at plough.

Secondly, these laws also ought to be designed for no other end ultimately but the good of the people.

Thirdly, they must not raise taxes on the property of the people without the consent of the people, given by themselves or their deputies. And this property concerns only such governments where the legislative is always in being, or at least where the people have not reserved any part of the legislative to deputies to be from time to time chosen by themselves.

Fourthly, the legislative neither must nor can transfer the power of making laws to anybody else, or place it anywhere but where the people have. . . .

## OF THE DISSOLUTION OF GOVERNMENT

The reason why men enter into society is the preservation of their property; and the end why they choose and authorize a legislative is that there may be laws made and rules set as guards and fences to the properties of all the members of the society to limit the power and moderate the dominion of every part and member of the society; for since it can never be supposed to be the will of the society that the legislative should have a power to destroy that which every one designs to secure by entering into society, and for which the people submitted themselves to legislators of their own making. Whenever the legislators endeavor to take away and destroy the property of the people, or to reduce them to slavery under arbitrary power, they put themselves into a state of war with the people who are thereupon absolved from any further obedience, and are left to the common refuge which God has provided for all men against force and violence. Whensoever, therefore, the legislative shall transgress this fundamental rule of society, and either by ambition, fear, folly, or corruption, endeavor to grasp themselves, or put into the hands of any other, an absolute power over the lives, liberties, and estates of the people, by this breach of trust they forfeit the power the people had put into their hands for quite contrary ends, and it devolves[7] to the people, who have a right to resume their original liberty and, by the establishment of a new legislative, such as they shall think fit, provide for their own safety and security, which is the end for which they are in society. What I have said here concerning the legislative in general holds true also concerning the supreme executor, who having a double trust put in him—both to have a part in the legislative and the supreme execution of the law—acts against both when he goes about to set up his own arbitrary will as the law of the society. . . .

To this perhaps it will be said that, the people being ignorant and always discontented, to lay the foundation of government in the unsteady opinion and uncertain humor[8] of the people is to expose it to certain ruin; and no government will be able long to subsist if the people may set up a new legislative whenever they take offense at the old one. To this I answer: Quite the contrary. People are not so easily got out of their old forms as some are apt to suggest. They are hardly to be prevailed with to amend the acknowledged faults in the frame they have been accustomed to. . . .

I answer, such revolutions happen not upon every little mismanagement in public affairs. Great mistakes in the ruling part, many wrong and inconvenient laws, and all the slips of human frailty will be born by the people without mutiny or murmur. But if a long train of abuses, prevarications,[9] and artifices,[10] all tending the same way, make the design visible to the people, and they cannot but feel what they lie under and see whither they are going, it is not to be wondererd that they should then rouse themselves and endeavor to put the rule into such hands which may secure to them the ends for which government was at first erected. . . .

If a controversy arise bet twixt a prince and some of the people in a matter where the law is silent or doubtful, and the thing be of great consequence, I should think the proper umpire in such a case should be the body of the people; for in cases where the prince has a trust reposed in him and is dispensed from the common ordinary rules of the law, there, if any men find themselves aggrieved and think the prince acts contrary to or beyond that trust, who so proper to judge as the body of the people (who, at first, lodged that trust in him) how far they meant it should extend? But if the prince, or whoever they be in the administration, decline that way of determination, the appeal then lies nowhere but to heaven; force between either persons who have no known superior on earth, or which permits no appeal to a judge on earth, being properly a state of war wherein the appeal lies only to heaven; and in that state the injured party must judge for himself when he will think fit to make use of that appeal and put himself upon it.

---

7.  devolves—passes.
8.  humor—mood.
9.  prevarications—lies, misrepresentations.
10. artifices—tricks.

To conclude, the power that every individual gave the society when he entered into it can never revert to the individuals again as long as the society lasts, but will always remain in the community, because without this there can be no community, no commonwealth, which is contrary to the original agreement; so also when the society has placed the legislative in any assembly of men, to continue in them and their successors with direction and authority for providing such successors, the legislative can never revert to the people while that government lasts because having provided a legislative with power to continue for ever, they have given up their political power to the legislative and cannot resume it. But if they have set limits to the duration of their legislative and made this supreme power in any person or assembly only temporary, or else when by the miscarriages of those in authority it is forfeited, upon the forefiture, or at the determination, of the time set, it reverts to the society, and the people have a right to act as supreme and continue the legislative in themselves, or erect a new form, or under the old form place it in new hands, as they think good.

# THE DECLARATION OF INDEPENDENCE

*Thomas Jefferson*

## A DECLARATION BY THE REPRESENTATIVES OF THE UNITED STATES OF AMERICA, IN GENERAL CONGRESS ASSEMBLED.

When in the Course of human events, it becomes necessary for **one** ~~a~~ people to

dissolve the political bands which have connected them with another

~~advance from that subordination in which they have hitherto remained~~, and

to assume among the powers of the earth, the **separate and** equal ~~and independent~~ station

to which the laws of nature and of nature's god entitle them, a decent respect

to the opinions of mankind requires that they should declare the causes

which impel them to the **separation** ~~change~~.

We hold these truths to be **self-evident,** ~~sacred and undeniable~~; that all men are created

equal ~~and independent~~; that **they are endowed by their Creator with certain** ~~from that equal creation they derive in rights~~

**unalienable rights, that** ~~inherent and inalienable~~, among **these** ~~which~~ are ~~the preservation of~~ life, ~~and~~

liberty and the pursuit of happiness; that to secure these ends, governments

are instituted among men, deriving their just powers from the consent of the

governed; that whenever any form of government ~~shall~~ become **s** destructive

of these ends, it is the right of the people to alter or to abolish it, and to

institute new government, laying its foundation on such principles and organizing its powers in such form, as to them shall seem most likely to

effect their safety and happiness. Prudence, indeed, will dictate that

governments long established should not be changed for light and transient

causes; and accordingly all experience hath shewn, that mankind are more

disposed to suffer, while evils are sufferable, than to right themselves by

abolishing the forms to which they are accustomed. But when a long train of

abuses and usurpations, ~~begun at a distinguished period, and~~ pursuing

**under absolute despotism**

invariably the same object, evinces a design to reduce them ^ ~~to arbitrary~~

~~power~~, it is their right, it is their duty, to throw off such government, and to

provide new guards for their future security. Such has been the patient

sufferance of these colonies; and such is now the necessity which constrains

**alter** **the present king of Great Britain**

them to ^ ~~expunge~~ their former systems of government. The history of ^ ~~his~~

**repeated**

~~present majesty~~ is a history of ^ ~~unremitting~~ injuries and usurpations, ~~among~~

~~which no one face stands single or solitary to contradict the uniform tenor of~~

**having**

~~the rest~~, all ^ ~~of which have~~ in direct object the establishment of an absolute

tyranny over these states. To prove this, let facts be submitted to a candid

world, ~~for the truth of which we pledge a faith yet unsullied by falsehood~~.

He has refused his assent to laws, the most wholesome and necessary for the

public good.

He has forbidden his governors to pass laws of immediate and pressing

importance, unless suspended in their operation till his assent should be

**utterly**

obtained; and when so suspended, he has ^ neglected ~~utterly~~ to attend to them.

He has refused to pass other laws for the accommodation of large districts of

people, unless those people would relinquish the right of representation in

the legislature, a right inestimable to them and formidable to tyrants only.

[He has called together legislative bodies at places unusual, uncomfortable, and distant from the depository of their public records, for the sole purpose

of fatiguing them into compliance with his measures.]

He has dissolved representative houses repeatedly and continually, for

opposing with manly firmness his invasions on the rights of the people.

**after such dissolutions**

He has refused for a long space of time, to cause others to be elected;

whereby the legislative powers, incapable of annihilation, have returned to

the people at large for their exercise, the state remaining in the meantime

exposed to all the dangers of invasion from without, and convulsions within.

He has endeavoured to prevent the population of these states; for that

purpose obstructing the laws of naturalization of foreigners; refusing to

pass others to encourage their migration hither; and raising the conditions of

new appropriations of lands.

**obstructed**

He has ~~suffered~~ the administration of justice ~~totally to cease in some of these~~

**by**

~~colonies,~~ refusing his assent to assent to laws for establishing judiciary

powers.

He has made ~~our~~ judges dependent on his will alone, for the tenure of their

**the      and payment**

offices, and amount of their salaries.

He has erected a multitude of new offices ~~by a self-assumed power~~, and sent

hither swarms of officers to harass our people, and eat out their substance.

**without the consent of our legislatures.**

He has kept among us, in times of peace, standing armies ~~and ships of war.~~

He has affected to render the military independent of and superior to the

civil power.

He has combined with others to subject us to a jurisdiction foreign to our

constitutions, and unacknowledged by our laws; giving his assent to their

**pretended**

~~pretended~~ acts of legislation:

For quartering large bodies of armed troops among us;

For protecting them, by a mock-trial, from punishment for any murders

which they should commit on the inhabitants of these states;

For cutting off **our** trade with all parts of the world;

For imposing taxes on us without our consent;

For depriving us **in many cases,** of the benefits of trial by jury;

For transporting us beyond seas to be tried for pretended offences;

[For abolishing the free system of English laws in a neighbouring province,

establishing therein an arbitrary government, and enlarging its boundaries

so as to render it at once an example and fit instrument for introducing the

same absolute rule into these colonies:]

For taking away our charters, **abolishing our most valuable laws** and altering fundamentally the forms of our

governments;

For suspending our own legislature, and declaring themselves invested

with power to legislate for us in all cases whatsoever.

He has abdicated government here, ~~withdrawing his governors, and~~ **by**

declaring us out of his ~~allegiance~~ and protection. **and waging war against us.**

He has plundered our seas, ravaged our coasts, burnt our towns, and

destroyed the lives of our people.

He is at this time transporting large armies of foreign mercenaries to

complete the works of death, desolation and tyranny, already begun with

circumstances of cruelty and **scarcely paralleled in the most barbarous ages, and** perfidy unworthy the head of a civilized nation.

[He has constrained our fellow citizens taken captive on the high seas to bear

arms against their country, to become the executioners of their friends and

brethren, or to fall themselves by their hands.]

**excited domestic insurrections amongst us and has**

He has⌃endeavoured to bring on the inhabitants of our frontiers, the merciless

less Indian savages, whose known rule of warfare, is an undistinguished

destruction of all ages, sexes and conditions ~~of existence~~.

~~He has incited treasonable insurrections of our fellow citizens, with the~~

~~allurements of forfeiture and confiscation of our property:~~

~~He has waged cruel war against human nature itself, violating its most~~

~~sacred rights of life and liberty in the persons of a distant people who never~~

~~offended him, captivating and carrying them into slavery in another~~

~~hemisphere, or to incur miserable death in their transportation thither. This~~

~~piratical warfare, the opprobrium of infidel powers, is the warfare of the~~

~~Christian king of Great Britain. Determined to keep open a market where~~

~~MEN should be bought and sold, he has prostituted his negative veto for~~

~~suppressing every legislative attempt to prohibit or to restrain this execrable~~

~~commerce: and that this assemblage of horrors might want no fact of distin-~~

~~guished die, he is now exciting those very people to rise in arms among us,~~

~~and to purchase that liberty of which he has deprived them, by murdering~~

~~the people upon whom he also obtruded them: thus paying off former~~

~~crimes committed against the liberties of one people, with crimes which he~~

~~urges them to commit against the lives of another.~~

In every stage of these oppressions we have petitioned for redress in the

**only**

most humble terms; our repeated petitions have been answered by⌃repeated

injury. A prince, whose character is thus marked by every act which may

**free**

define a tyrant, is unfit to be the ruler of a⌃people ~~who mean to be free~~.

~~Future ages will scarce believe that the hardiness of one man, adventured~~

~~within the short compass of twelve years only, on so many sets of tyranny~~

~~without a mask, over a people fostered and fixed in principles of liberty.~~

Nor have we been wanting in attentions to our British brethren. We have

warned them from time to time of attempts by their legislature to extend

**an unwarranted  us.**
a jurisdiction over ~~these our states~~. We have reminded them of the

circumstances of our emigration and settlement here, ~~no one of which could~~

~~warrant so strange a pretension: that these were effected at the expense of~~

~~our own blood and treasure, unassisted by the wealth or the strength of~~

~~Great Britain: that in constituting indeed our several forms of government,~~

~~we had adopted one common king, thereby laying a foundation for~~

~~perpetual league and amity with them: but that submission to their~~

~~parliament was no part of our constitution, nor ever in idea, if history may~~
                         **have**
~~be credited~~: and we appealed to their native justice and magnanimity,

**and we have conjured them by**
~~as well as to~~ the ties of our common kindred to disavow these usurpations,

    **would inevitably         connections and correspondence**
which ~~were likely to~~ interrupt our ~~correspondence and connection~~. They too

have been deaf to the voice of justice and of consanguinity, ~~and when~~

~~occassions have been given them, by the regular course of their laws, of~~

~~removing from their councils the disturbers of our harmony, they have by~~

~~their free election re-established them in power. At this very time too they are~~

~~permitting their chief magistrate to send over not only soldiers of our~~

~~common blood, but Scotch and foreign merceneries to invade and deluge us~~

~~in blood. These facts have given the last stab to agonizing affection, and~~

~~manly spirit bids us to renounce forever these unfeeling brethren~~. We

    **therefore, acquiesce in the necessity, which denounces our separation,**
must ~~endeavor to forget our former love for them~~, and ~~to~~ hold them as we

hold the rest of mankind, enemies in war, in peace friends. ~~We might have~~

~~been a free and a great people altogether; but a communication of grandeur~~

~~and of freedom it seems is below their dignity. Be it so, since they will have~~

~~it: the road to happiness and to glory is open to us too; we will climb it apart~~

~~from the, and acquiesce in the necessity which denounces our eternal~~

~~separation!~~

We, therefore, the representatives of the United States of America, in General
**appealing to the Supreme Judge of the world for the rectitude of our intentions**
Congress assembled do, in the name, and by authority of the good people of

**solumnly publish and declare, that these United Colonies are, and of a right**
these colonies ~~and reject and renounce all allegiance and subjection to the~~

**ought to be free and independent states; they are absolved from all**
~~kings of Great Britain and all others who may hereafter claim by, through, or~~

**allegiance to the British Crown, and that all**
~~under them; we utterly dissolve and break off all~~ political connection ~~which~~
**them**                                                                 **state**
~~may have heretofore subsisted~~ between us and the ~~people or parliament~~ of

**is and ought to be totally dissolved,**
Great Britain; and ~~finally we do assert and declare these colonies to be free~~

~~and independent states,~~ and that as free and independent states they ~~shall~~

~~hereafter~~ have full power to levy war, conclude peace, contract alliances,

establish commerce, and to do all other acts and things which independent
**with a firm reliance on the protection of divine Providence**
states may of right do. And for the support of this declaration we mutually

pledge to each other our lives, our fortunes, and our sacred honour.

# THE VIRGINIA DECLARATION OF RIGHTS

*George Mason*

A DECLARATION OF RIGHTS made by the Representatives of the good people of VIRGINIA, assembled in full and free Convention; which rights do pertain to them and their posterity, as the basis and foundation of Government.

1. That all men are by nature equally free and independent, and have certain inherent rights, of which, when they enter into a state of society, they cannot, by any compact, deprive or divest their posterity; namely, the enjoyment of life and liberty, with the means of acquiring and possessing property, and pursuing and obtaining happiness and safety.

2. That all power is vested in, and consequently derived from, the People; that magistrates are their trustees and servants, and at all times amenable to them.

3. That Government is, or ought to be, instituted for the common benefit, protection, and security of the people, nation, or community;—of all the various modes and forms of Government that is best which is capable of producing the greatest degree of happiness and safety, and is most effectually secured against the danger of mal-administration;—and that, whenever any Government shall be found inadequate or contrary to these purposes, a majority of the community hath an indubitable, unalienable, and indefeasible right, to reform, alter, or abolish it, in such manner as shall be judged most conducive to the publick weal.

4. That no man, or set of men, are entitled to exclusive or separate emoluments or privileges from the community, but in consideration of publick services; which, not being descendible neither ought the offices of Magistrate, Legislator, or Judge, to be hereditary.

5. That the Legislative and Executive powers of the State should be separate and distinct from the Judicative; and, that the members of the two first may be restrained from oppression, by feeling and participating the burdens of the people, they should, at fixed periods, be reduced to a private station, return into that body from which they were originally taken, and the vacancies be supplied by frequent, certain, and regular elections, in which all, or

any part of the former members, to be again eligible, or ineligible, as the law shall direct.

6. That elections of members to serve as Representatives of the people, in Assembly, ought to be free; and that all men, having sufficient evidence of permanent common interest with, and attachment to, the community, have the right of suffrage, and cannot be taxed or deprived of their property for publick uses without their own consent or that of their Representative so elected, nor bound by any law to which they have not, in like manner, assented, for the public good.

7. That all power of suspending laws, or the execution of laws, by any authority, without consent of the Representatives of the people, is injurious to their rights, and ought not to be exercised.

8. That in all capital or criminal prosecutions a man hath a right to demand the cause and nature of his accusation, to be confronted with the accusers and witnesses, to call for evidence in his favour, and to a speedy trial by an impartial jury of his vicinage, without whose unanimous consent he cannot be found guilty, nor can he be compelled to give evidence against himself; that no man be deprived of his liberty except by the law of the land, or the judgment of his peers.

9. That excessive bail ought not to be required, nor excessive fines imposed, nor cruel and unusual punishments inflicted.

10. That general warrants, whereby any officer or messenger may be commanded to search suspected places without evidence of a fact committed, or to seize any person or persons not named, or whose offence is not particularly described and supported by evidence, are grievous and oppressive, and ought not to be granted.

11. That in controversies respecting property, and in suits between man and man, the ancient trial by Jury is preferable to any other, and ought to be held sacred.

12. That the freedom of the Press is one of the great bulwarks of liberty, and can never be restrained but by despotick Governments.

13. That a well-regulated Militia, composed of the body of the people, trained to arms, is the proper, natural, and safe defence of a free State; that Standing Armies, in time of peace, should be avoided as dangerous to liberty; and that, in all cases, the military should be under strict subordination to, and governed by, the civil power.

14. That the people have a right to uniform Government; and, therefore, that no Government separate from, or independent of, the Government of *Virginia*, ought to be erected or established within the limits thereof.

15. That no free Government, or the blessing of liberty, can be preserved to any people but by a firm adherence to justice, moderation, temperance, frugality, and virtue, and by frequent recurrence to fundamental principles.

16. That Religion, or the duty which we owe to our *Creator*, and the manner of discharging it, can be directed only by reason and conviction, not by force or violence; and, therefore, all men are equally entitled to the free exercise of religion, according to the dictates of conscience; and that it is the mutual duty of all to practise Christian forbearance, love, and charity, towards each other.

# THE FEDERAL BILL OF RIGHTS

**ARTICLE I**

Congress shall make no law respecting an establishment of religion, or prohibiting the free exercise thereof; or abridging the freedom of speech, or of the press; or the right of the people peacably to assemble, and to petition the Government for a redress of grievances.

**ARTICLE II**

A well-regulated militia, being necessary to the security of a free State, the right of the people to keep and bear arms, shall not be infringed.

**ARTICLE III**

No soldier shall, in time of peace be quartered in any house, without the consent of the owner, nor in time of war, but in a manner to be prescribed by law.

**ARTICLE IV**

The right of the people to be secure in their persons, houses, papers, and effects, against unreasonable searches and seizures, shall not be violated, and no warrants shall issue, but upon probable cause, supported by oath or affirmation, and particularly describing the place to be searched, and the persons or things to be seized.

**ARTICLE V**

No person shall be held to answer for a capital, or otherwise infamous crime, unless on a presentment or indictment of a Grand Jury, except in cases arising in the land or naval forces, or in the militia, when in actual service in time of war or public danger; nor shall any person be subject for the same offence to be twice put in jeopardy of life or limb; nor shall be compelled in any criminal case to be a witness against himself, nor be deprived of life, liberty, or property, without due process of law; nor shall private property be taken for public use without just compensation.

**ARTICLE VI**

In all criminal prosecutions, the accused shall enjoy the right to a speedy and public trial, by an impartial jury of the State and district wherein the crime shall have been committed, which district shall have been previously ascertained by law, and to be informed of the nature and cause of the accusation; to be confronted with the witnesses against him; to have compulsory process for obtaining witnesses in his favor, and to have the assistance of counsel for his defence.

### ARTICLE VII

In suits at common law, where the value in controversy shall exceed twenty dollars, the right of trial by jury shall be preserved, and no fact tried by a jury shall be otherwise re-examined in any court of the United States, than according to the rules of the common law.

### ARTICLE VIII

Excessive bail shall not be required, nor excessive fines imposed, nor cruel and unusual punishments inflicted.

### ARTICLE IX

The enumeration in the Constitution, of certain rights, shall not be construed to deny or disparage others retained by the people.

### ARTICLE X

The powers not delegated to the United States by the Constitution, nor prohibited by it to the States, are preserved to the States respectively, or to the people.